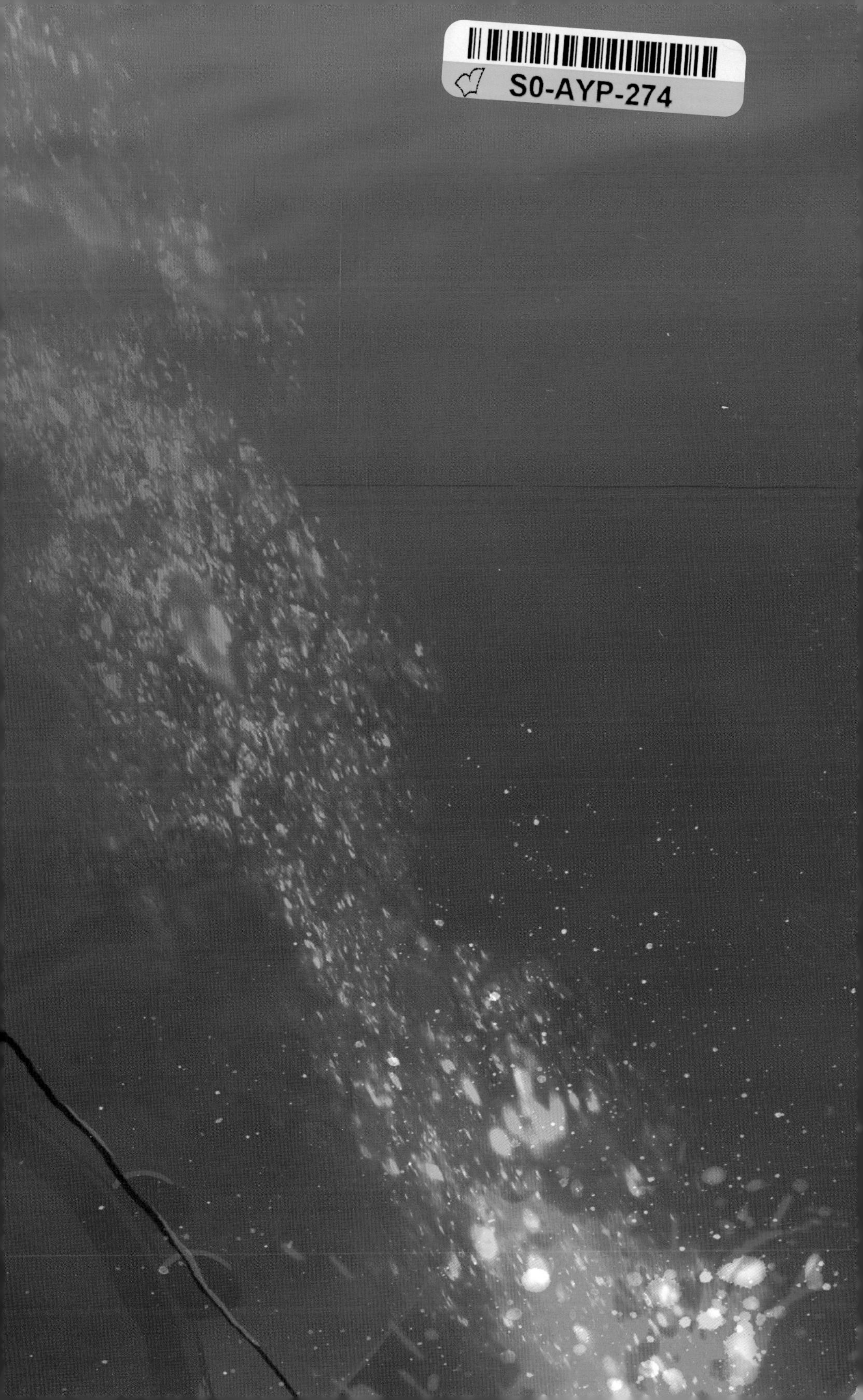

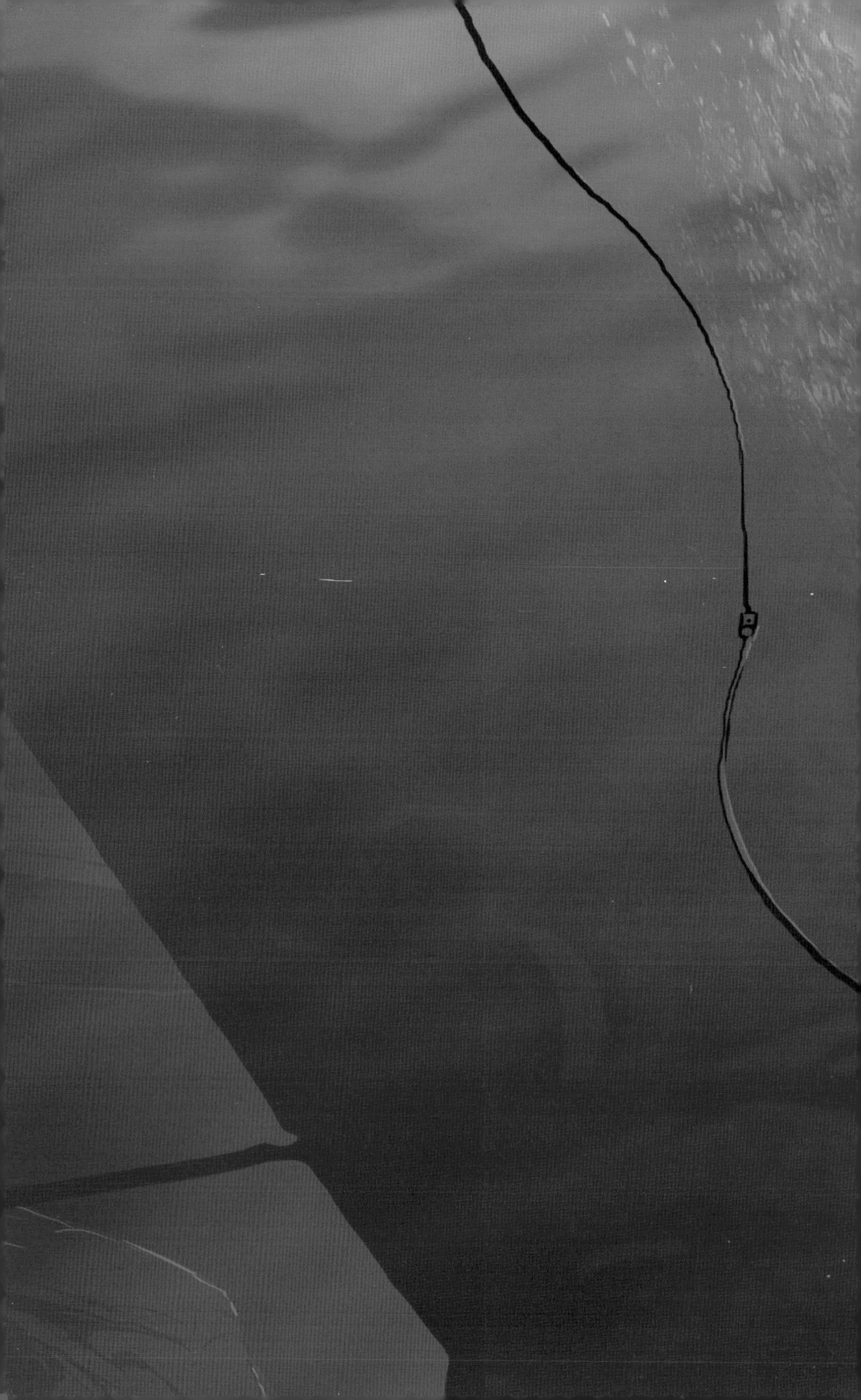

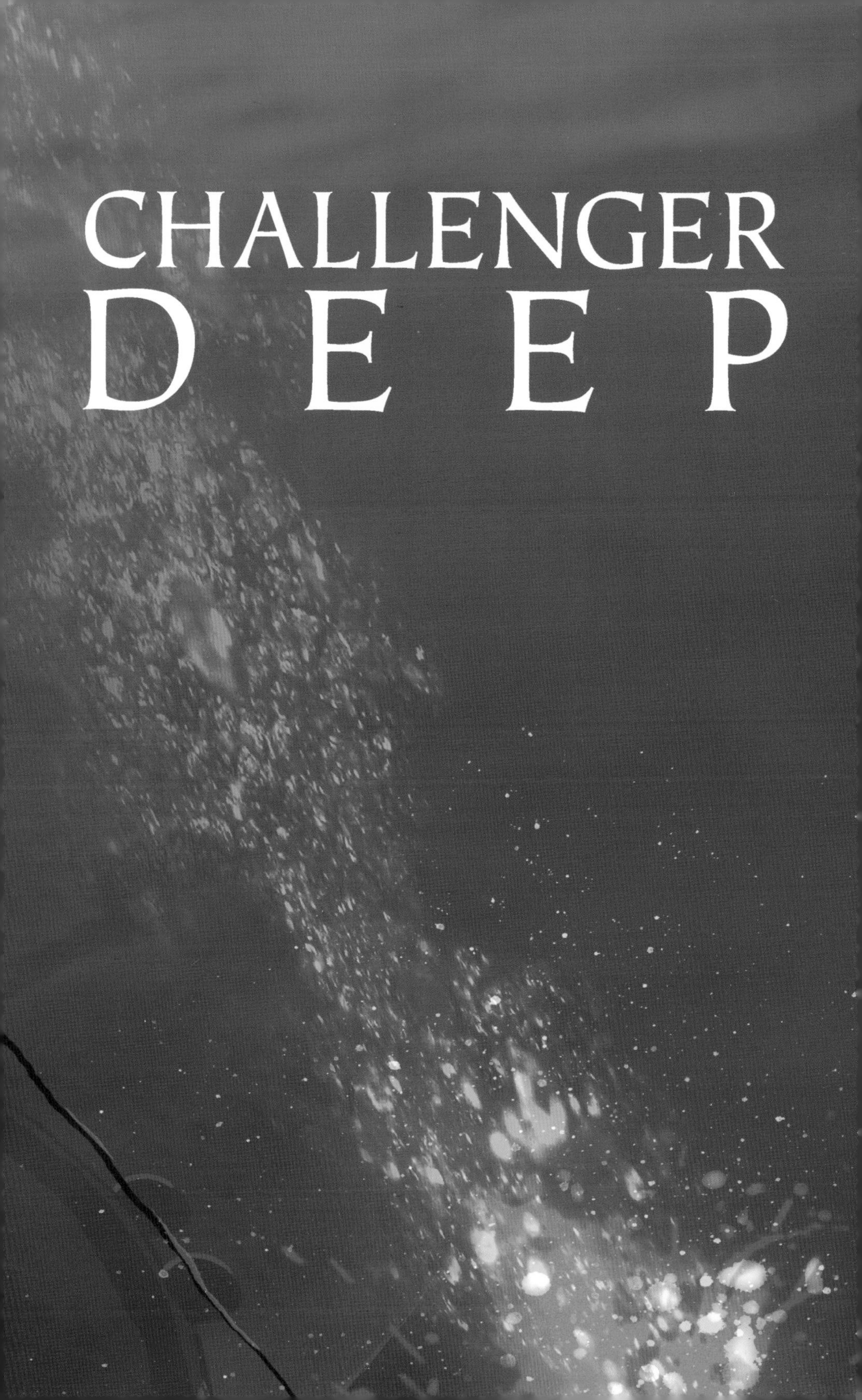
CHALLENGER
DEEP

**ROSS RICHIE**
chief executive officer

**MARK WAID**
editor-in-chief

**ADAM FORTIER**
vice president,
publishing

**CHIP MOSHER**
marketing director

**MATT GAGNON**
managing editor

**JENNY CHRISTOPHER**
sales director

First Edition: January 2009

10 9 8 7 6 5 4 3 2 1
PRINTED IN KOREA

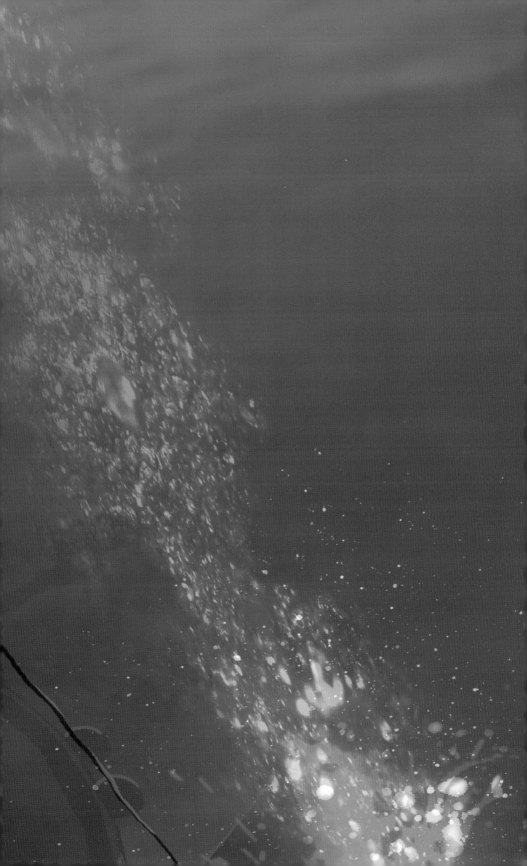

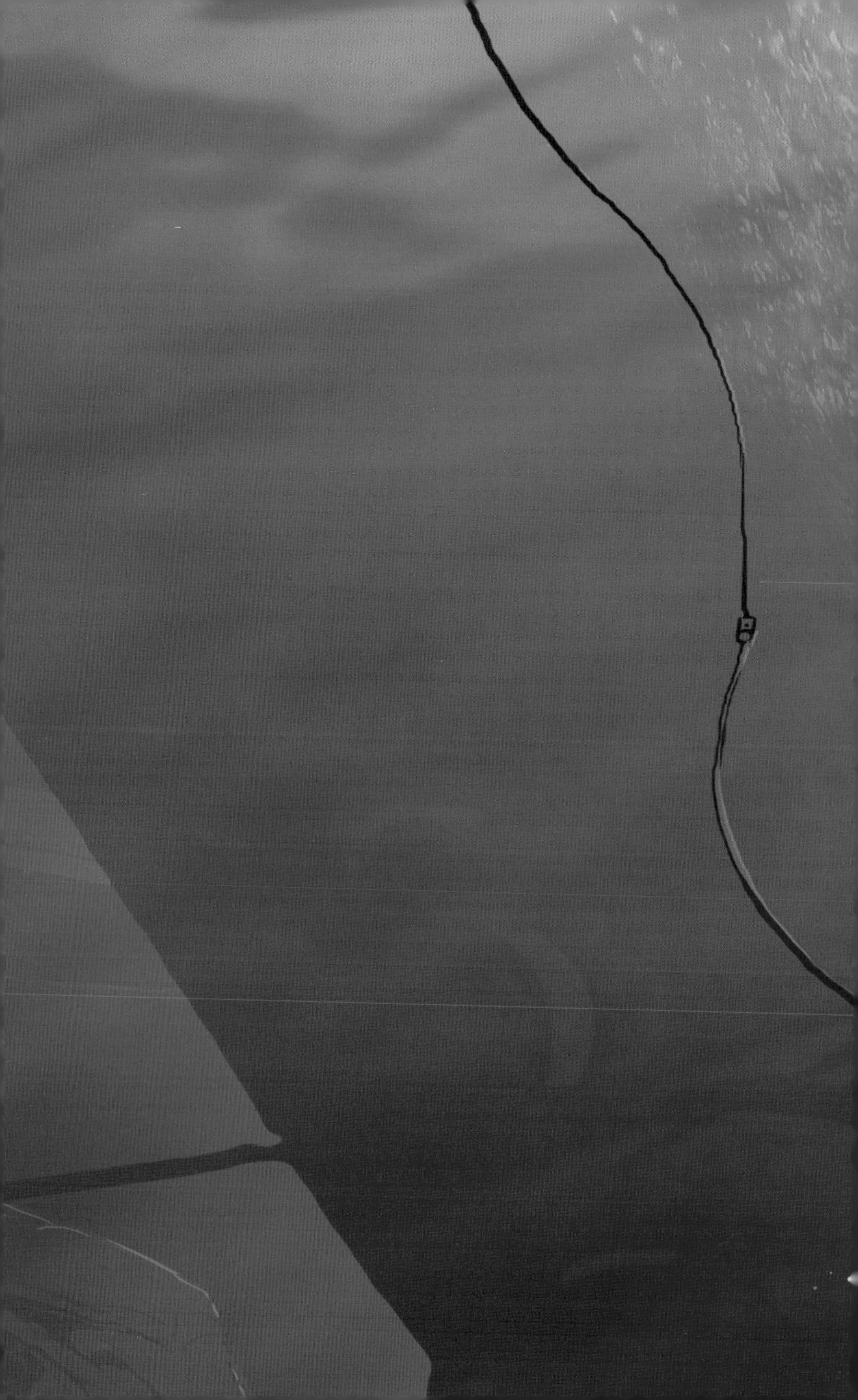

Story by **ANDREW COSBY** and **ANDY SCHMIDT**

Script by **ANDY SCHMIDT**

Art by **CHEE**

## ANDREW DALHOUSE
Colorist

## MARSHALL DILLON
Letterer

## MARK WAID
editor

## KODY CHAMBERLAIN
Cover Artist

# CHAPTER 1

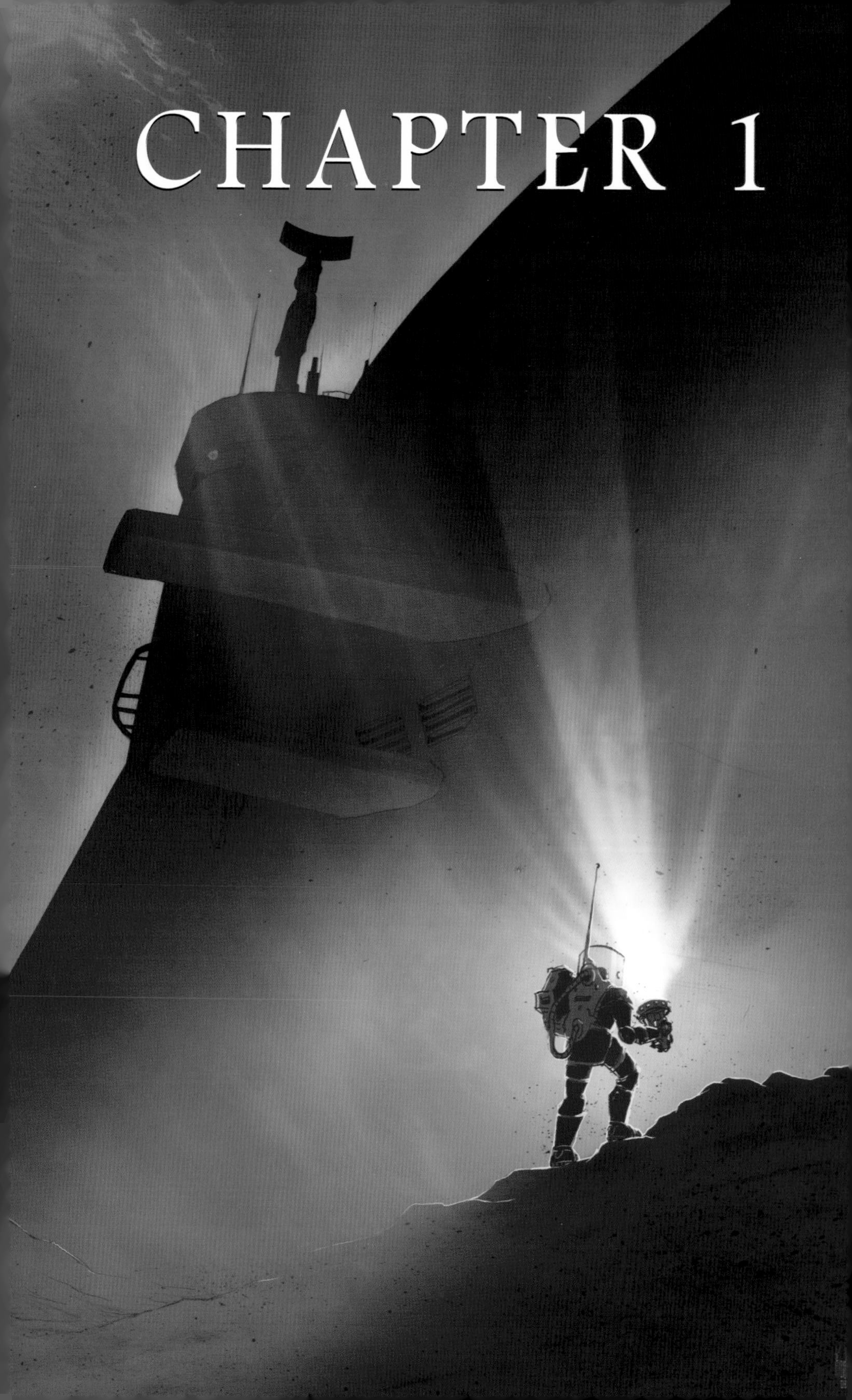

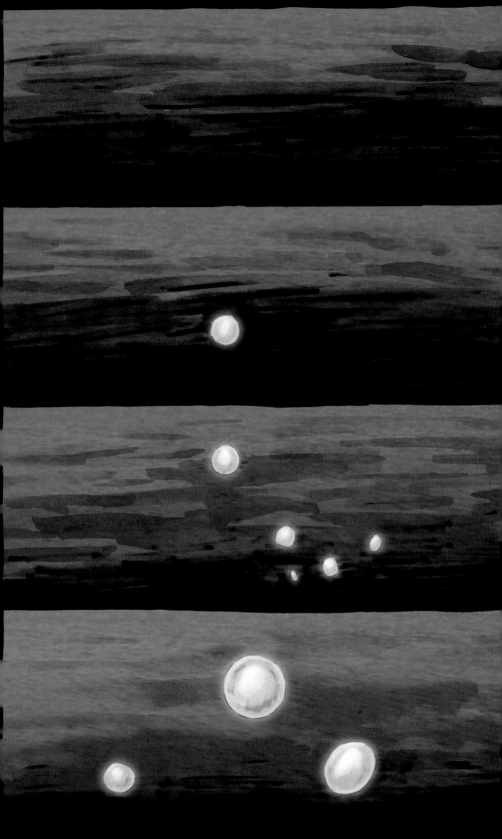

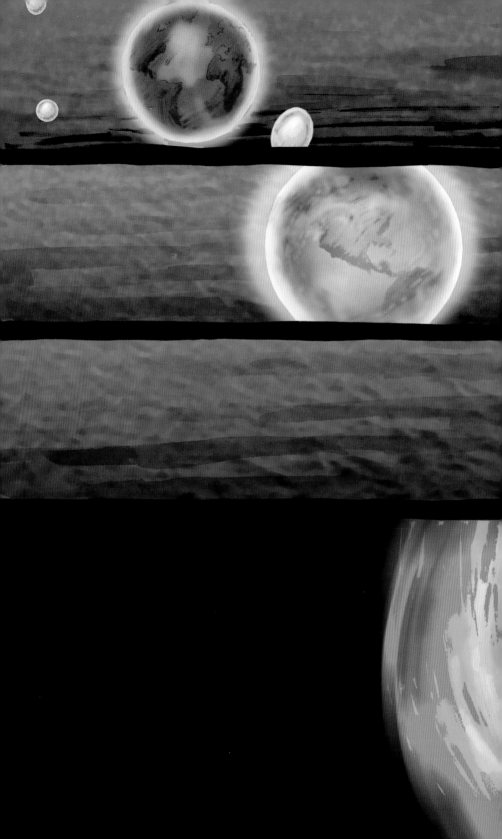

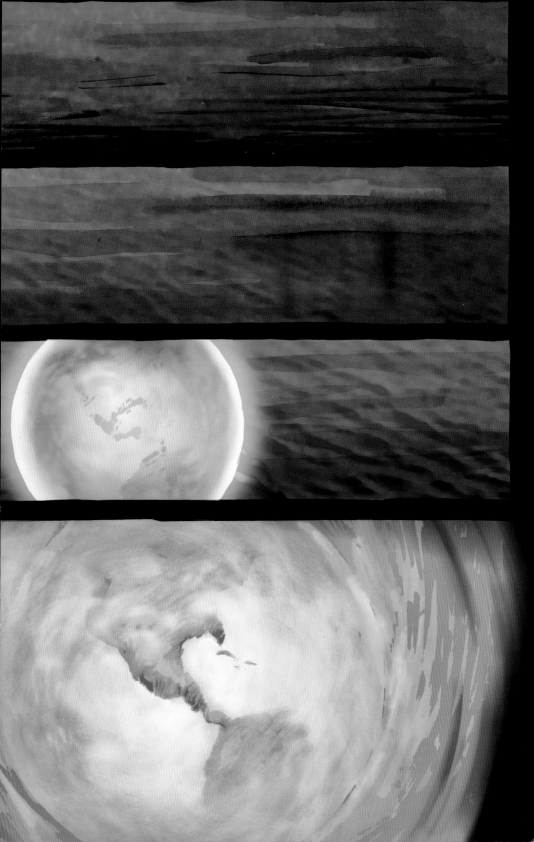

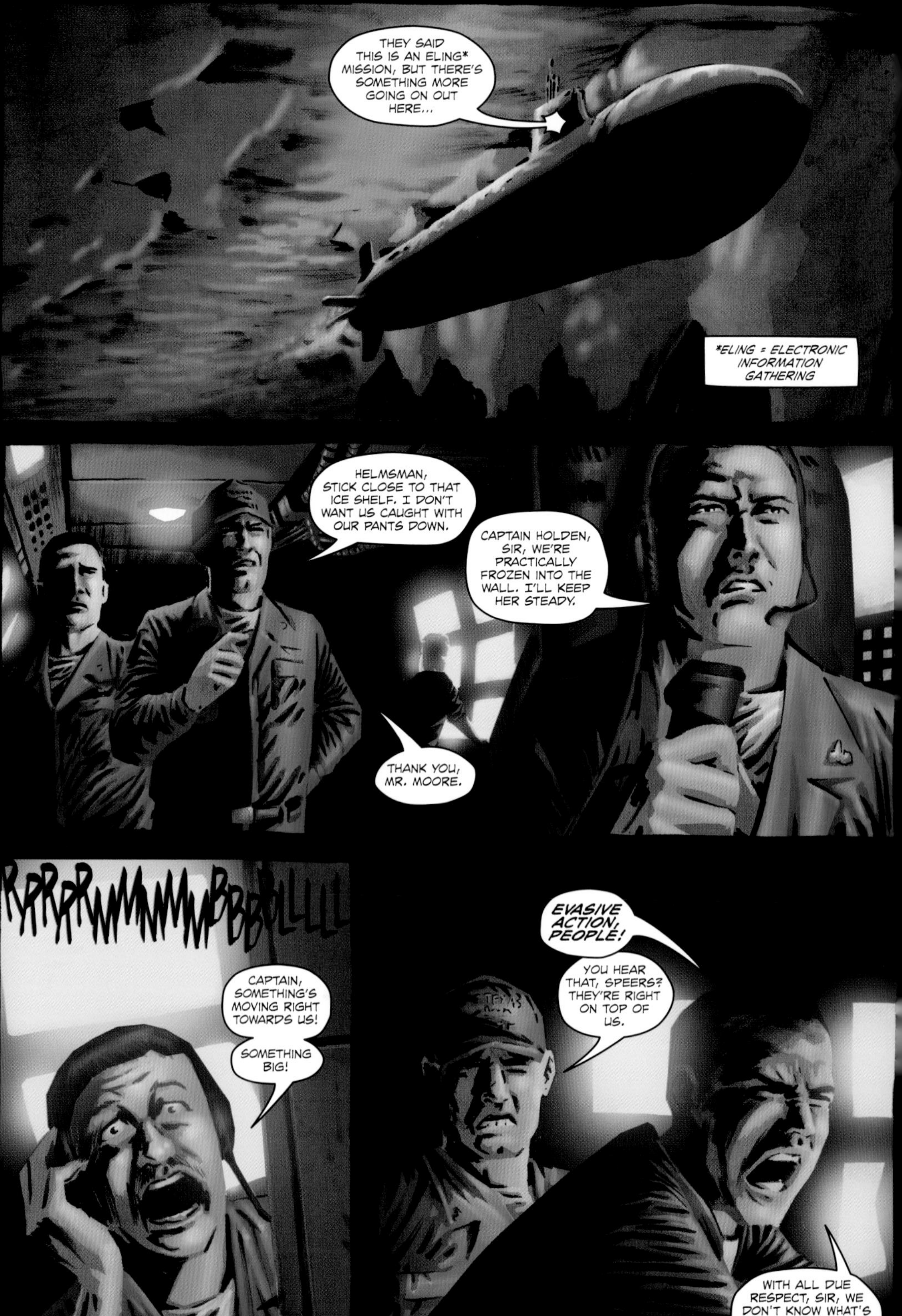
THEY SAID THIS IS AN ELING* MISSION, BUT THERE'S SOMETHING MORE GOING ON OUT HERE...
*ELING = ELECTRONIC INFORMATION GATHERING
HELMSMAN, STICK CLOSE TO THAT ICE SHELF. I DON'T WANT US CAUGHT WITH OUR PANTS DOWN.
CAPTAIN HOLDEN, SIR, WE'RE PRACTICALLY FROZEN INTO THE WALL. I'LL KEEP HER STEADY.
THANK YOU, MR. MOORE.
RRRRRMMMMMBBBLLLLL
CAPTAIN, SOMETHING'S MOVING RIGHT TOWARDS US!
SOMETHING BIG!
EVASIVE ACTION, PEOPLE!
YOU HEAR THAT, SPEERS? THEY'RE RIGHT ON TOP OF US.
WITH ALL DUE RESPECT, SIR, WE DON'T KNOW WHAT'S HITTING US, BUT AT THIS DEPTH, IT'S NOT AN ENEMY CRAFT!

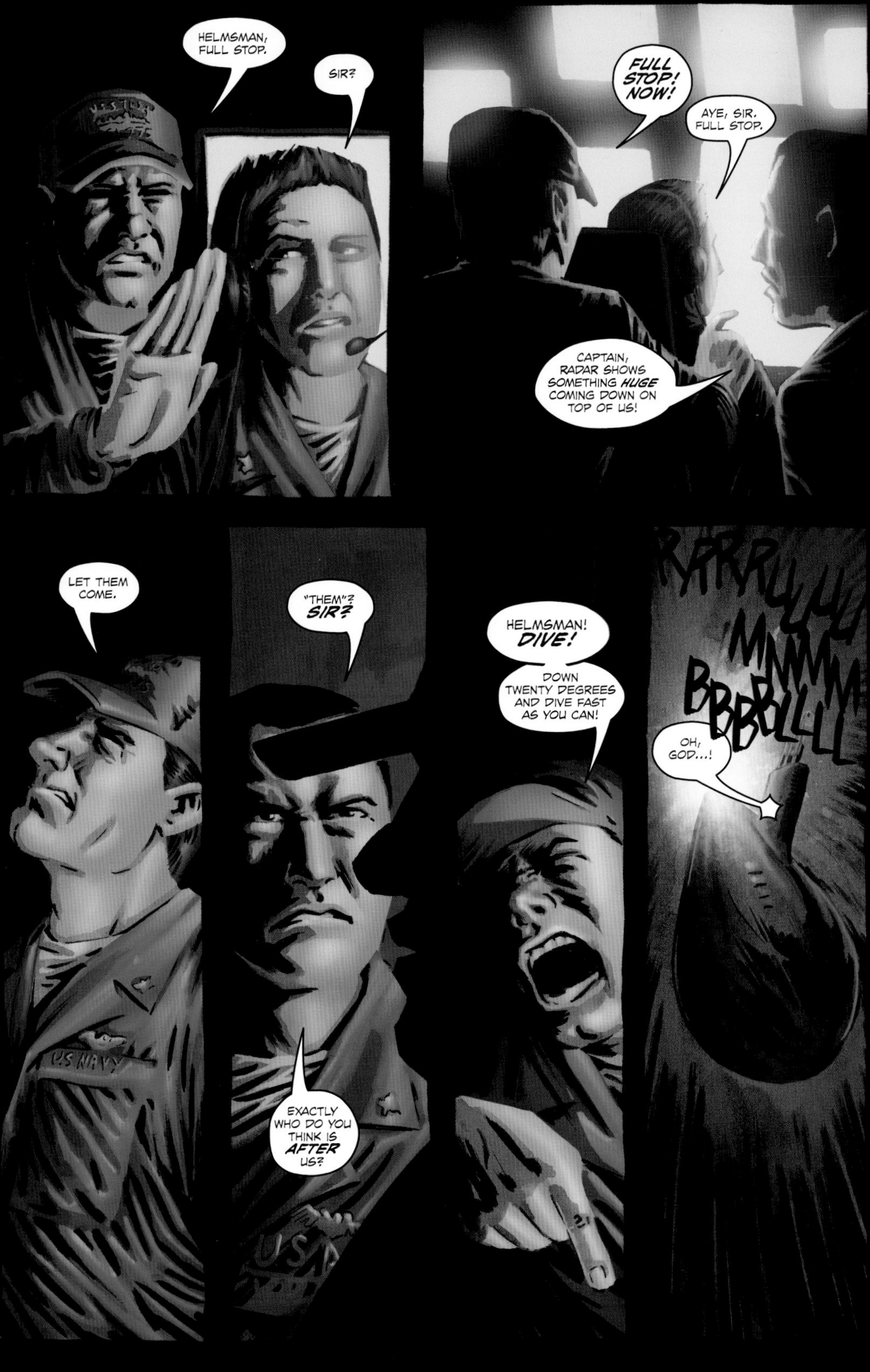
HELMSMAN, FULL STOP.
SIR?
FULL STOP! NOW!
AYE, SIR. FULL STOP.
CAPTAIN, RADAR SHOWS SOMETHING HUGE COMING DOWN ON TOP OF US!
LET THEM COME.
"THEM"? SIR?
EXACTLY WHO DO YOU THINK IS AFTER US?
HELMSMAN! DIVE!
DOWN TWENTY DEGREES AND DIVE FAST AS YOU CAN!
RRRRUUU MMMM BBBBLLLL
OH, GOD...!

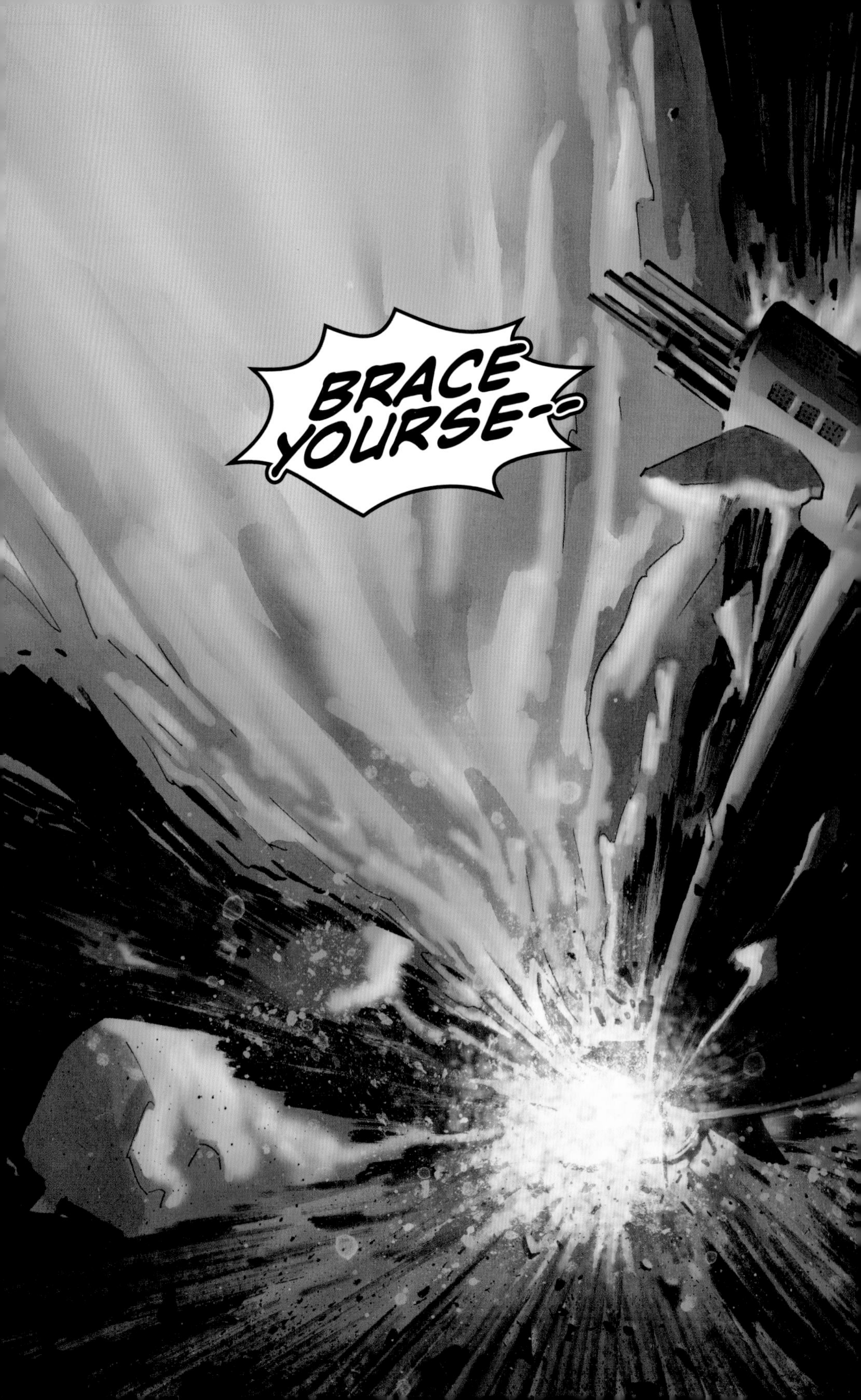
BRACE YOURSE--

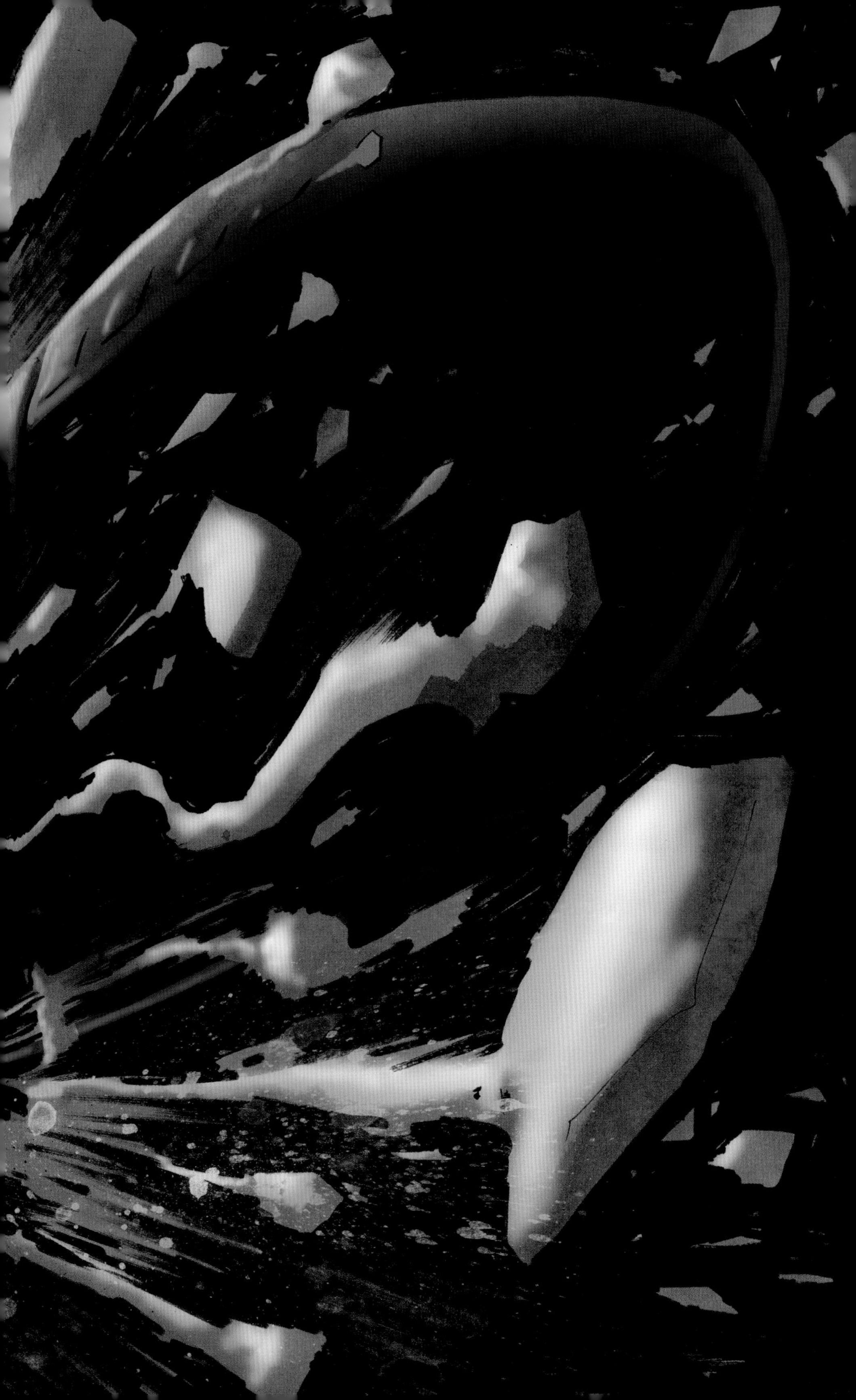

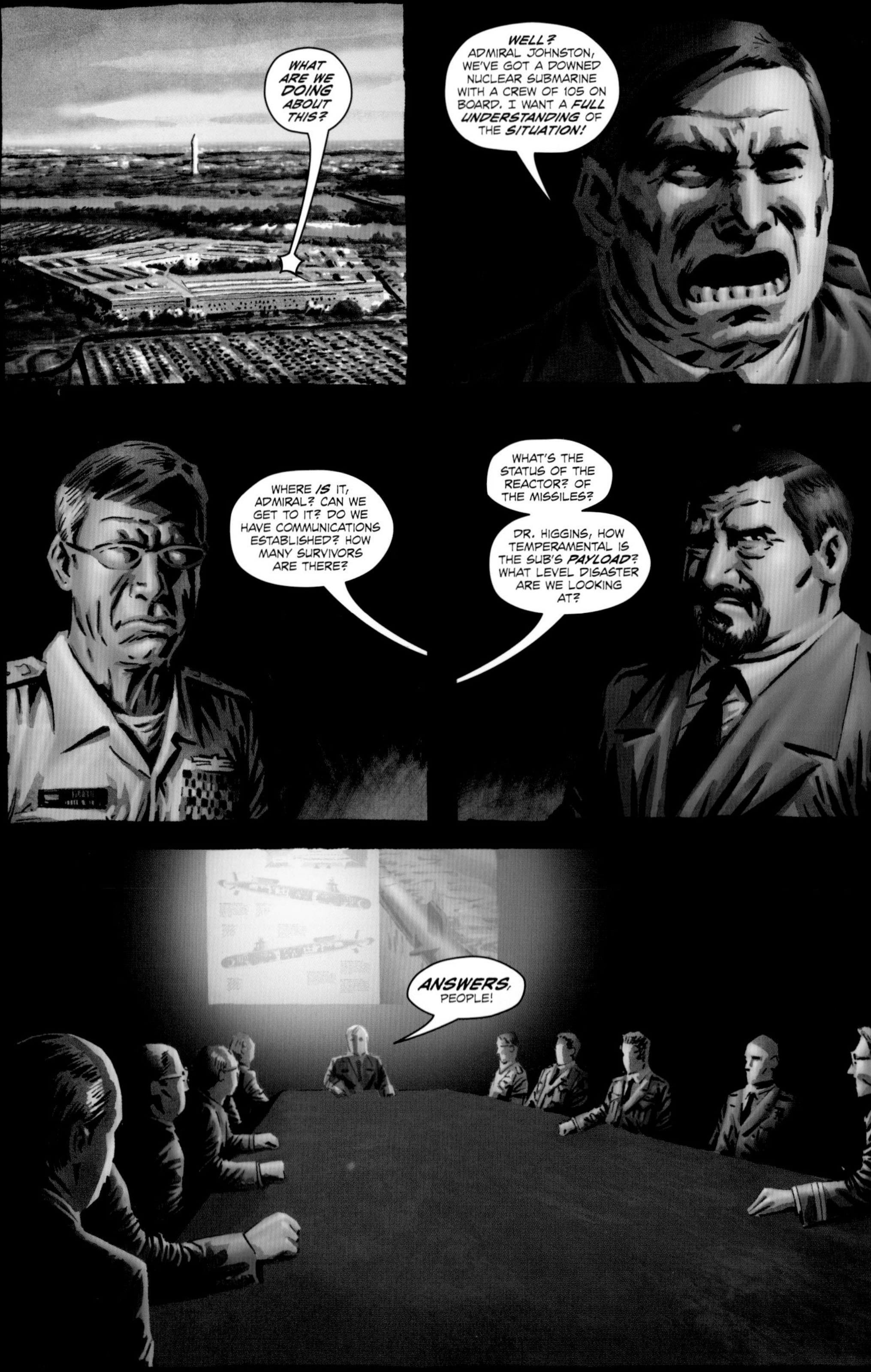
WHAT ARE WE DOING ABOUT THIS?
WELL? ADMIRAL JOHNSTON, WE'VE GOT A DOWNED NUCLEAR SUBMARINE WITH A CREW OF 105 ON BOARD. I WANT A FULL UNDERSTANDING OF THE SITUATION!
WHERE IS IT, ADMIRAL? CAN WE GET TO IT? DO WE HAVE COMMUNICATIONS ESTABLISHED? HOW MANY SURVIVORS ARE THERE?
WHAT'S THE STATUS OF THE REACTOR? OF THE MISSILES?
DR. HIGGINS, HOW TEMPERAMENTAL IS THE SUB'S PAYLOAD? WHAT LEVEL DISASTER ARE WE LOOKING AT?
ANSWERS, PEOPLE!

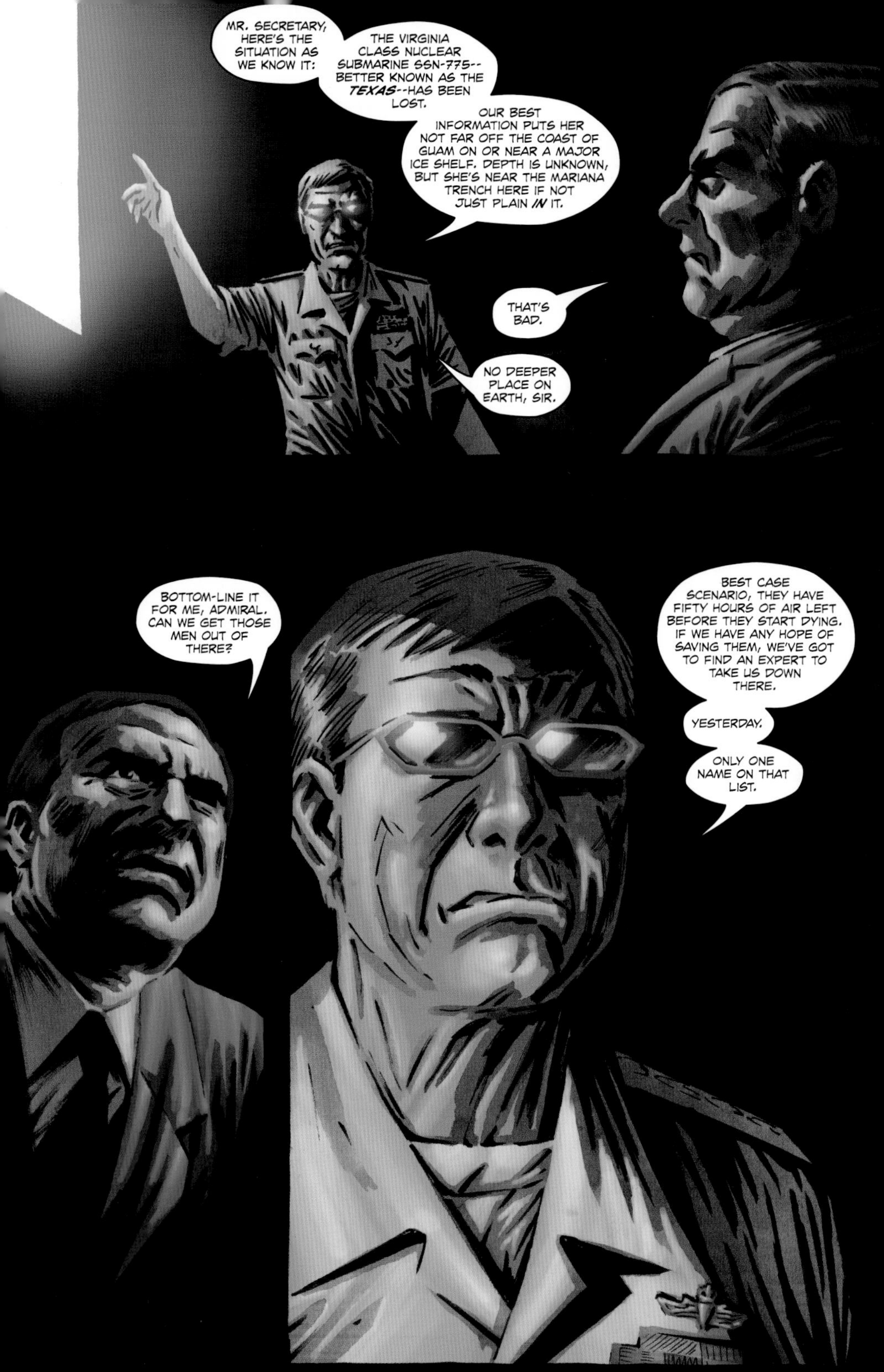
MR. SECRETARY, HERE'S THE SITUATION AS WE KNOW IT:
THE VIRGINIA CLASS NUCLEAR SUBMARINE SSN-775-- BETTER KNOWN AS THE *TEXAS*--HAS BEEN LOST.
OUR BEST INFORMATION PUTS HER NOT FAR OFF THE COAST OF GUAM ON OR NEAR A MAJOR ICE SHELF. DEPTH IS UNKNOWN, BUT SHE'S NEAR THE MARIANA TRENCH HERE IF NOT JUST PLAIN *IN* IT.
THAT'S BAD.
NO DEEPER PLACE ON EARTH, SIR.
BOTTOM-LINE IT FOR ME, ADMIRAL. CAN WE GET THOSE MEN OUT OF THERE?
BEST CASE SCENARIO, THEY HAVE FIFTY HOURS OF AIR LEFT BEFORE THEY START DYING. IF WE HAVE ANY HOPE OF SAVING THEM, WE'VE GOT TO FIND AN EXPERT TO TAKE US DOWN THERE.
YESTERDAY.
ONLY ONE NAME ON THAT LIST.

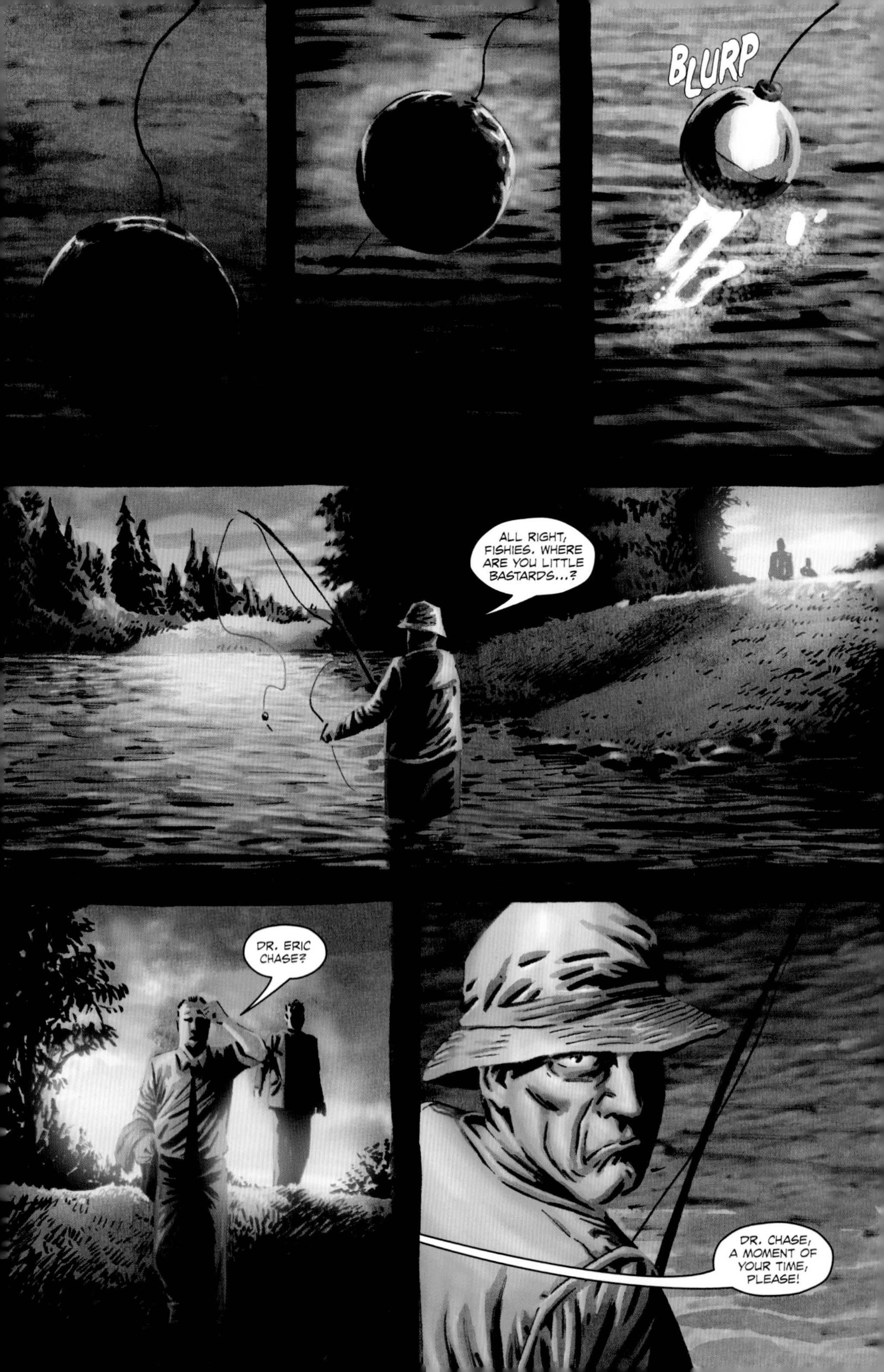
BLURP
ALL RIGHT, FISHIES. WHERE ARE YOU LITTLE BASTARDS...?
DR. ERIC CHASE?
DR. CHASE, A MOMENT OF YOUR TIME, PLEASE!

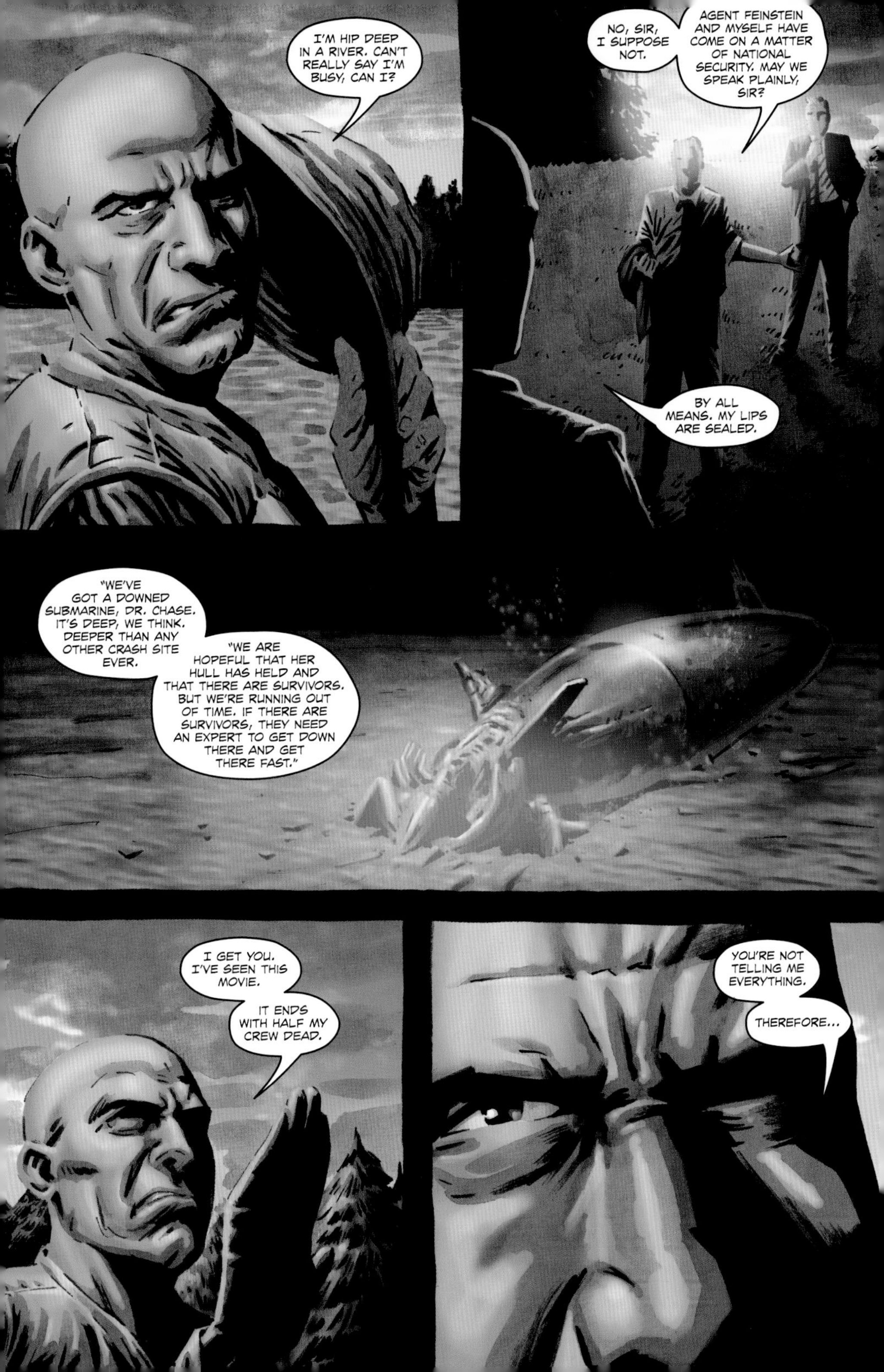
I'M HIP DEEP IN A RIVER. CAN'T REALLY SAY I'M BUSY, CAN I?
NO, SIR, I SUPPOSE NOT.
AGENT FEINSTEIN AND MYSELF HAVE COME ON A MATTER OF NATIONAL SECURITY. MAY WE SPEAK PLAINLY, SIR?
BY ALL MEANS. MY LIPS ARE SEALED.
"WE'VE GOT A DOWNED SUBMARINE, DR. CHASE. IT'S DEEP, WE THINK. DEEPER THAN ANY OTHER CRASH SITE EVER.
"WE ARE HOPEFUL THAT HER HULL HAS HELD AND THAT THERE ARE SURVIVORS. BUT WE'RE RUNNING OUT OF TIME. IF THERE ARE SURVIVORS, THEY NEED AN EXPERT TO GET DOWN THERE AND GET THERE FAST."
I GET YOU. I'VE SEEN THIS MOVIE.
IT ENDS WITH HALF MY CREW DEAD.
YOU'RE NOT TELLING ME EVERYTHING.
THEREFORE...

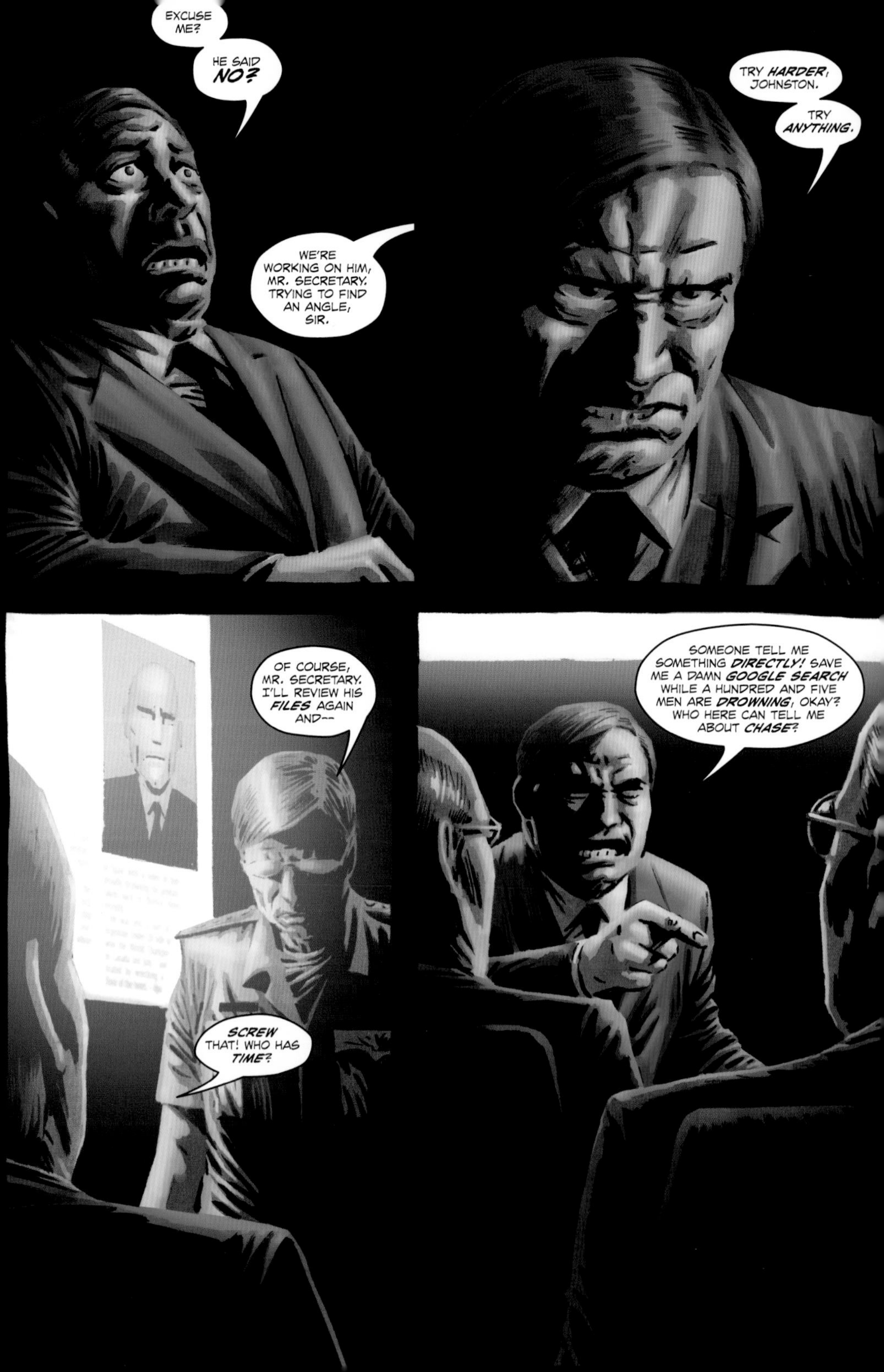
EXCUSE ME?
HE SAID NO?
WE'RE WORKING ON HIM, MR. SECRETARY. TRYING TO FIND AN ANGLE, SIR.
TRY HARDER, JOHNSTON.
TRY ANYTHING.
OF COURSE, MR. SECRETARY. I'LL REVIEW HIS FILES AGAIN AND--
SCREW THAT! WHO HAS TIME?
SOMEONE TELL ME SOMETHING DIRECTLY! SAVE ME A DAMN GOOGLE SEARCH WHILE A HUNDRED AND FIVE MEN ARE DROWNING, OKAY? WHO HERE CAN TELL ME ABOUT CHASE?

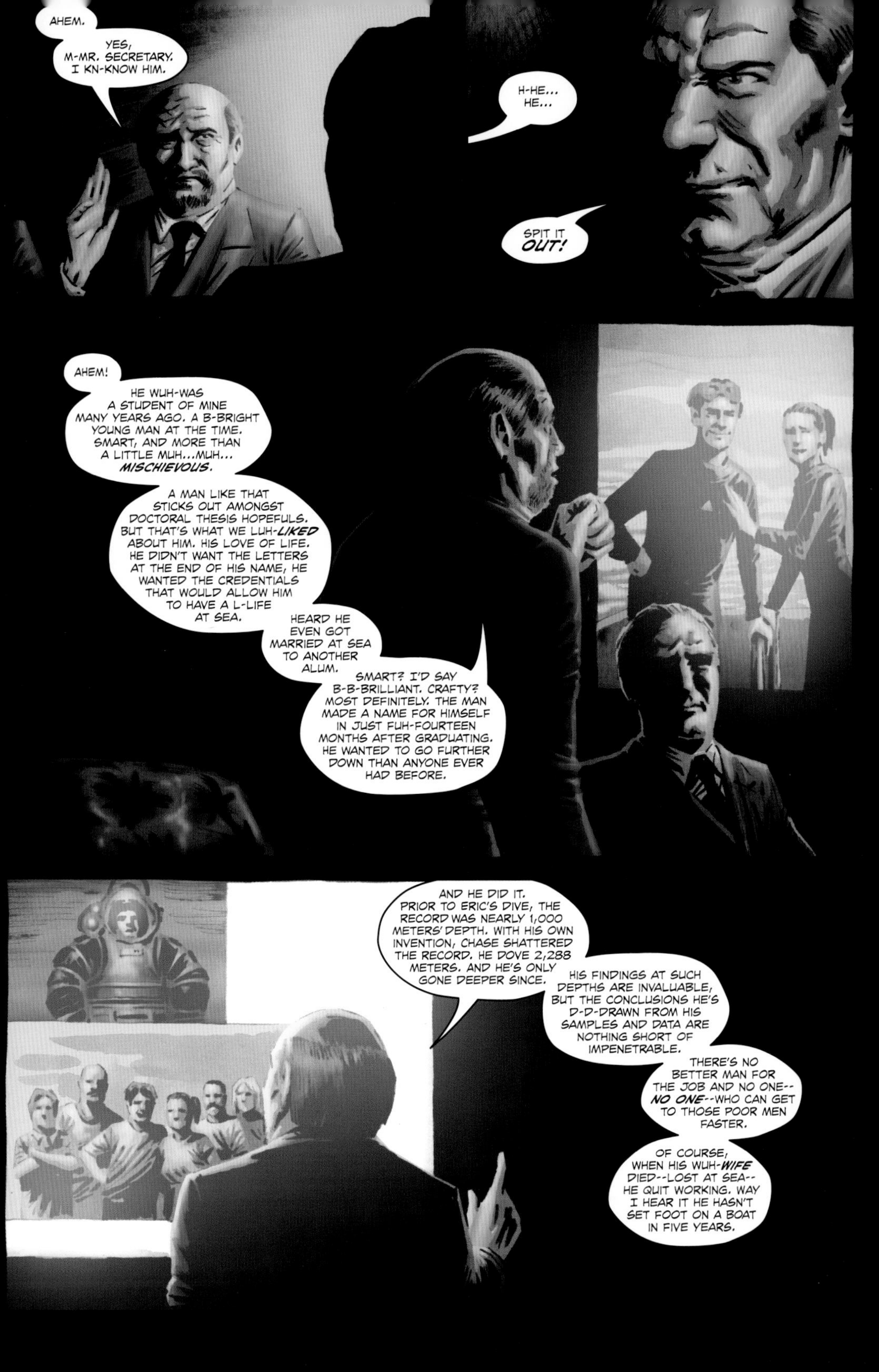
AHEM.
YES, M-MR. SECRETARY. I KN-KNOW HIM.
H-HE... HE...
SPIT IT OUT!
AHEM!
HE WUH-WAS A STUDENT OF MINE MANY YEARS AGO. A B-BRIGHT YOUNG MAN AT THE TIME. SMART, AND MORE THAN A LITTLE MUH...MUH... MISCHIEVOUS.
A MAN LIKE THAT STICKS OUT AMONGST DOCTORAL THESIS HOPEFULS. BUT THAT'S WHAT WE LUH-LIKED ABOUT HIM. HIS LOVE OF LIFE. HE DIDN'T WANT THE LETTERS AT THE END OF HIS NAME, HE WANTED THE CREDENTIALS THAT WOULD ALLOW HIM TO HAVE A L-LIFE AT SEA.
HEARD HE EVEN GOT MARRIED AT SEA TO ANOTHER ALUM.
SMART? I'D SAY B-B-BRILLIANT. CRAFTY? MOST DEFINITELY. THE MAN MADE A NAME FOR HIMSELF IN JUST FUH-FOURTEEN MONTHS AFTER GRADUATING. HE WANTED TO GO FURTHER DOWN THAN ANYONE EVER HAD BEFORE.
AND HE DID IT. PRIOR TO ERIC'S DIVE, THE RECORD WAS NEARLY 1,000 METERS' DEPTH. WITH HIS OWN INVENTION, CHASE SHATTERED THE RECORD. HE DOVE 2,288 METERS. AND HE'S ONLY GONE DEEPER SINCE.
HIS FINDINGS AT SUCH DEPTHS ARE INVALUABLE, BUT THE CONCLUSIONS HE'S D-D-DRAWN FROM HIS SAMPLES AND DATA ARE NOTHING SHORT OF IMPENETRABLE.
THERE'S NO BETTER MAN FOR THE JOB AND NO ONE-- NO ONE--WHO CAN GET TO THOSE POOR MEN FASTER.
OF COURSE, WHEN HIS WUH-WIFE DIED--LOST AT SEA-- HE QUIT WORKING. WAY I HEAR IT HE HASN'T SET FOOT ON A BOAT IN FIVE YEARS.

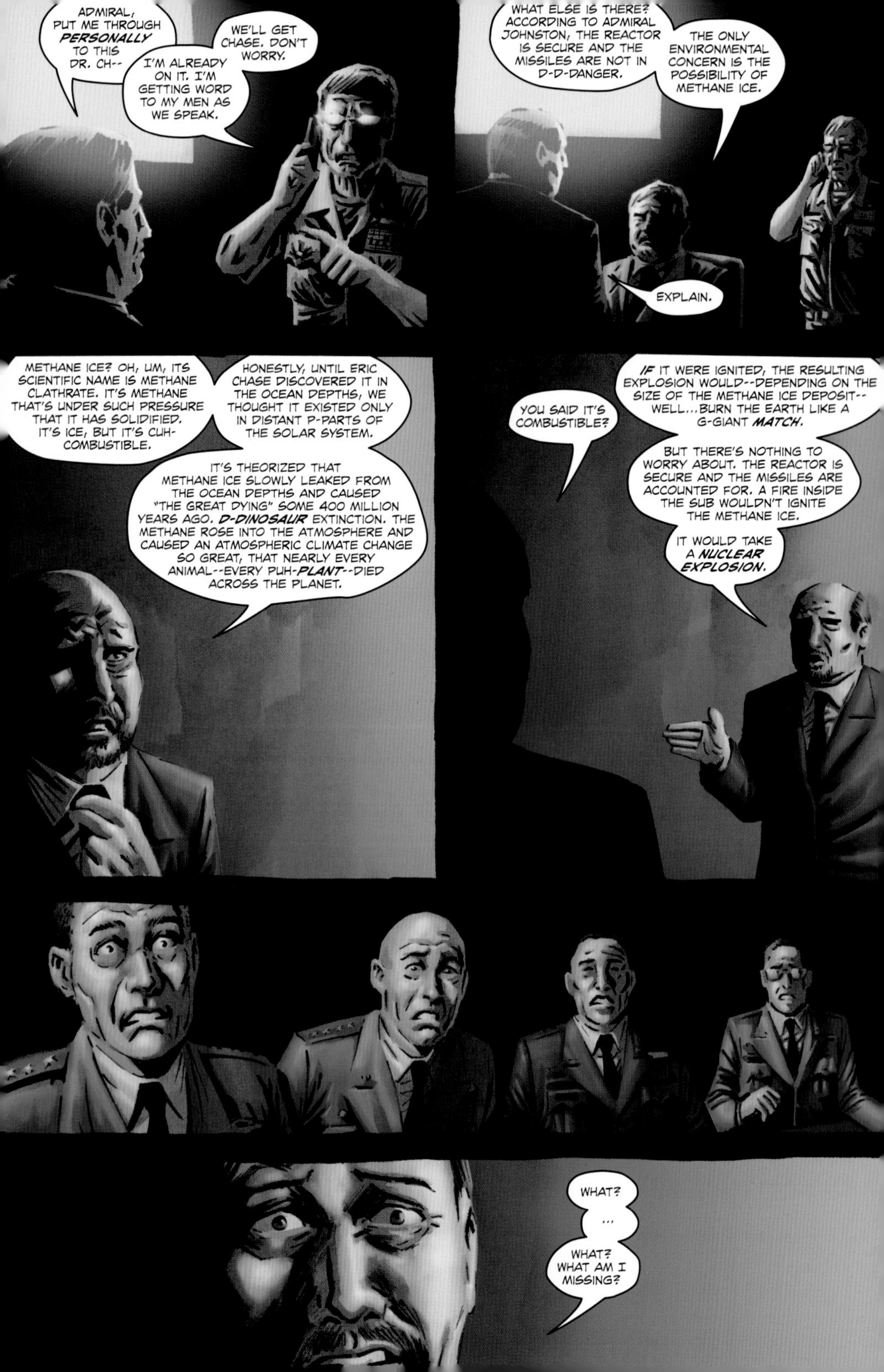
ADMIRAL, PUT ME THROUGH PERSONALLY TO THIS DR. CH--
WE'LL GET CHASE. DON'T WORRY.
I'M ALREADY ON IT. I'M GETTING WORD TO MY MEN AS WE SPEAK.
WHAT ELSE IS THERE? ACCORDING TO ADMIRAL JOHNSTON, THE REACTOR IS SECURE AND THE MISSILES ARE NOT IN D-D-DANGER.
THE ONLY ENVIRONMENTAL CONCERN IS THE POSSIBILITY OF METHANE ICE.
EXPLAIN.
METHANE ICE? OH, UM, ITS SCIENTIFIC NAME IS METHANE CLATHRATE. IT'S METHANE THAT'S UNDER SUCH PRESSURE THAT IT HAS SOLIDIFIED. IT'S ICE, BUT IT'S CUH-COMBUSTIBLE.
HONESTLY, UNTIL ERIC CHASE DISCOVERED IT IN THE OCEAN DEPTHS, WE THOUGHT IT EXISTED ONLY IN DISTANT P-PARTS OF THE SOLAR SYSTEM.
IT'S THEORIZED THAT METHANE ICE SLOWLY LEAKED FROM THE OCEAN DEPTHS AND CAUSED "THE GREAT DYING" SOME 400 MILLION YEARS AGO. D-DINOSAUR EXTINCTION. THE METHANE ROSE INTO THE ATMOSPHERE AND CAUSED AN ATMOSPHERIC CLIMATE CHANGE SO GREAT, THAT NEARLY EVERY ANIMAL--EVERY PUH-PLANT--DIED ACROSS THE PLANET.
YOU SAID IT'S COMBUSTIBLE?
IF IT WERE IGNITED, THE RESULTING EXPLOSION WOULD--DEPENDING ON THE SIZE OF THE METHANE ICE DEPOSIT--WELL...BURN THE EARTH LIKE A G-GIANT MATCH.
BUT THERE'S NOTHING TO WORRY ABOUT. THE REACTOR IS SECURE AND THE MISSILES ARE ACCOUNTED FOR. A FIRE INSIDE THE SUB WOULDN'T IGNITE THE METHANE ICE.
IT WOULD TAKE A NUCLEAR EXPLOSION.
WHAT?
...
WHAT? WHAT AM I MISSING?

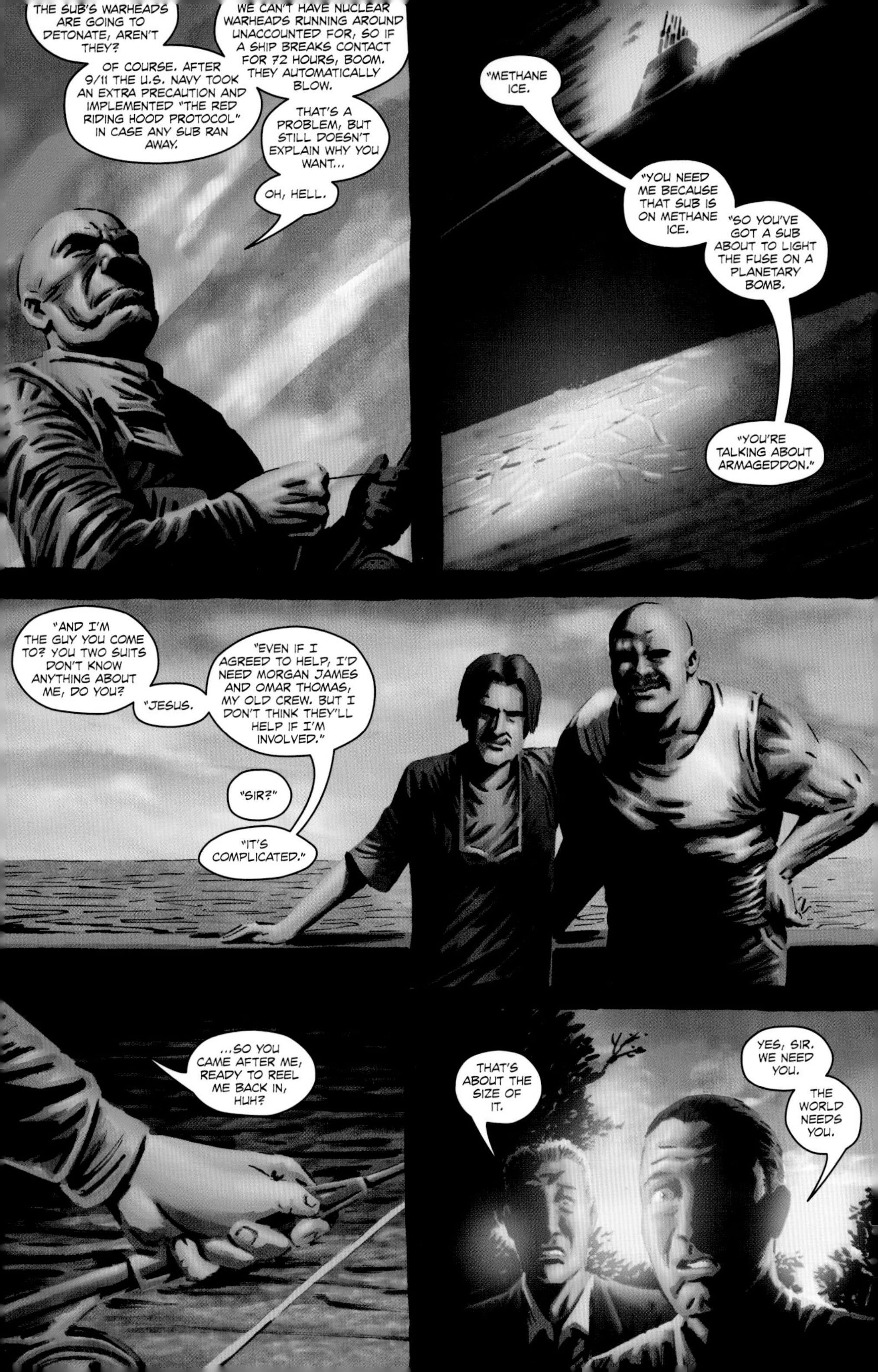
THE SUB'S WARHEADS ARE GOING TO DETONATE, AREN'T THEY?
OF COURSE. AFTER 9/11 THE U.S. NAVY TOOK AN EXTRA PRECAUTION AND IMPLEMENTED "THE RED RIDING HOOD PROTOCOL" IN CASE ANY SUB RAN AWAY.
WE CAN'T HAVE NUCLEAR WARHEADS RUNNING AROUND UNACCOUNTED FOR, SO IF A SHIP BREAKS CONTACT FOR 72 HOURS, BOOM. THEY AUTOMATICALLY BLOW.
THAT'S A PROBLEM, BUT STILL DOESN'T EXPLAIN WHY YOU WANT...
OH, HELL.
"METHANE ICE.
"YOU NEED ME BECAUSE THAT SUB IS ON METHANE ICE.
"SO YOU'VE GOT A SUB ABOUT TO LIGHT THE FUSE ON A PLANETARY BOMB.
"YOU'RE TALKING ABOUT ARMAGEDDON."
"AND I'M THE GUY YOU COME TO? YOU TWO SUITS DON'T KNOW ANYTHING ABOUT ME, DO YOU?
"JESUS.
"EVEN IF I AGREED TO HELP, I'D NEED MORGAN JAMES AND OMAR THOMAS, MY OLD CREW. BUT I DON'T THINK THEY'LL HELP IF I'M INVOLVED."
"SIR?"
"IT'S COMPLICATED."
...SO YOU CAME AFTER ME, READY TO REEL ME BACK IN, HUH?
THAT'S ABOUT THE SIZE OF IT.
YES, SIR. WE NEED YOU.
THE WORLD NEEDS YOU.

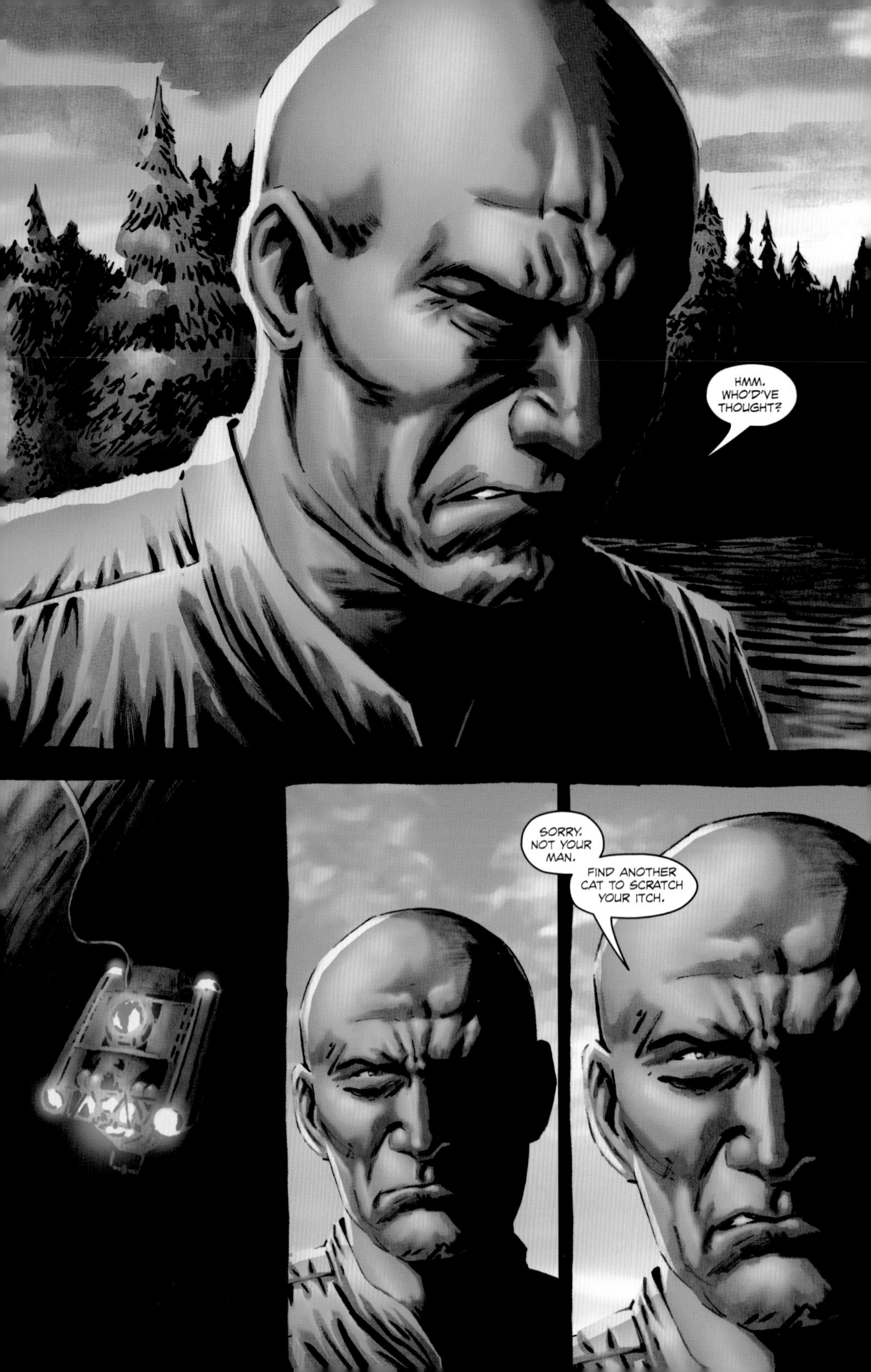
HMM. WHO'D'VE THOUGHT?
SORRY. NOT YOUR MAN.
FIND ANOTHER CAT TO SCRATCH YOUR ITCH.

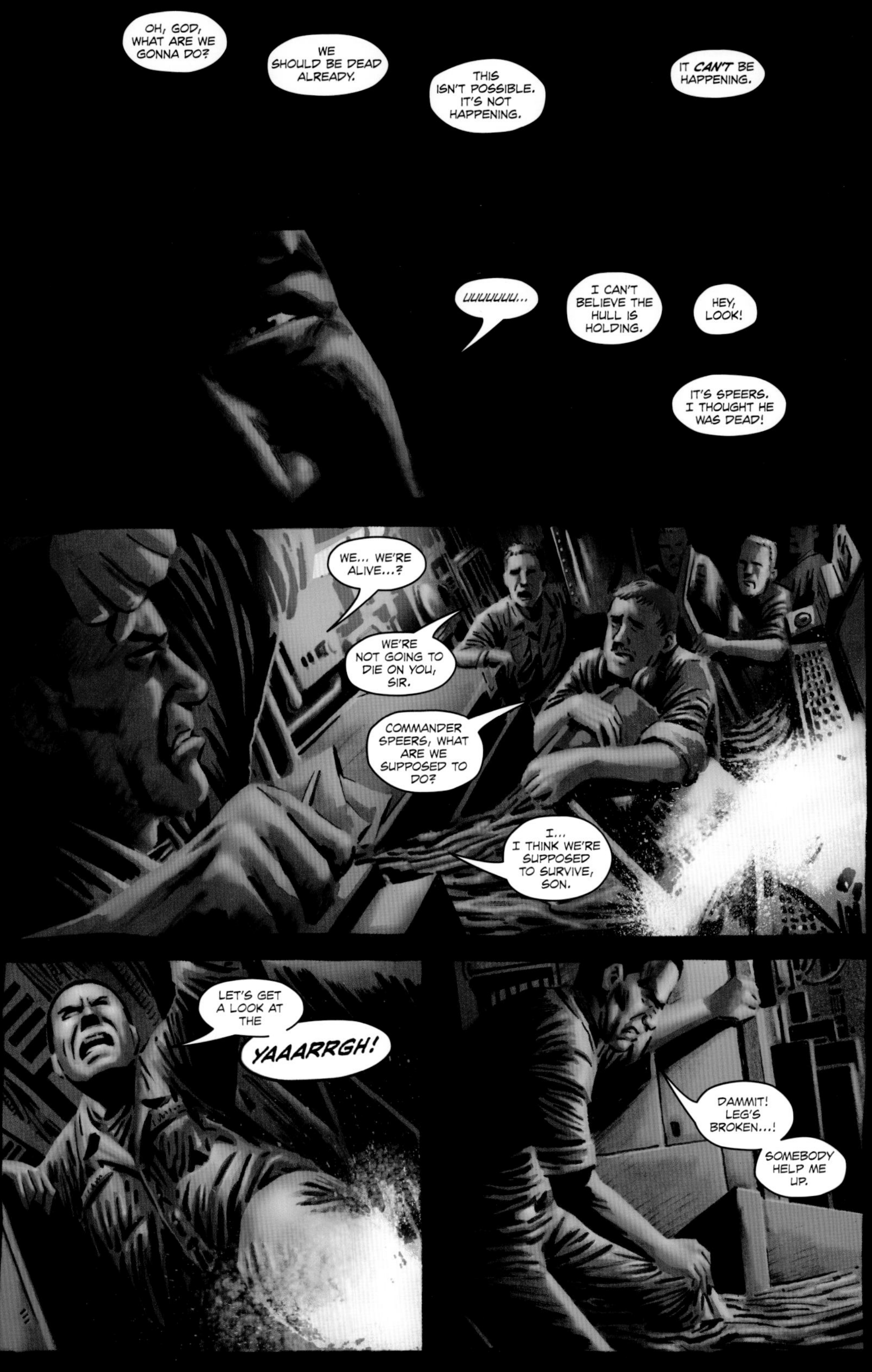
OH, GOD, WHAT ARE WE GONNA DO?
WE SHOULD BE DEAD ALREADY.
THIS ISN'T POSSIBLE. IT'S NOT HAPPENING.
IT *CAN'T* BE HAPPENING.
*UUUUUUU...*
I CAN'T BELIEVE THE HULL IS HOLDING.
HEY, LOOK!
IT'S SPEERS. I THOUGHT HE WAS DEAD!
WE... WE'RE ALIVE...?
WE'RE NOT GOING TO DIE ON YOU, SIR.
COMMANDER SPEERS, WHAT ARE WE SUPPOSED TO DO?
I... I THINK WE'RE SUPPOSED TO SURVIVE, SON.
LET'S GET A LOOK AT THE
*YAAARRGH!*
DAMMIT! LEG'S BROKEN...!
SOMEBODY HELP ME UP.

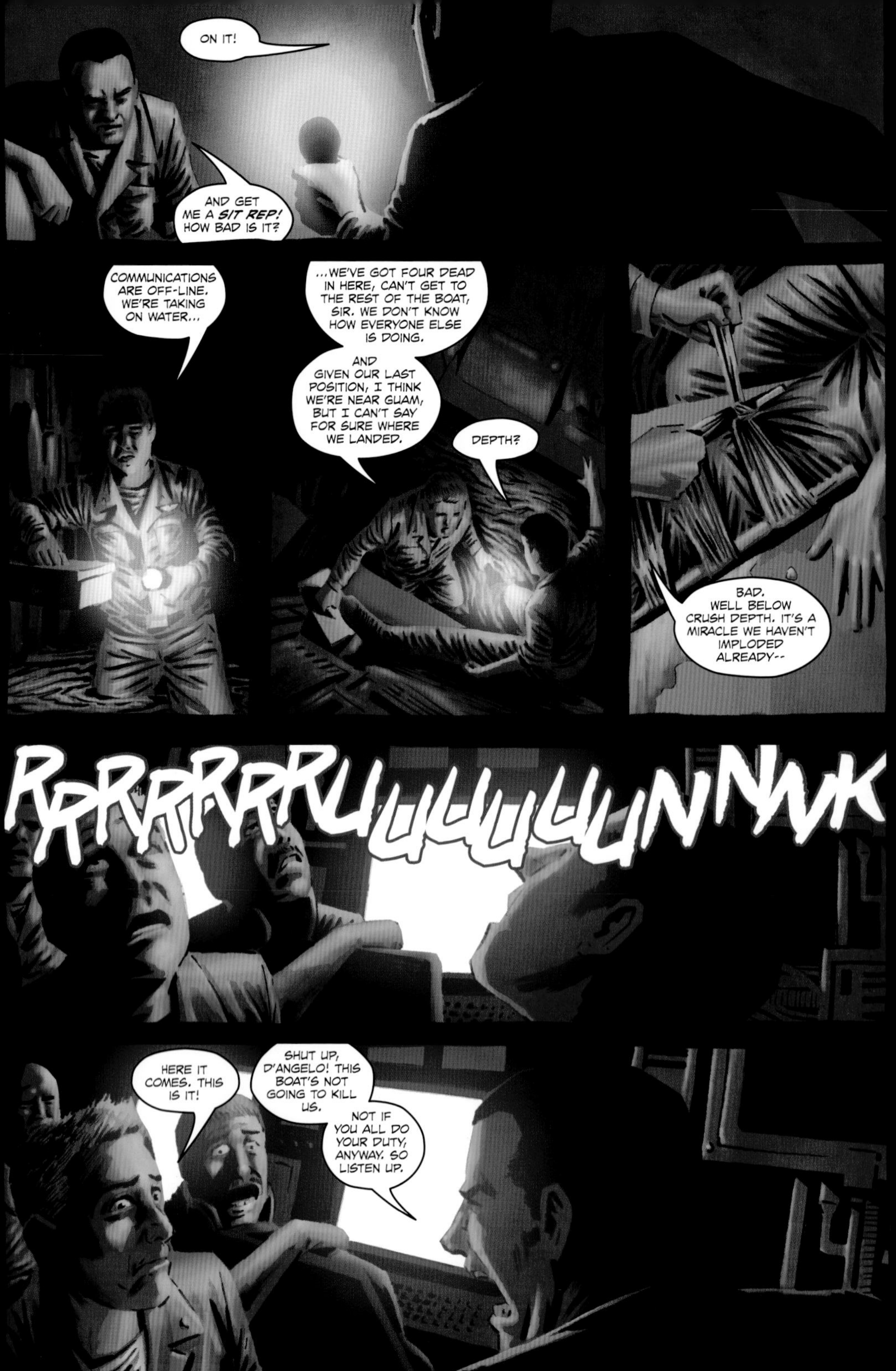
ON IT!
AND GET ME A SIT REP! HOW BAD IS IT?
COMMUNICATIONS ARE OFF-LINE. WE'RE TAKING ON WATER...
...WE'VE GOT FOUR DEAD IN HERE, CAN'T GET TO THE REST OF THE BOAT, SIR. WE DON'T KNOW HOW EVERYONE ELSE IS DOING.
AND GIVEN OUR LAST POSITION, I THINK WE'RE NEAR GUAM, BUT I CAN'T SAY FOR SURE WHERE WE LANDED.
DEPTH?
BAD. WELL BELOW CRUSH DEPTH. IT'S A MIRACLE WE HAVEN'T IMPLODED ALREADY--
RRRRRRUUUUUUNNWK
HERE IT COMES. THIS IS IT!
SHUT UP, D'ANGELO! THIS BOAT'S NOT GOING TO KILL US.
NOT IF YOU ALL DO YOUR DUTY, ANYWAY. SO LISTEN UP.

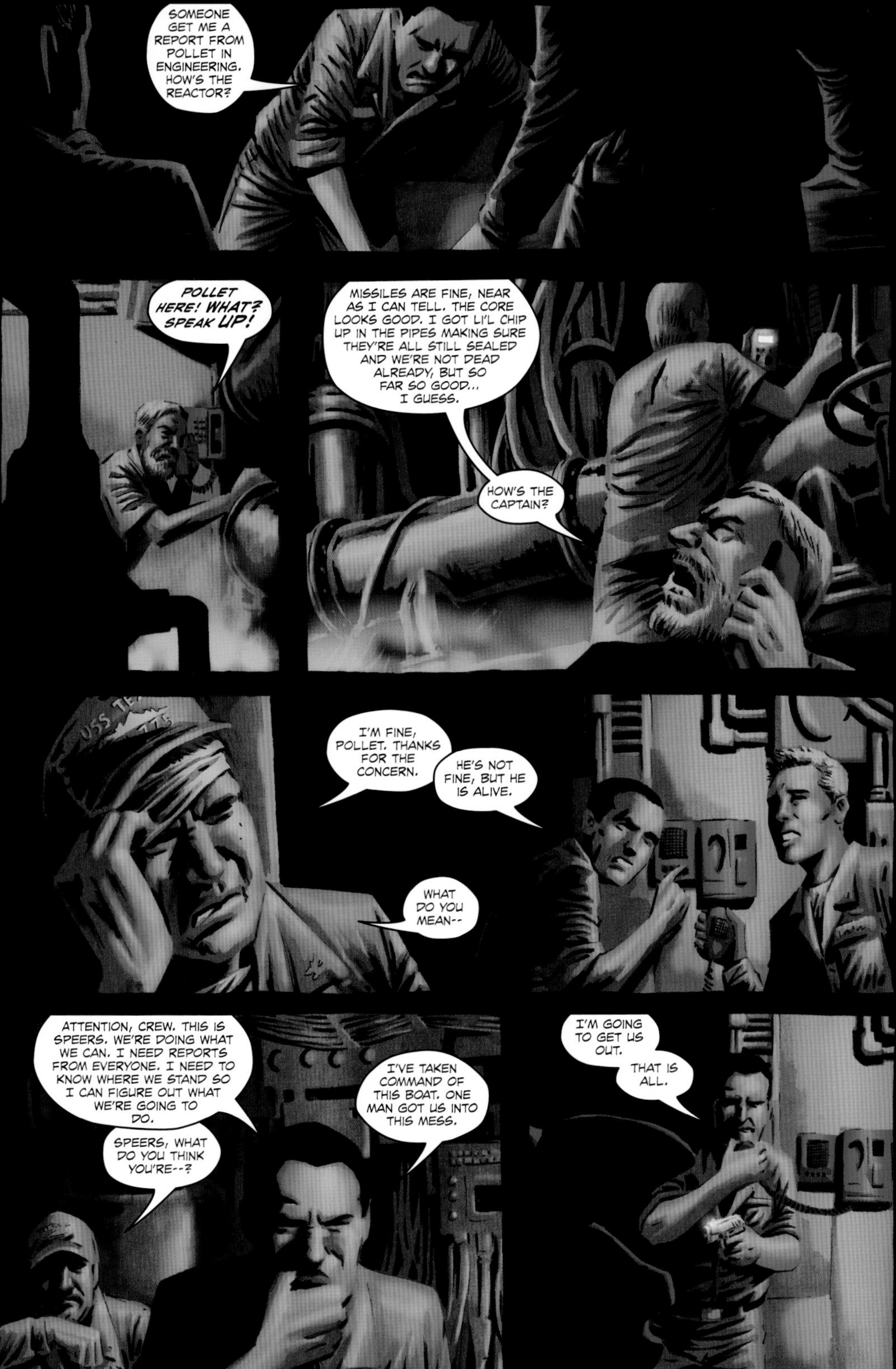
SOMEONE GET ME A REPORT FROM POLLET IN ENGINEERING. HOW'S THE REACTOR?
POLLET HERE! WHAT? SPEAK UP!
MISSILES ARE FINE, NEAR AS I CAN TELL. THE CORE LOOKS GOOD. I GOT LI'L CHIP UP IN THE PIPES MAKING SURE THEY'RE ALL STILL SEALED AND WE'RE NOT DEAD ALREADY, BUT SO FAR SO GOOD... I GUESS.
HOW'S THE CAPTAIN?
I'M FINE, POLLET. THANKS FOR THE CONCERN.
HE'S NOT FINE, BUT HE IS ALIVE.
WHAT DO YOU MEAN--
ATTENTION, CREW. THIS IS SPEERS. WE'RE DOING WHAT WE CAN. I NEED REPORTS FROM EVERYONE. I NEED TO KNOW WHERE WE STAND SO I CAN FIGURE OUT WHAT WE'RE GOING TO DO.
SPEERS, WHAT DO YOU THINK YOU'RE--?
I'VE TAKEN COMMAND OF THIS BOAT. ONE MAN GOT US INTO THIS MESS.
I'M GOING TO GET US OUT.
THAT IS ALL.

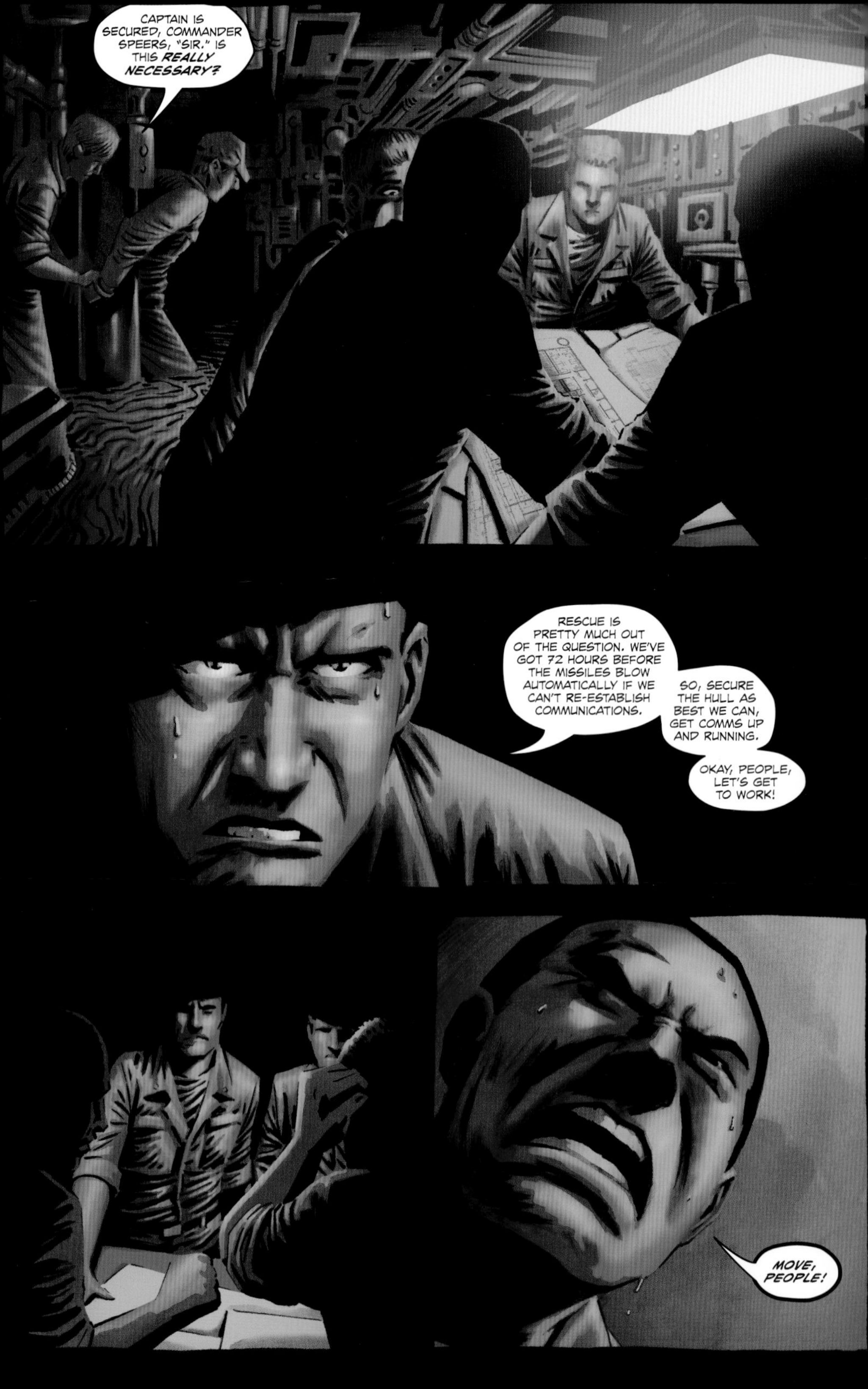
CAPTAIN IS SECURED, COMMANDER SPEERS, "SIR." IS THIS REALLY NECESSARY?
RESCUE IS PRETTY MUCH OUT OF THE QUESTION. WE'VE GOT 72 HOURS BEFORE THE MISSILES BLOW AUTOMATICALLY IF WE CAN'T RE-ESTABLISH COMMUNICATIONS.
SO, SECURE THE HULL AS BEST WE CAN, GET COMMS UP AND RUNNING.
OKAY, PEOPLE, LET'S GET TO WORK!
MOVE, PEOPLE!

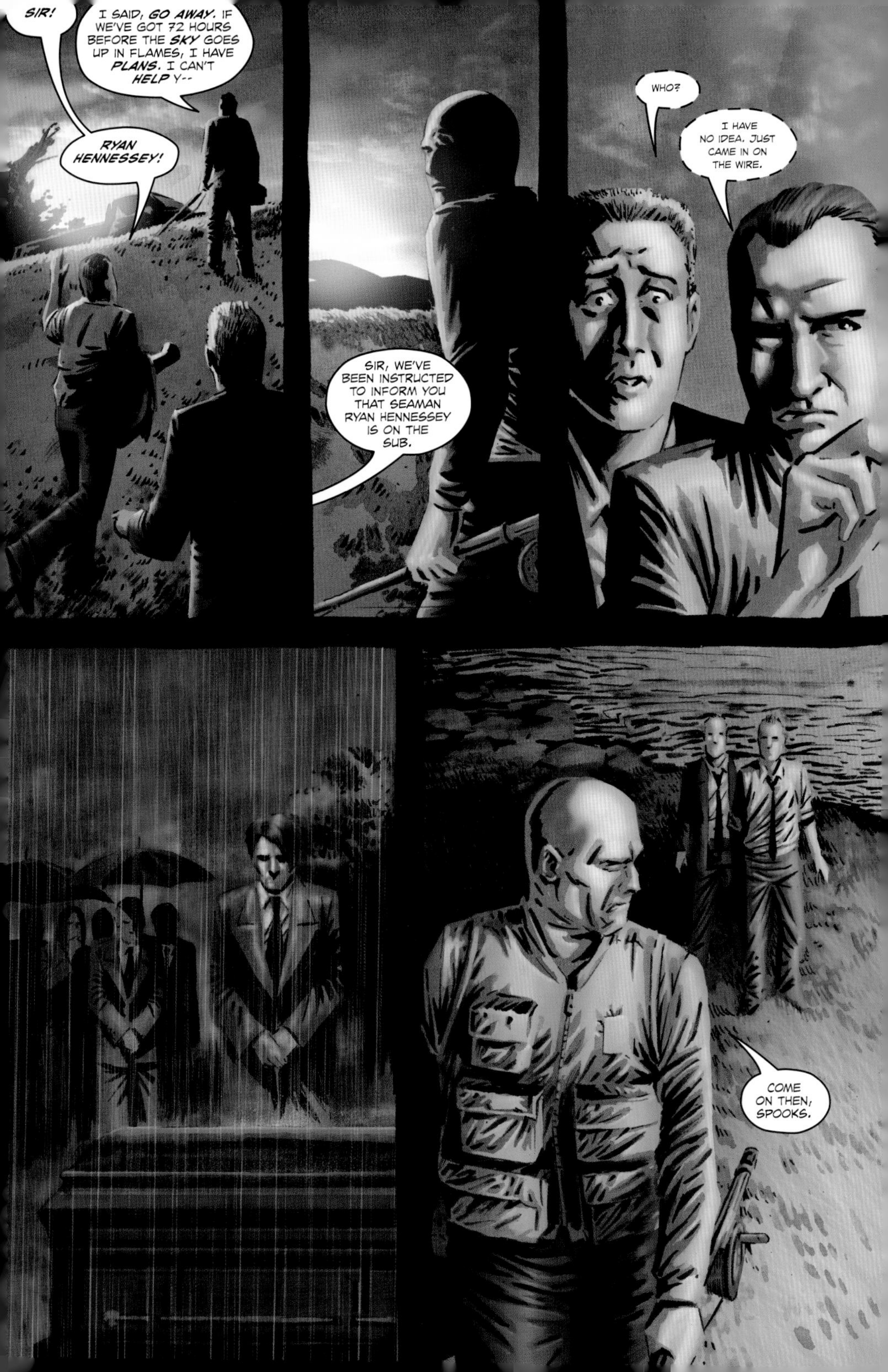
SIR!
I SAID, GO AWAY. IF WE'VE GOT 72 HOURS BEFORE THE SKY GOES UP IN FLAMES, I HAVE PLANS. I CAN'T HELP Y--
RYAN HENNESSEY!
SIR, WE'VE BEEN INSTRUCTED TO INFORM YOU THAT SEAMAN RYAN HENNESSEY IS ON THE SUB.
WHO?
I HAVE NO IDEA. JUST CAME IN ON THE WIRE.
COME ON THEN, SPOOKS.

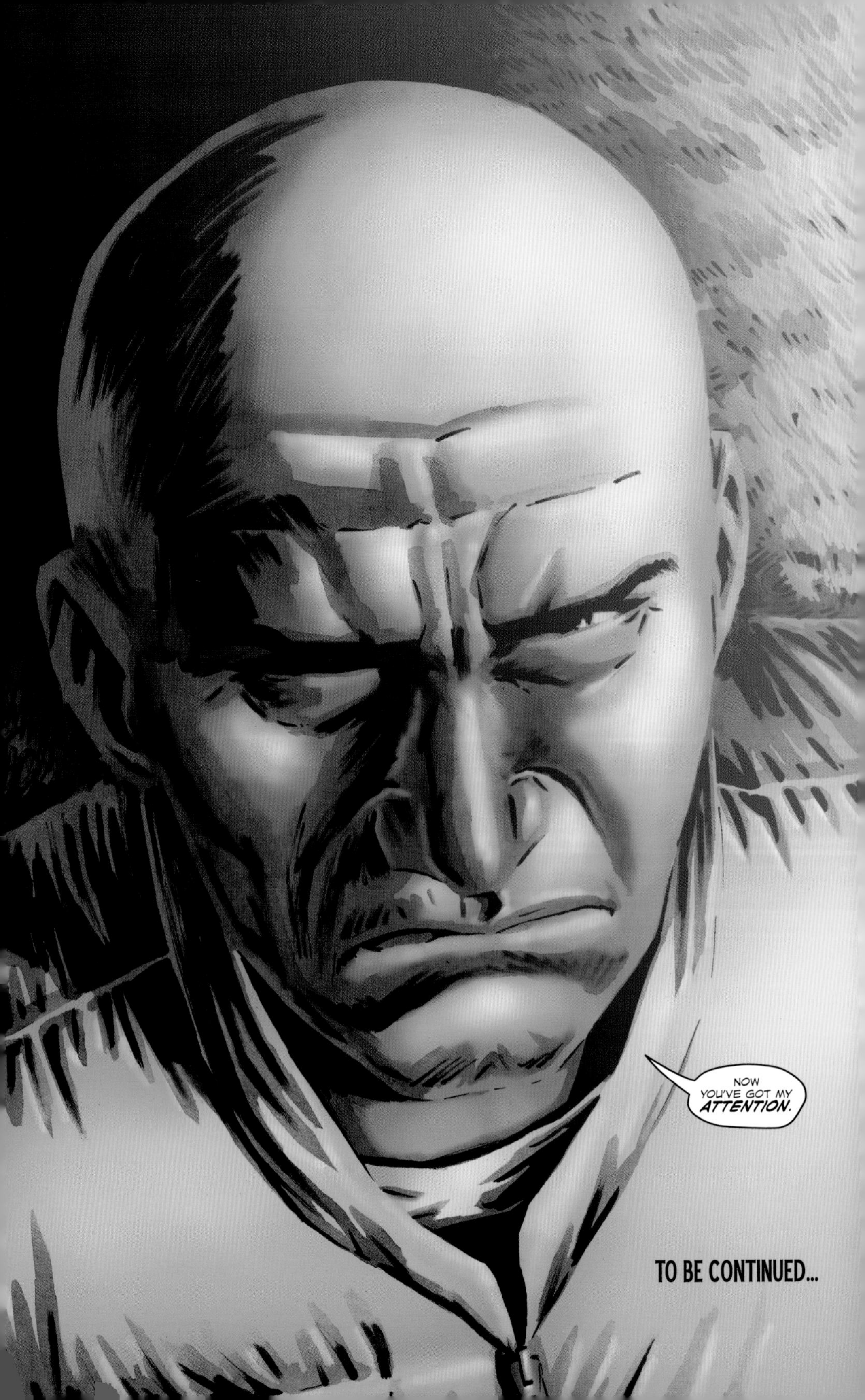
NOW YOU'VE GOT MY ATTENTION.
TO BE CONTINUED...

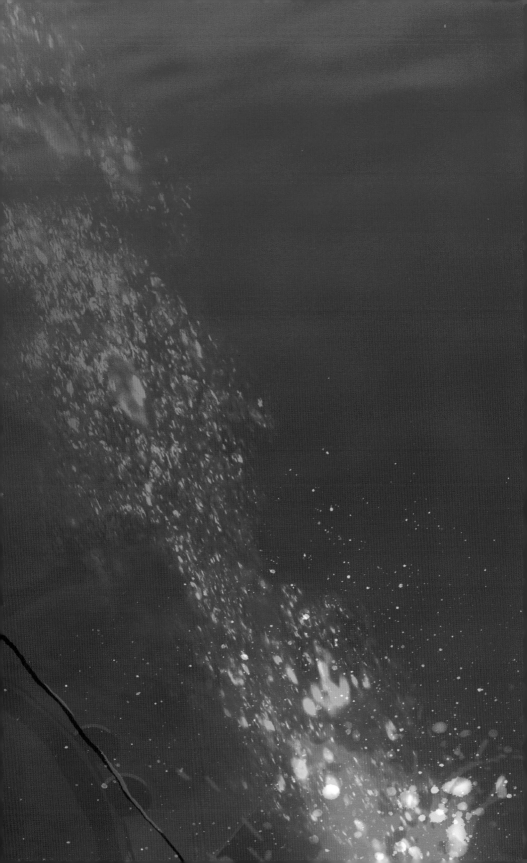

# CHAPTER 2

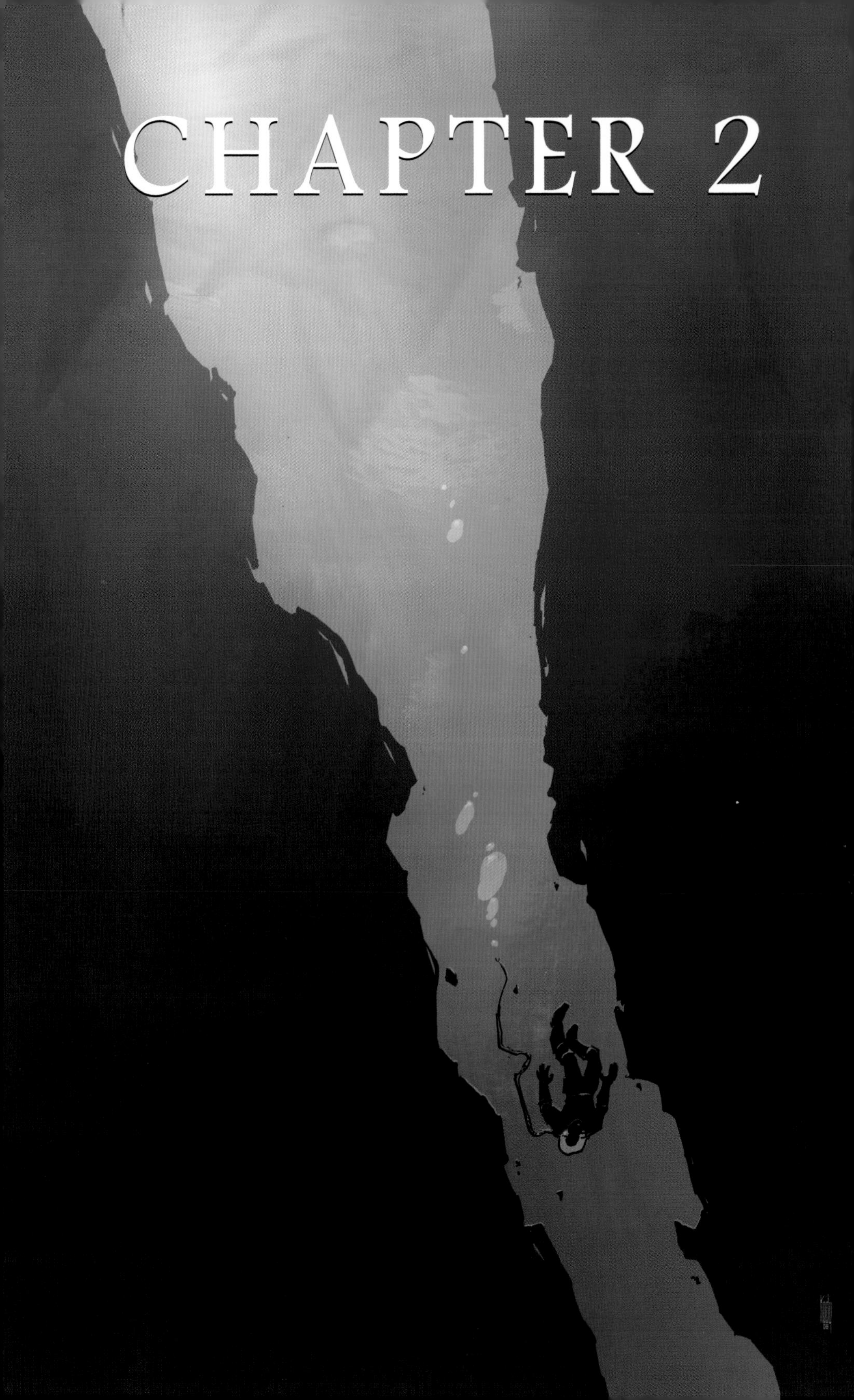

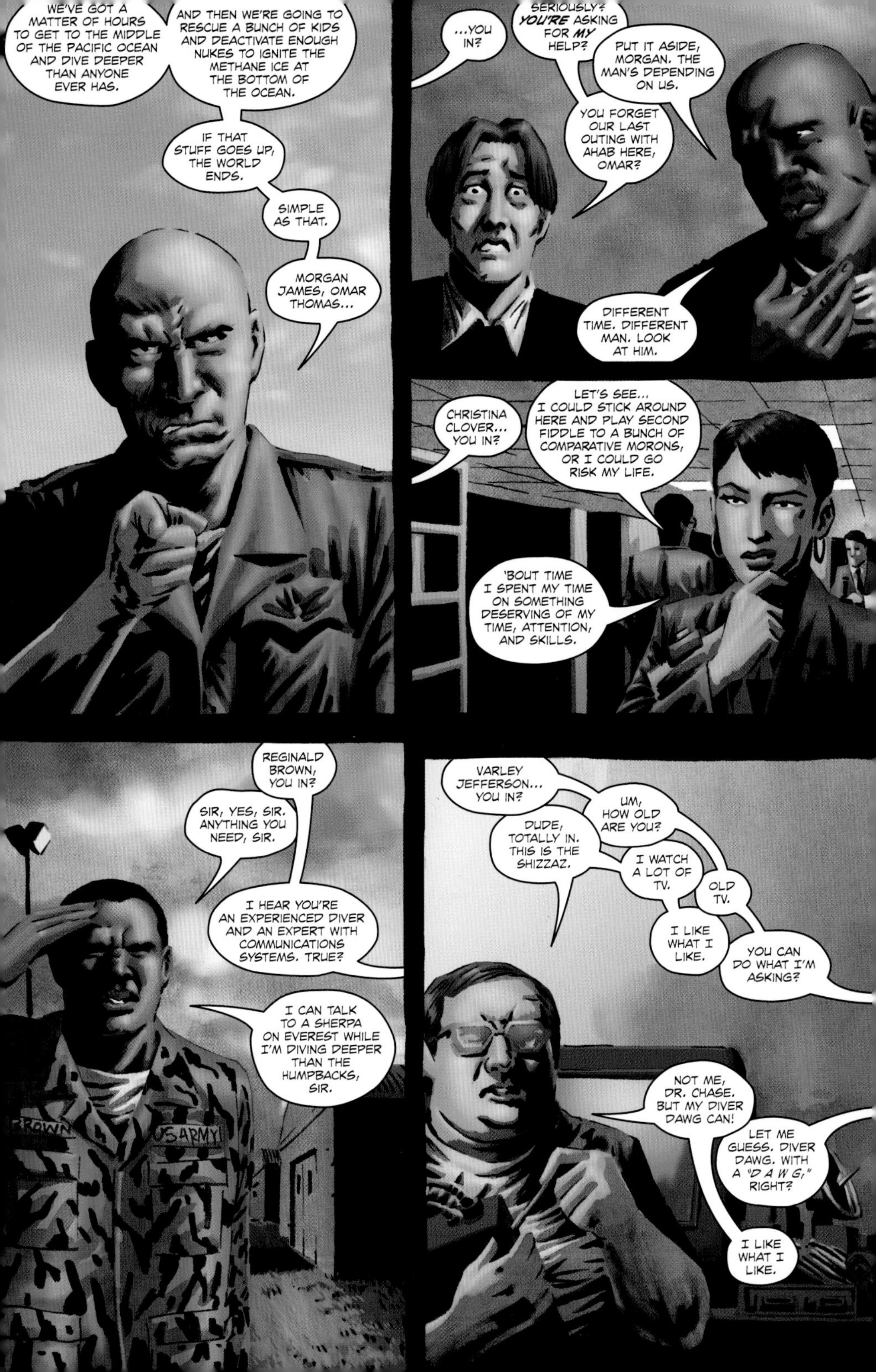
WE'VE GOT A MATTER OF HOURS TO GET TO THE MIDDLE OF THE PACIFIC OCEAN AND DIVE DEEPER THAN ANYONE EVER HAS.
AND THEN WE'RE GOING TO RESCUE A BUNCH OF KIDS AND DEACTIVATE ENOUGH NUKES TO IGNITE THE METHANE ICE AT THE BOTTOM OF THE OCEAN.
IF THAT STUFF GOES UP, THE WORLD ENDS.
SIMPLE AS THAT.
MORGAN JAMES, OMAR THOMAS...
...YOU IN?
SERIOUSLY? ***YOU'RE*** ASKING FOR ***MY*** HELP?
PUT IT ASIDE, MORGAN. THE MAN'S DEPENDING ON US.
YOU FORGET OUR LAST OUTING WITH AHAB HERE, OMAR?
DIFFERENT TIME. DIFFERENT MAN. LOOK AT HIM.
CHRISTINA CLOVER... YOU IN?
LET'S SEE... I COULD STICK AROUND HERE AND PLAY SECOND FIDDLE TO A BUNCH OF COMPARATIVE MORONS, OR I COULD GO RISK MY LIFE.
'BOUT TIME I SPENT MY TIME ON SOMETHING DESERVING OF MY TIME, ATTENTION, AND SKILLS.
REGINALD BROWN, YOU IN?
SIR, YES, SIR. ANYTHING YOU NEED, SIR.
I HEAR YOU'RE AN EXPERIENCED DIVER AND AN EXPERT WITH COMMUNICATIONS SYSTEMS. TRUE?
I CAN TALK TO A SHERPA ON EVEREST WHILE I'M DIVING DEEPER THAN THE HUMPBACKS, SIR.
BROWN
US ARMY
VARLEY JEFFERSON... YOU IN?
DUDE, TOTALLY IN. THIS IS THE SHIZZAZ.
UM, HOW OLD ARE YOU?
I WATCH A LOT OF TV.
OLD TV.
I LIKE WHAT I LIKE.
YOU CAN DO WHAT I'M ASKING?
NOT ME, DR. CHASE. BUT MY DIVER DAWG CAN!
LET ME GUESS. DIVER DAWG. WITH A "D A W G," RIGHT?
I LIKE WHAT I LIKE.

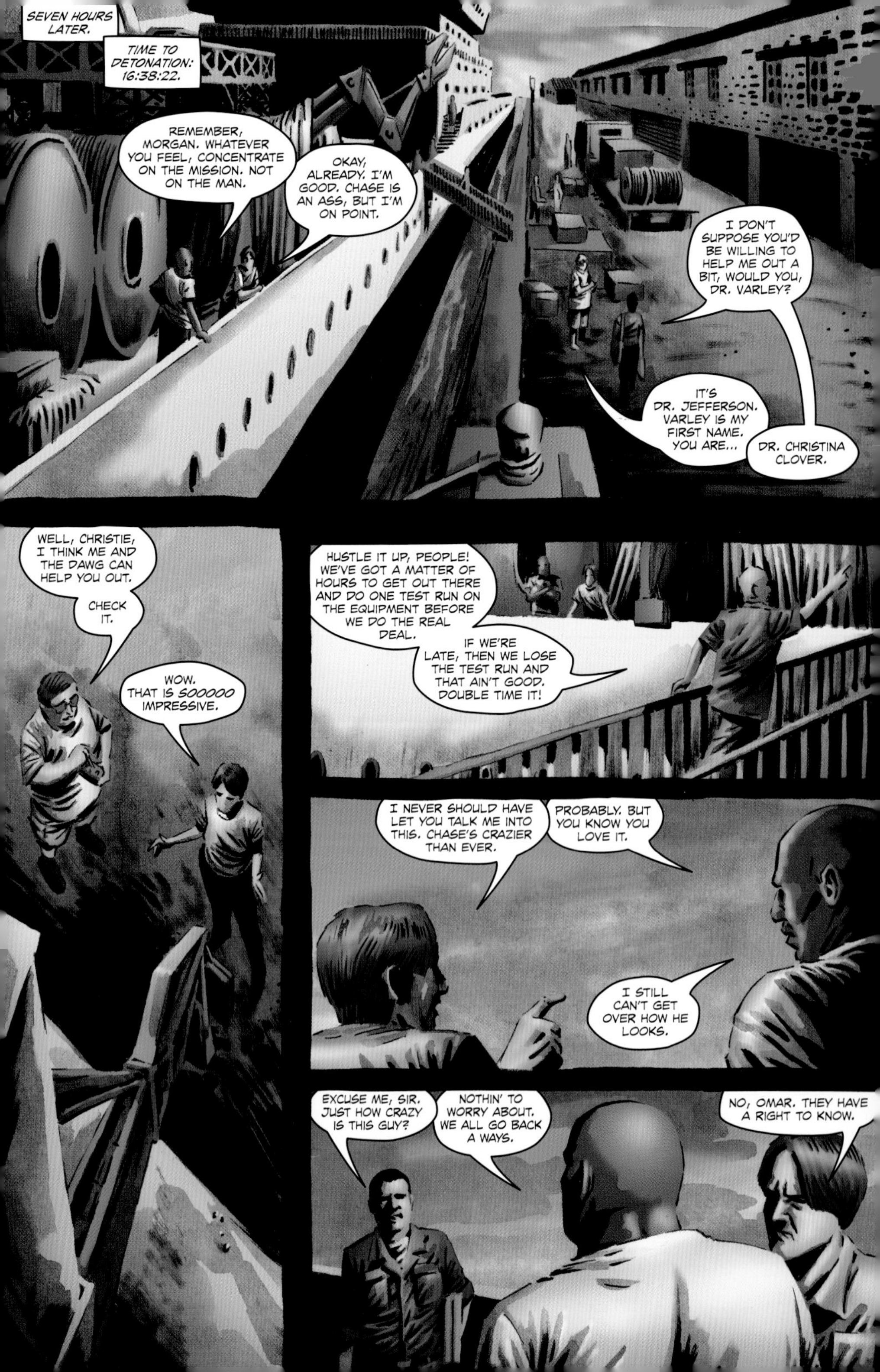
SEVEN HOURS LATER.
TIME TO DETONATION: 16:38:22.
REMEMBER, MORGAN. WHATEVER YOU FEEL, CONCENTRATE ON THE MISSION. NOT ON THE MAN.
OKAY, ALREADY. I'M GOOD. CHASE IS AN ASS, BUT I'M ON POINT.
I DON'T SUPPOSE YOU'D BE WILLING TO HELP ME OUT A BIT, WOULD YOU, DR. VARLEY?
IT'S DR. JEFFERSON. VARLEY IS MY FIRST NAME. YOU ARE...
DR. CHRISTINA CLOVER.
WELL, CHRISTIE, I THINK ME AND THE DAWG CAN HELP YOU OUT.
CHECK IT.
WOW. THAT IS *SOOOOO* IMPRESSIVE.
HUSTLE IT UP, PEOPLE! WE'VE GOT A MATTER OF HOURS TO GET OUT THERE AND DO ONE TEST RUN ON THE EQUIPMENT BEFORE WE DO THE REAL DEAL.
IF WE'RE LATE, THEN WE LOSE THE TEST RUN AND THAT AIN'T GOOD. DOUBLE TIME IT!
I NEVER SHOULD HAVE LET YOU TALK ME INTO THIS. CHASE'S CRAZIER THAN EVER.
PROBABLY. BUT YOU KNOW YOU LOVE IT.
I STILL CAN'T GET OVER HOW HE LOOKS.
EXCUSE ME, SIR. JUST HOW CRAZY IS THIS GUY?
NOTHIN' TO WORRY ABOUT. WE ALL GO BACK A WAYS.
NO, OMAR. THEY HAVE A RIGHT TO KNOW.

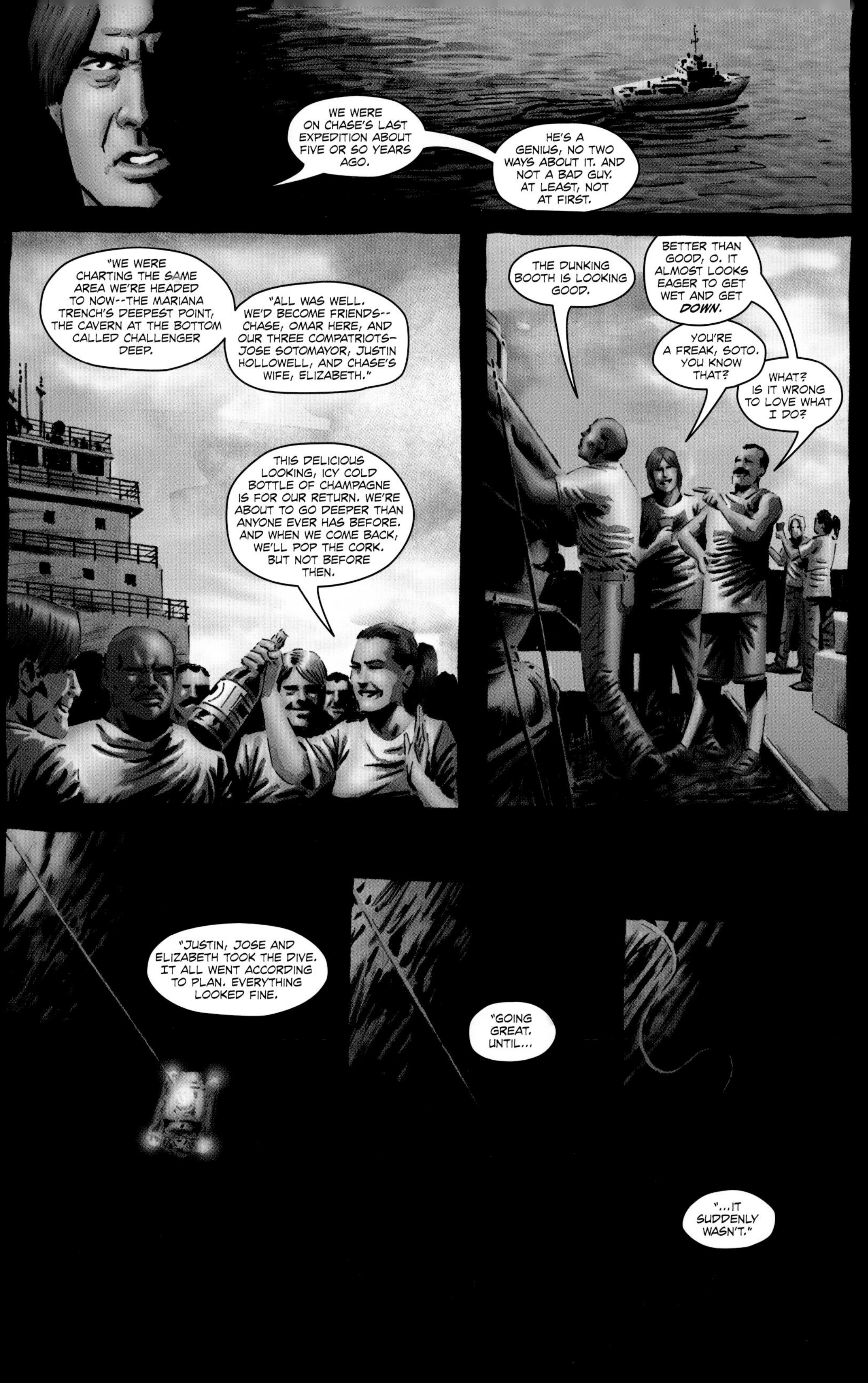

WE WERE ON CHASE'S LAST EXPEDITION ABOUT FIVE OR SO YEARS AGO.
HE'S A GENIUS, NO TWO WAYS ABOUT IT. AND NOT A BAD GUY. AT LEAST, NOT AT FIRST.
"WE WERE CHARTING THE SAME AREA WE'RE HEADED TO NOW--THE MARIANA TRENCH'S DEEPEST POINT, THE CAVERN AT THE BOTTOM CALLED CHALLENGER DEEP.
"ALL WAS WELL. WE'D BECOME FRIENDS--CHASE, OMAR HERE, AND OUR THREE COMPATRIOTS-JOSE SOTOMAYOR, JUSTIN HOLLOWELL, AND CHASE'S WIFE, ELIZABETH."
THIS DELICIOUS LOOKING, ICY COLD BOTTLE OF CHAMPAGNE IS FOR OUR RETURN. WE'RE ABOUT TO GO DEEPER THAN ANYONE EVER HAS BEFORE. AND WHEN WE COME BACK, WE'LL POP THE CORK. BUT NOT BEFORE THEN.
THE DUNKING BOOTH IS LOOKING GOOD.
BETTER THAN GOOD, O. IT ALMOST LOOKS EAGER TO GET WET AND GET ***DOWN***.
YOU'RE A FREAK, SOTO. YOU KNOW THAT?
WHAT? IS IT WRONG TO LOVE WHAT I DO?
"JUSTIN, JOSE AND ELIZABETH TOOK THE DIVE. IT ALL WENT ACCORDING TO PLAN. EVERYTHING LOOKED FINE.
"GOING GREAT. UNTIL...
"...IT SUDDENLY WASN'T."

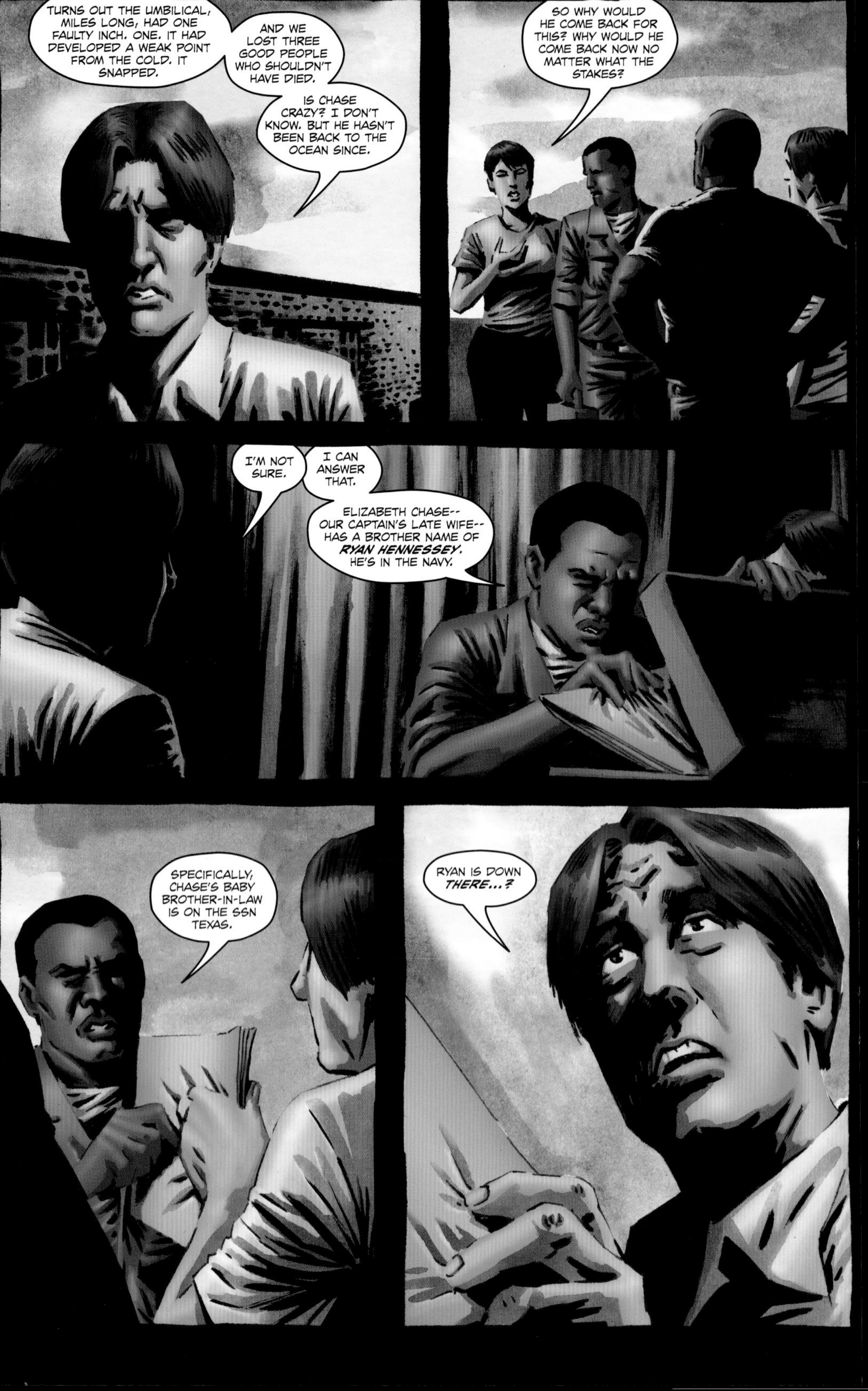
TURNS OUT THE UMBILICAL, MILES LONG, HAD ONE FAULTY INCH. ONE. IT HAD DEVELOPED A WEAK POINT FROM THE COLD. IT SNAPPED.
AND WE LOST THREE GOOD PEOPLE WHO SHOULDN'T HAVE DIED.
IS CHASE CRAZY? I DON'T KNOW. BUT HE HASN'T BEEN BACK TO THE OCEAN SINCE.
SO WHY WOULD HE COME BACK FOR THIS? WHY WOULD HE COME BACK NOW NO MATTER WHAT THE STAKES?
I'M NOT SURE.
I CAN ANSWER THAT.
ELIZABETH CHASE-- OUR CAPTAIN'S LATE WIFE-- HAS A BROTHER NAME OF *RYAN HENNESSEY*. HE'S IN THE NAVY.
SPECIFICALLY, CHASE'S BABY BROTHER-IN-LAW IS ON THE SSN TEXAS.
RYAN IS DOWN *THERE...?*

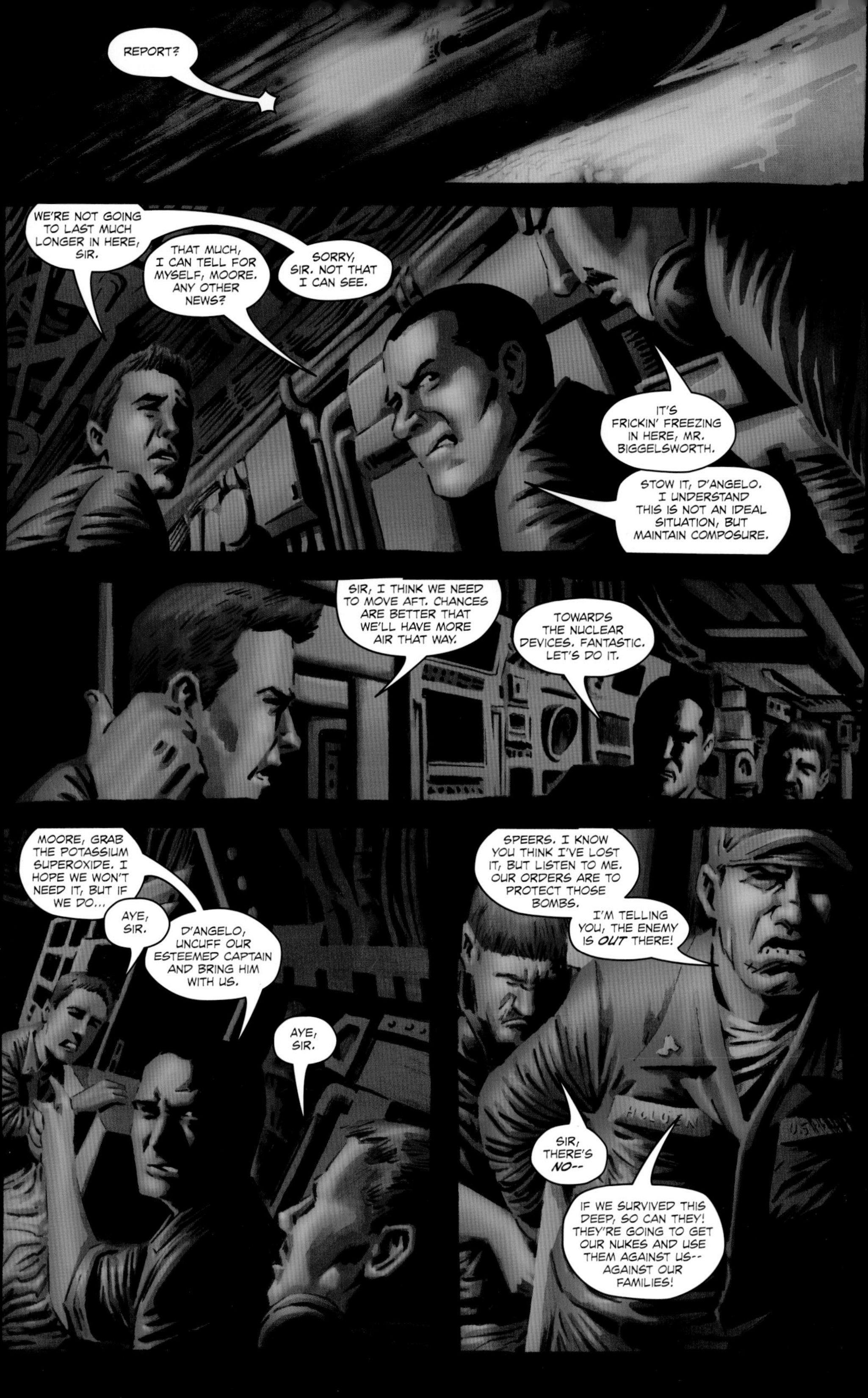
REPORT?
WE'RE NOT GOING TO LAST MUCH LONGER IN HERE, SIR.
THAT MUCH, I CAN TELL FOR MYSELF, MOORE. ANY OTHER NEWS?
SORRY, SIR. NOT THAT I CAN SEE.
IT'S FRICKIN' FREEZING IN HERE, MR. BIGGELSWORTH.
STOW IT, D'ANGELO. I UNDERSTAND THIS IS NOT AN IDEAL SITUATION, BUT MAINTAIN COMPOSURE.
SIR, I THINK WE NEED TO MOVE AFT. CHANCES ARE BETTER THAT WE'LL HAVE MORE AIR THAT WAY.
TOWARDS THE NUCLEAR DEVICES. FANTASTIC. LET'S DO IT.
MOORE, GRAB THE POTASSIUM SUPEROXIDE. I HOPE WE WON'T NEED IT, BUT IF WE DO...
AYE, SIR.
D'ANGELO, UNCUFF OUR ESTEEMED CAPTAIN AND BRING HIM WITH US.
AYE, SIR.
SPEERS. I KNOW YOU THINK I'VE LOST IT, BUT LISTEN TO ME. OUR ORDERS ARE TO PROTECT THOSE BOMBS.
I'M TELLING YOU, THE ENEMY IS *OUT* THERE!
SIR, THERE'S *NO--*
IF WE SURVIVED THIS DEEP, SO CAN THEY! THEY'RE GOING TO GET OUR NUKES AND USE THEM AGAINST US-- AGAINST OUR FAMILIES!

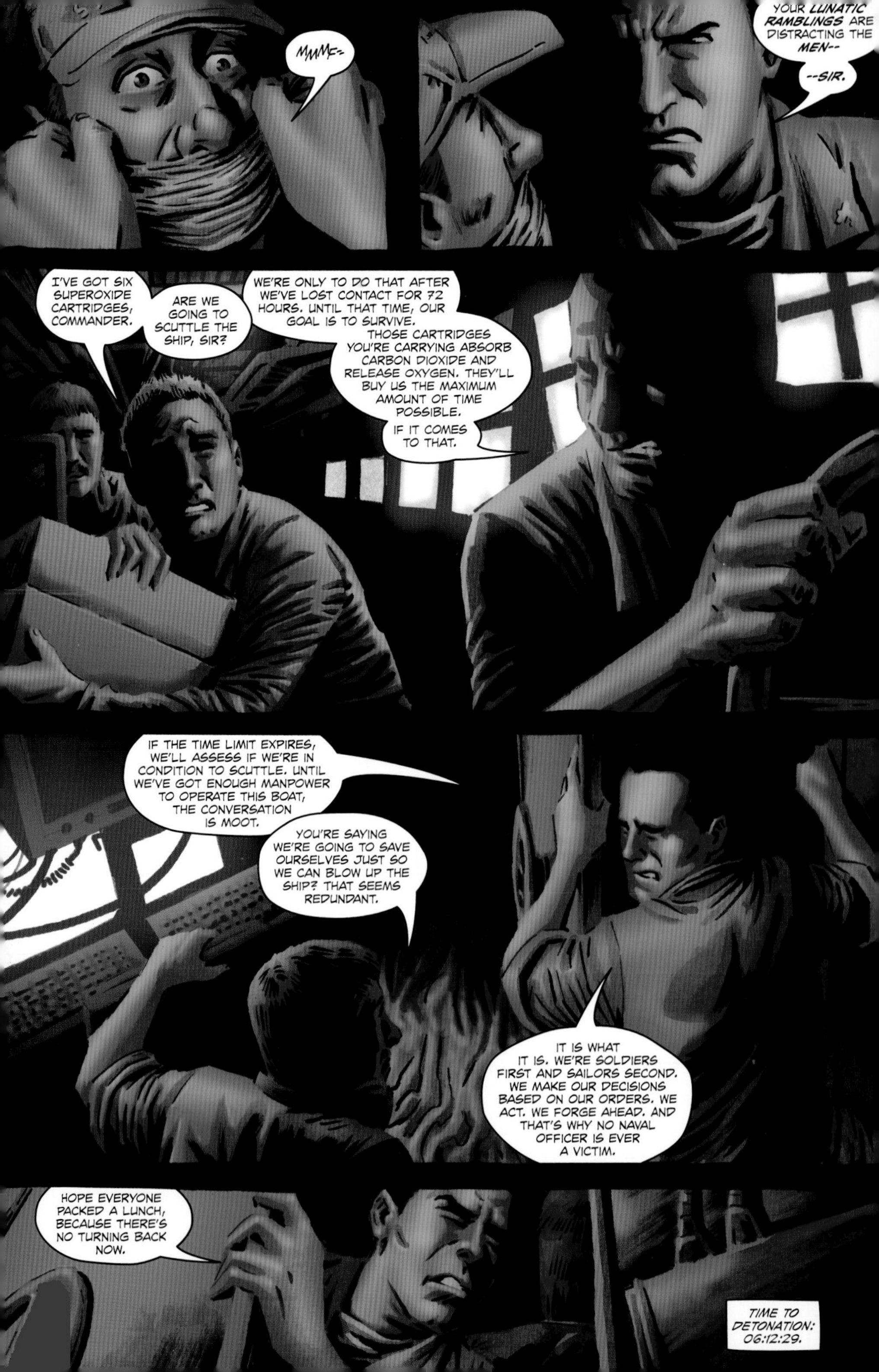
MMMF--
YOUR LUNATIC RAMBLINGS ARE DISTRACTING THE MEN--
--SIR.
I'VE GOT SIX SUPEROXIDE CARTRIDGES, COMMANDER.
ARE WE GOING TO SCUTTLE THE SHIP, SIR?
WE'RE ONLY TO DO THAT AFTER WE'VE LOST CONTACT FOR 72 HOURS. UNTIL THAT TIME, OUR GOAL IS TO SURVIVE.
THOSE CARTRIDGES YOU'RE CARRYING ABSORB CARBON DIOXIDE AND RELEASE OXYGEN. THEY'LL BUY US THE MAXIMUM AMOUNT OF TIME POSSIBLE.
IF IT COMES TO THAT.
IF THE TIME LIMIT EXPIRES, WE'LL ASSESS IF WE'RE IN CONDITION TO SCUTTLE. UNTIL WE'VE GOT ENOUGH MANPOWER TO OPERATE THIS BOAT, THE CONVERSATION IS MOOT.
YOU'RE SAYING WE'RE GOING TO SAVE OURSELVES JUST SO WE CAN BLOW UP THE SHIP? THAT SEEMS REDUNDANT.
IT IS WHAT IT IS. WE'RE SOLDIERS FIRST AND SAILORS SECOND. WE MAKE OUR DECISIONS BASED ON OUR ORDERS. WE ACT. WE FORGE AHEAD. AND THAT'S WHY NO NAVAL OFFICER IS EVER A VICTIM.
HOPE EVERYONE PACKED A LUNCH, BECAUSE THERE'S NO TURNING BACK NOW.
TIME TO DETONATION: 06:12:29.

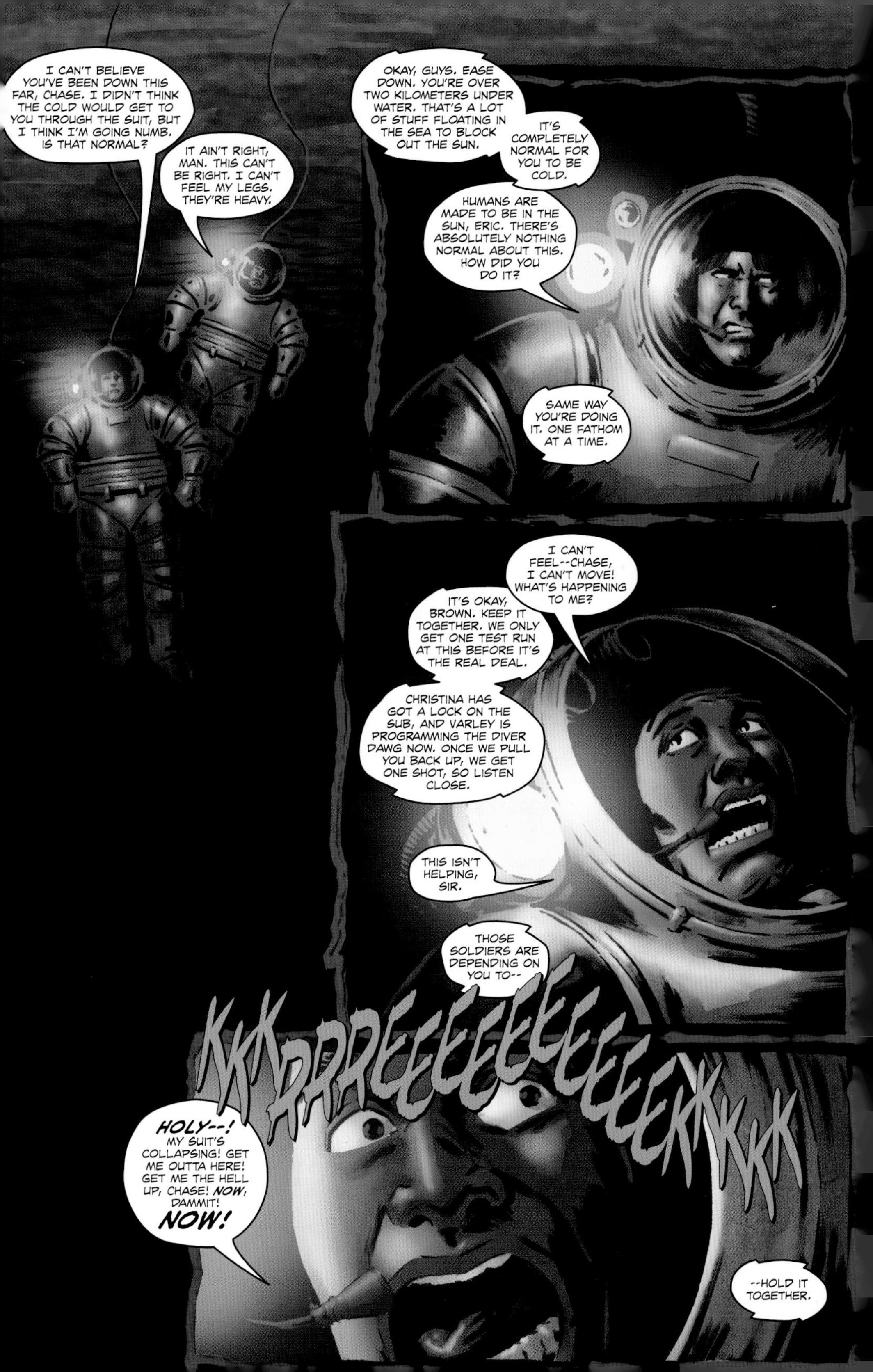
I CAN'T BELIEVE YOU'VE BEEN DOWN THIS FAR, CHASE. I DIDN'T THINK THE COLD WOULD GET TO YOU THROUGH THE SUIT, BUT I THINK I'M GOING NUMB. IS THAT NORMAL?
IT AIN'T RIGHT, MAN. THIS CAN'T BE RIGHT. I CAN'T FEEL MY LEGS. THEY'RE HEAVY.
OKAY, GUYS. EASE DOWN. YOU'RE OVER TWO KILOMETERS UNDER WATER. THAT'S A LOT OF STUFF FLOATING IN THE SEA TO BLOCK OUT THE SUN.
IT'S COMPLETELY NORMAL FOR YOU TO BE COLD.
HUMANS ARE MADE TO BE IN THE SUN, ERIC. THERE'S ABSOLUTELY NOTHING NORMAL ABOUT THIS. HOW DID YOU DO IT?
SAME WAY YOU'RE DOING IT. ONE FATHOM AT A TIME.
I CAN'T FEEL--CHASE, I CAN'T MOVE! WHAT'S HAPPENING TO ME?
IT'S OKAY, BROWN. KEEP IT TOGETHER. WE ONLY GET ONE TEST RUN AT THIS BEFORE IT'S THE REAL DEAL.
CHRISTINA HAS GOT A LOCK ON THE SUB, AND VARLEY IS PROGRAMMING THE DIVER DAWG NOW. ONCE WE PULL YOU BACK UP, WE GET ONE SHOT, SO LISTEN CLOSE.
THIS ISN'T HELPING, SIR.
THOSE SOLDIERS ARE DEPENDING ON YOU TO--
KKKRRREEEEEEEEEEEEEEEEKKKK
HOLY--! MY SUIT'S COLLAPSING! GET ME OUTTA HERE! GET ME THE HELL UP, CHASE! NOW, DAMMIT! NOW!
--HOLD IT TOGETHER.

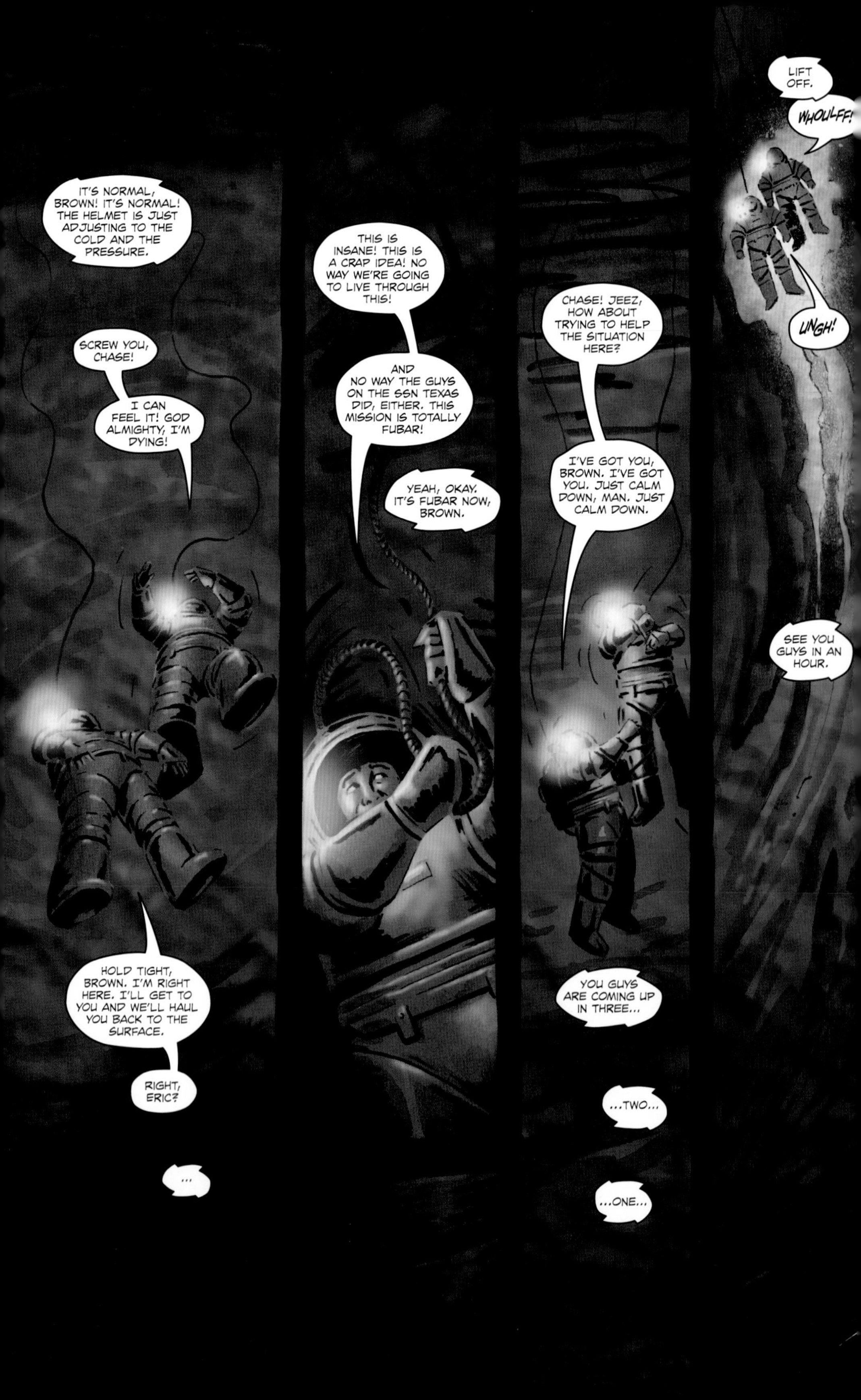
IT'S NORMAL, BROWN! IT'S NORMAL! THE HELMET IS JUST ADJUSTING TO THE COLD AND THE PRESSURE.
SCREW YOU, CHASE!
I CAN FEEL IT! GOD ALMIGHTY, I'M DYING!
HOLD TIGHT, BROWN. I'M RIGHT HERE. I'LL GET TO YOU AND WE'LL HAUL YOU BACK TO THE SURFACE.
RIGHT, ERIC?
...
THIS IS INSANE! THIS IS A CRAP IDEA! NO WAY WE'RE GOING TO LIVE THROUGH THIS!
AND NO WAY THE GUYS ON THE SSN TEXAS DID, EITHER. THIS MISSION IS TOTALLY FUBAR!
YEAH, OKAY. IT'S FUBAR NOW, BROWN.
CHASE! JEEZ, HOW ABOUT TRYING TO HELP THE SITUATION HERE?
I'VE GOT YOU, BROWN. I'VE GOT YOU. JUST CALM DOWN, MAN. JUST CALM DOWN.
YOU GUYS ARE COMING UP IN THREE...
...TWO...
...ONE...
LIFT OFF.
WHOULFF!
UNGH!
SEE YOU GUYS IN AN HOUR.

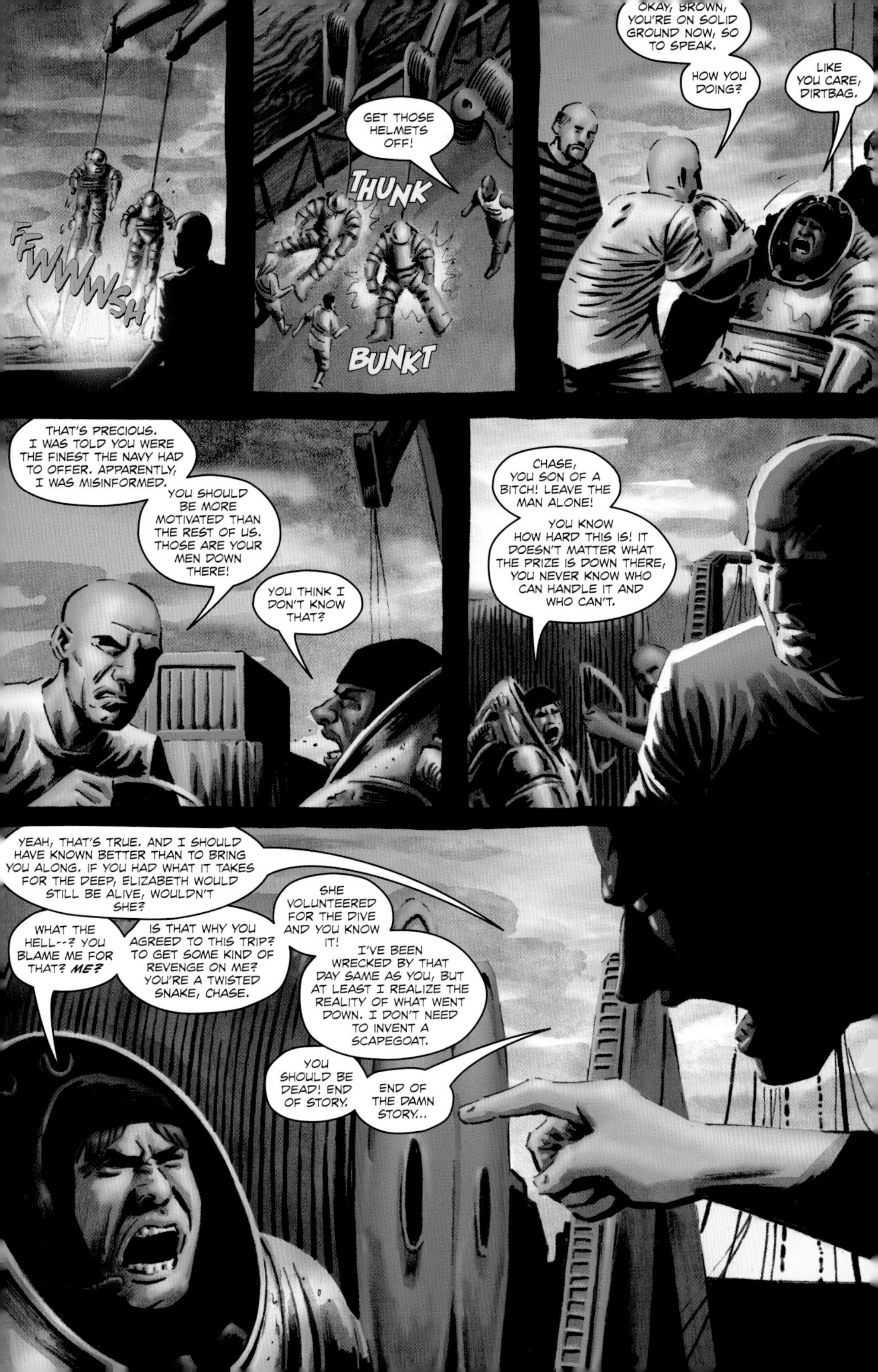
FFWWWNSH
GET THOSE HELMETS OFF!
THUNK
BUNKT
OKAY, BROWN, YOU'RE ON SOLID GROUND NOW, SO TO SPEAK.
HOW YOU DOING?
LIKE YOU CARE, DIRTBAG.
THAT'S PRECIOUS. I WAS TOLD YOU WERE THE FINEST THE NAVY HAD TO OFFER. APPARENTLY, I WAS MISINFORMED.
YOU SHOULD BE MORE MOTIVATED THAN THE REST OF US. THOSE ARE YOUR MEN DOWN THERE!
YOU THINK I DON'T KNOW THAT?
CHASE, YOU SON OF A BITCH! LEAVE THE MAN ALONE!
YOU KNOW HOW HARD THIS IS! IT DOESN'T MATTER WHAT THE PRIZE IS DOWN THERE, YOU NEVER KNOW WHO CAN HANDLE IT AND WHO CAN'T.
YEAH, THAT'S TRUE. AND I SHOULD HAVE KNOWN BETTER THAN TO BRING YOU ALONG. IF YOU HAD WHAT IT TAKES FOR THE DEEP, ELIZABETH WOULD STILL BE ALIVE, WOULDN'T SHE?
WHAT THE HELL--? YOU BLAME ME FOR THAT? ME?
IS THAT WHY YOU AGREED TO THIS TRIP? TO GET SOME KIND OF REVENGE ON ME? YOU'RE A TWISTED SNAKE, CHASE.
SHE VOLUNTEERED FOR THE DIVE AND YOU KNOW IT!
I'VE BEEN WRECKED BY THAT DAY SAME AS YOU, BUT AT LEAST I REALIZE THE REALITY OF WHAT WENT DOWN. I DON'T NEED TO INVENT A SCAPEGOAT.
YOU SHOULD BE DEAD! END OF STORY.
END OF THE DAMN STORY...

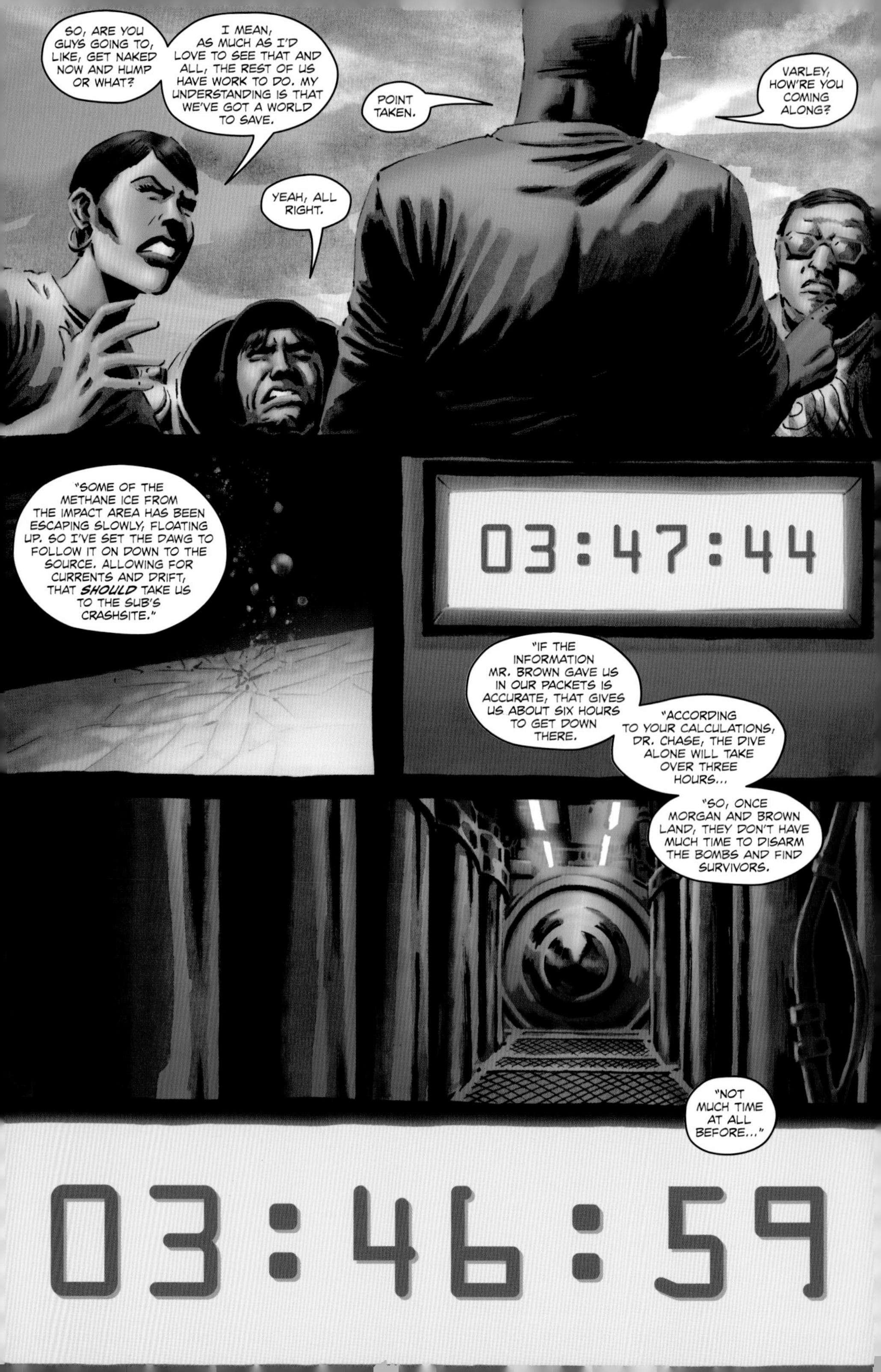
SO, ARE YOU GUYS GOING TO, LIKE, GET NAKED NOW AND HUMP OR WHAT?
I MEAN, AS MUCH AS I'D LOVE TO SEE THAT AND ALL, THE REST OF US HAVE WORK TO DO. MY UNDERSTANDING IS THAT WE'VE GOT A WORLD TO SAVE.
YEAH, ALL RIGHT.
POINT TAKEN.
VARLEY, HOW'RE YOU COMING ALONG?
"SOME OF THE METHANE ICE FROM THE IMPACT AREA HAS BEEN ESCAPING SLOWLY, FLOATING UP. SO I'VE SET THE DAWG TO FOLLOW IT ON DOWN TO THE SOURCE. ALLOWING FOR CURRENTS AND DRIFT, THAT ***SHOULD*** TAKE US TO THE SUB'S CRASHSITE."
03:47:44
"IF THE INFORMATION MR. BROWN GAVE US IN OUR PACKETS IS ACCURATE, THAT GIVES US ABOUT SIX HOURS TO GET DOWN THERE.
"ACCORDING TO YOUR CALCULATIONS, DR. CHASE, THE DIVE ALONE WILL TAKE OVER THREE HOURS...
"SO, ONCE MORGAN AND BROWN LAND, THEY DON'T HAVE MUCH TIME TO DISARM THE BOMBS AND FIND SURVIVORS.
"NOT MUCH TIME AT ALL BEFORE..."
03:46:59

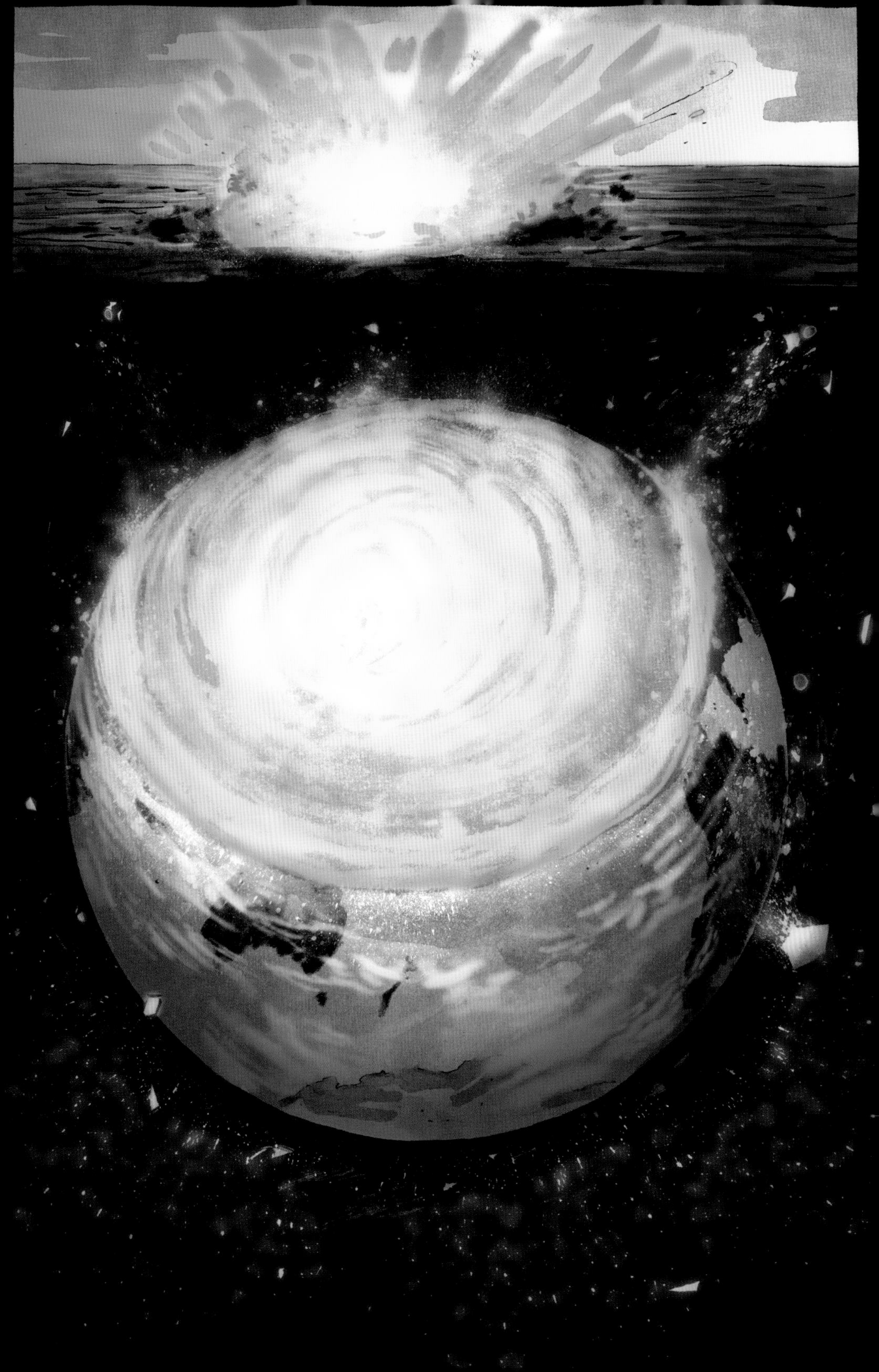

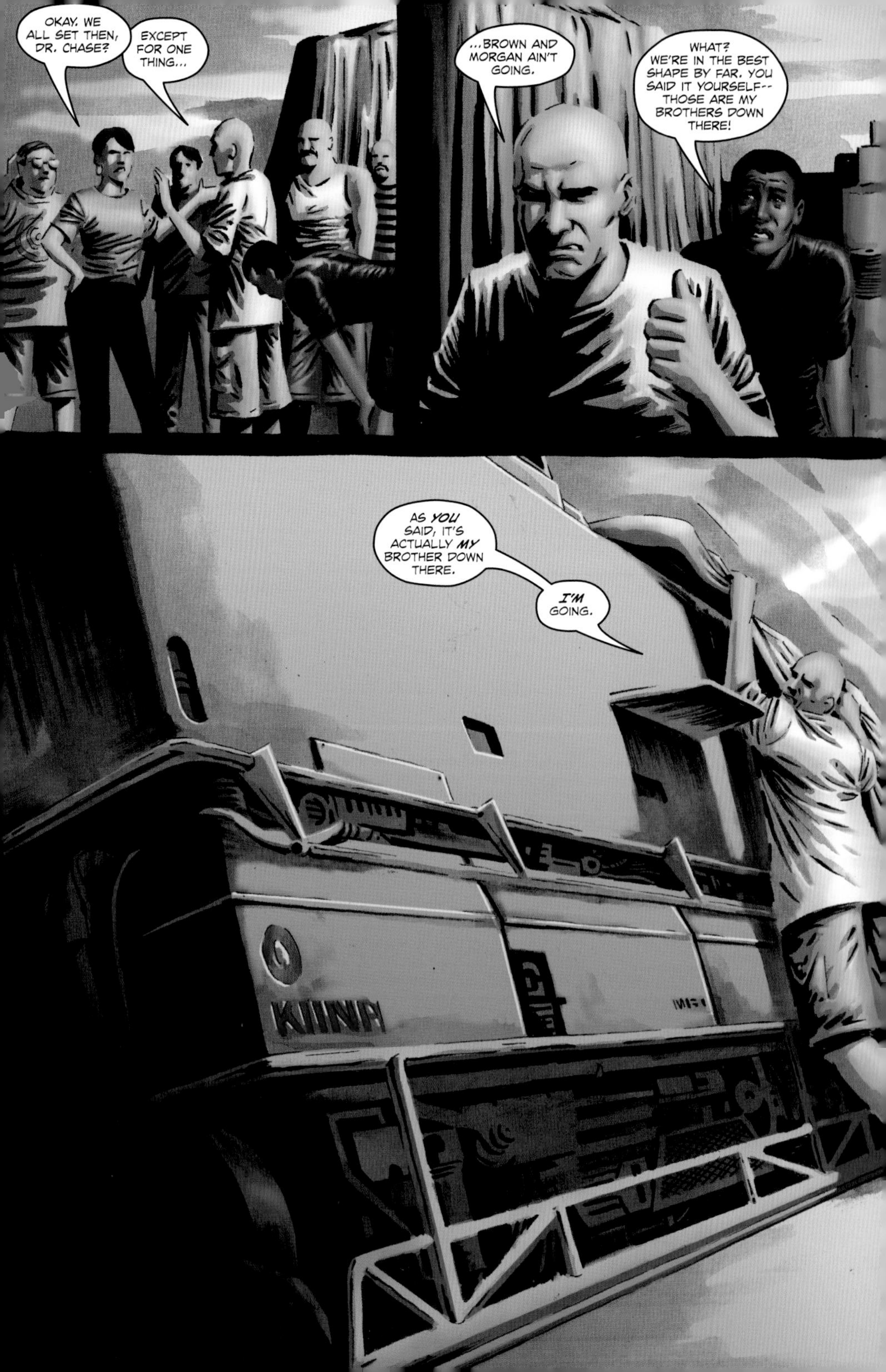
OKAY. WE ALL SET THEN, DR. CHASE?
EXCEPT FOR ONE THING...
...BROWN AND MORGAN AIN'T GOING.
WHAT? WE'RE IN THE BEST SHAPE BY FAR. YOU SAID IT YOURSELF-- THOSE ARE MY BROTHERS DOWN THERE!
AS *YOU* SAID, IT'S ACTUALLY *MY* BROTHER DOWN THERE.
*I'M* GOING.

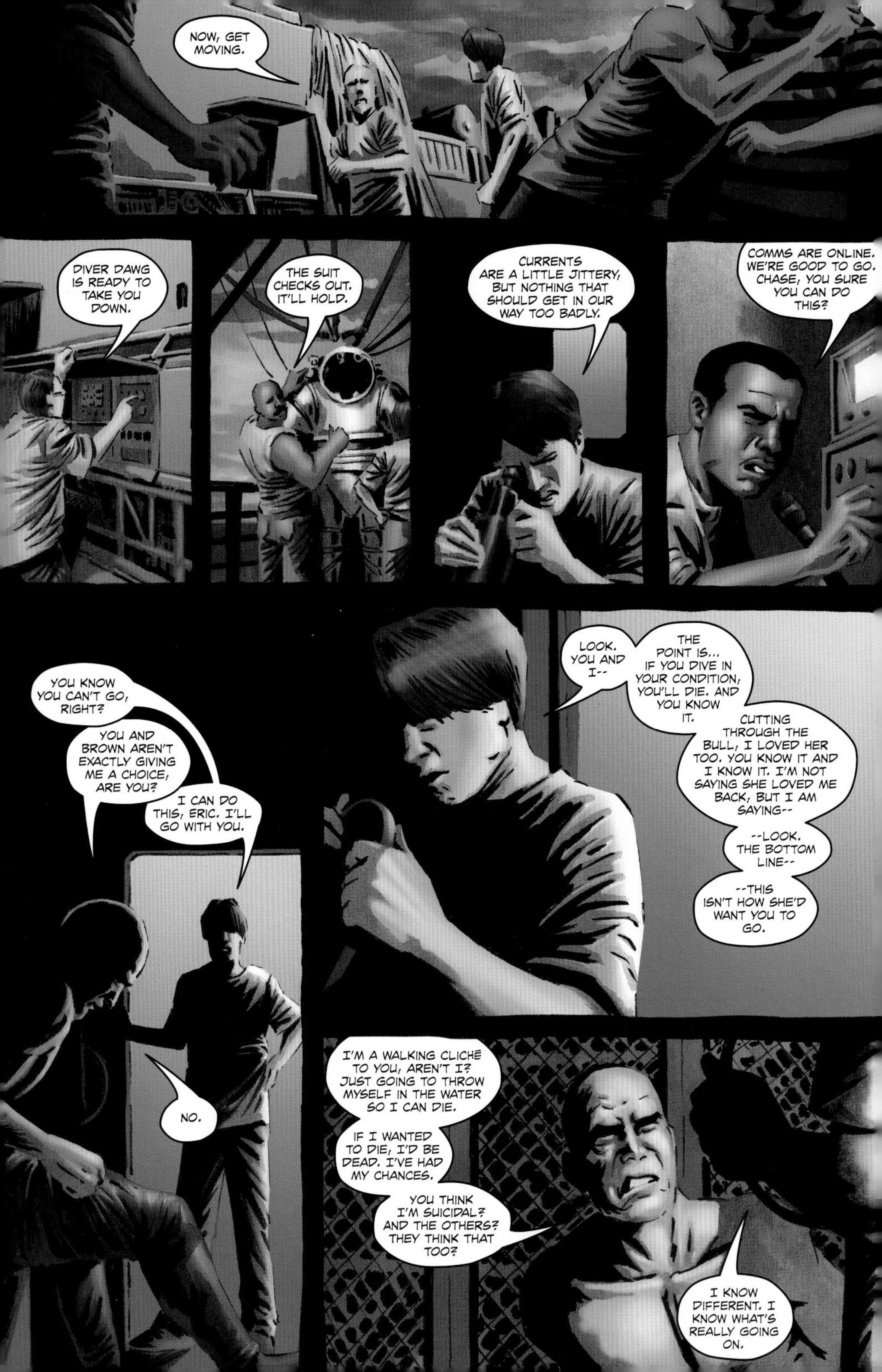

NOW, GET MOVING.
DIVER DAWG IS READY TO TAKE YOU DOWN.
THE SUIT CHECKS OUT. IT'LL HOLD.
CURRENTS ARE A LITTLE JITTERY, BUT NOTHING THAT SHOULD GET IN OUR WAY TOO BADLY.
COMMS ARE ONLINE. WE'RE GOOD TO GO. CHASE, YOU SURE YOU CAN DO THIS?
YOU KNOW YOU CAN'T GO, RIGHT?
YOU AND BROWN AREN'T EXACTLY GIVING ME A CHOICE, ARE YOU?
I CAN DO THIS, ERIC. I'LL GO WITH YOU.
NO.
LOOK. YOU AND I--
THE POINT IS... IF YOU DIVE IN YOUR CONDITION, YOU'LL DIE. AND YOU KNOW IT.
CUTTING THROUGH THE BULL, I LOVED HER TOO. YOU KNOW IT AND I KNOW IT. I'M NOT SAYING SHE LOVED ME BACK, BUT I AM SAYING--
--LOOK. THE BOTTOM LINE--
--THIS ISN'T HOW SHE'D WANT YOU TO GO.
I'M A WALKING CLICHE TO YOU, AREN'T I? JUST GOING TO THROW MYSELF IN THE WATER SO I CAN DIE.
IF I WANTED TO DIE, I'D BE DEAD. I'VE HAD MY CHANCES.
YOU THINK I'M SUICIDAL? AND THE OTHERS? THEY THINK THAT TOO?
I KNOW DIFFERENT. I KNOW WHAT'S REALLY GOING ON.

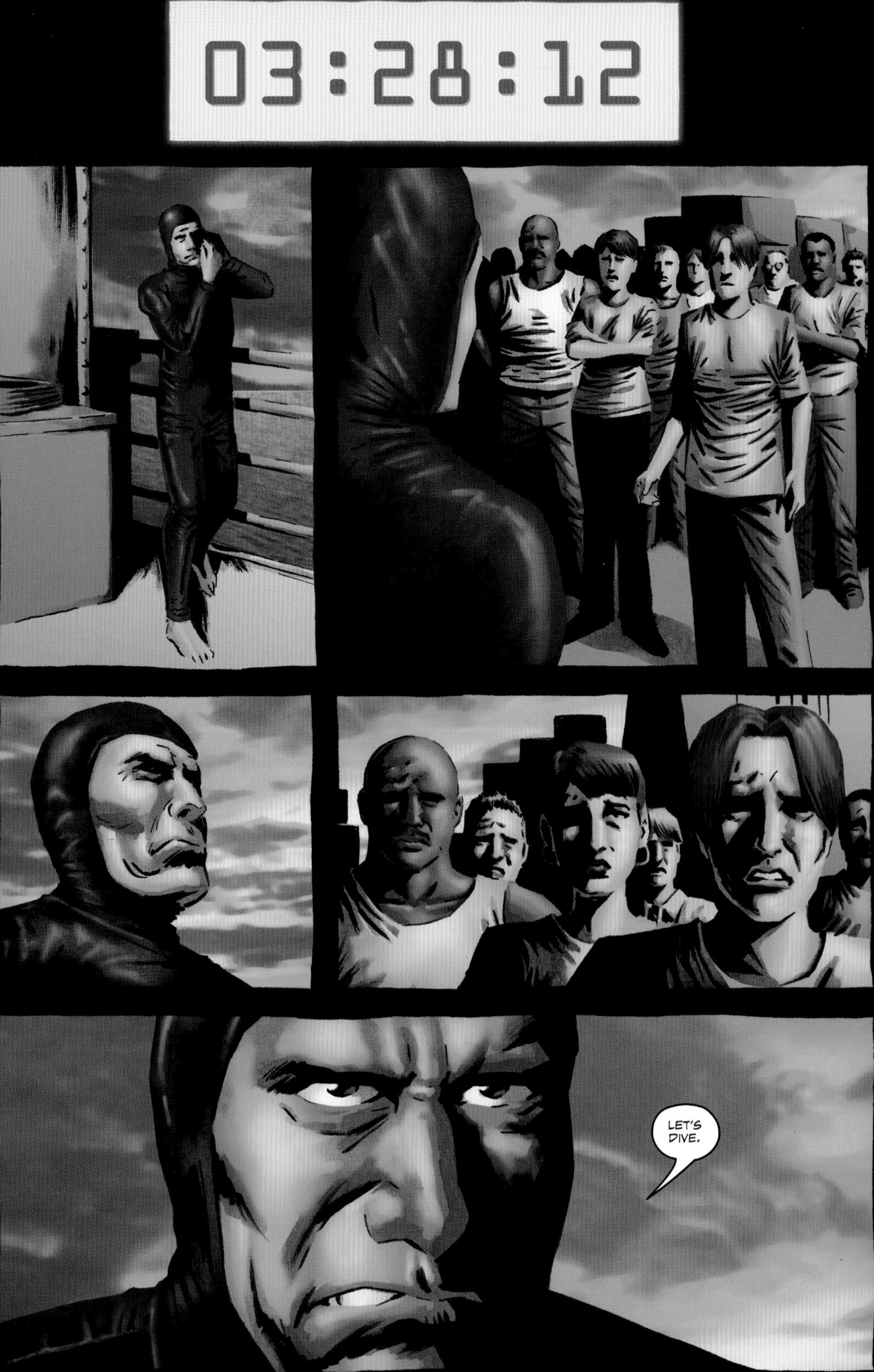
03:28:12
LET'S DIVE.

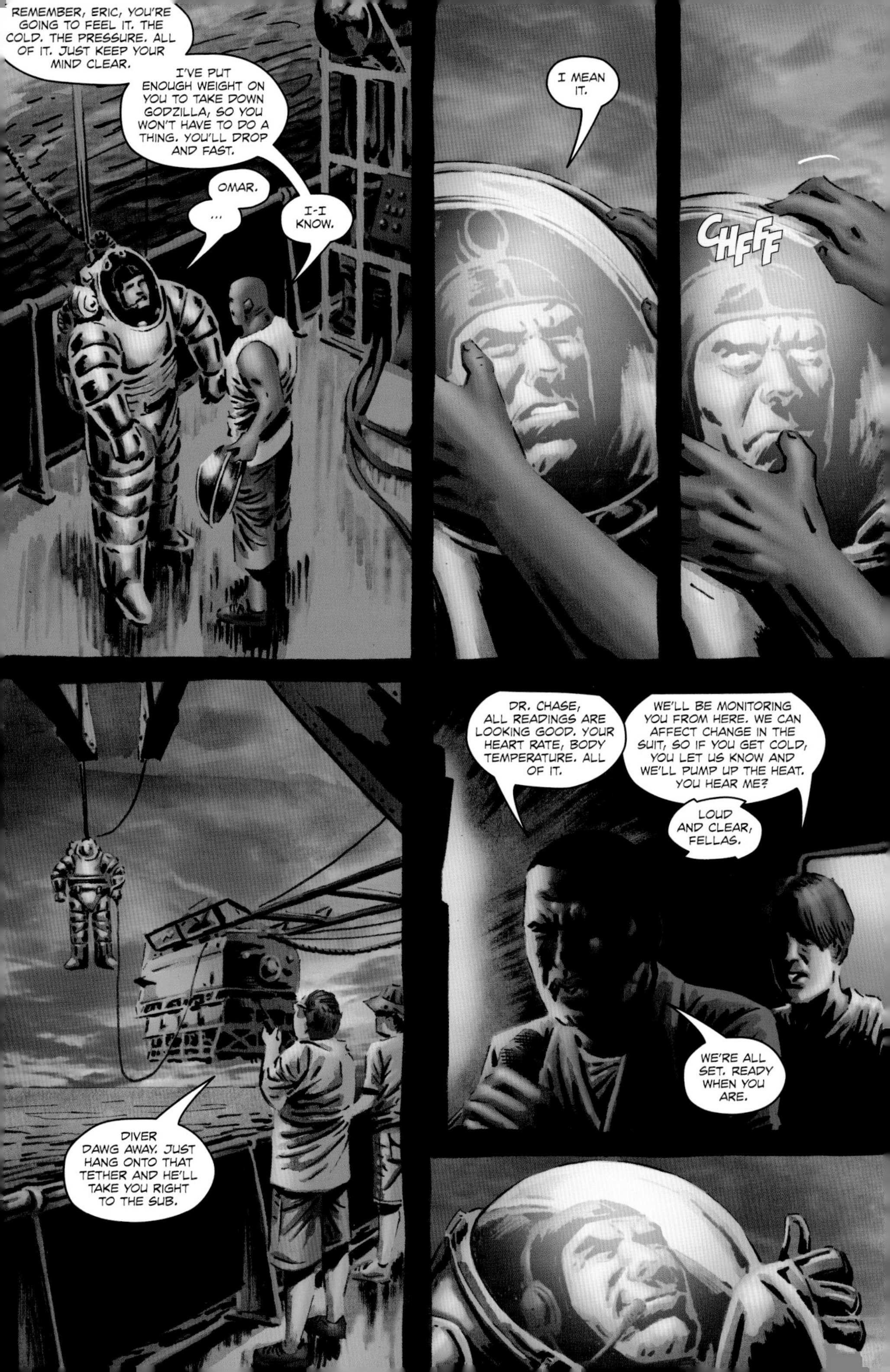
REMEMBER, ERIC, YOU'RE GOING TO FEEL IT. THE COLD. THE PRESSURE. ALL OF IT. JUST KEEP YOUR MIND CLEAR.
I'VE PUT ENOUGH WEIGHT ON YOU TO TAKE DOWN GODZILLA, SO YOU WON'T HAVE TO DO A THING. YOU'LL DROP AND FAST.
OMAR.
...
I-I KNOW.
I MEAN IT.
CHFFF
DIVER DAWG AWAY. JUST HANG ONTO THAT TETHER AND HE'LL TAKE YOU RIGHT TO THE SUB.
DR. CHASE, ALL READINGS ARE LOOKING GOOD. YOUR HEART RATE, BODY TEMPERATURE. ALL OF IT.
WE'LL BE MONITORING YOU FROM HERE. WE CAN AFFECT CHANGE IN THE SUIT, SO IF YOU GET COLD, YOU LET US KNOW AND WE'LL PUMP UP THE HEAT. YOU HEAR ME?
LOUD AND CLEAR, FELLAS.
WE'RE ALL SET. READY WHEN YOU ARE.

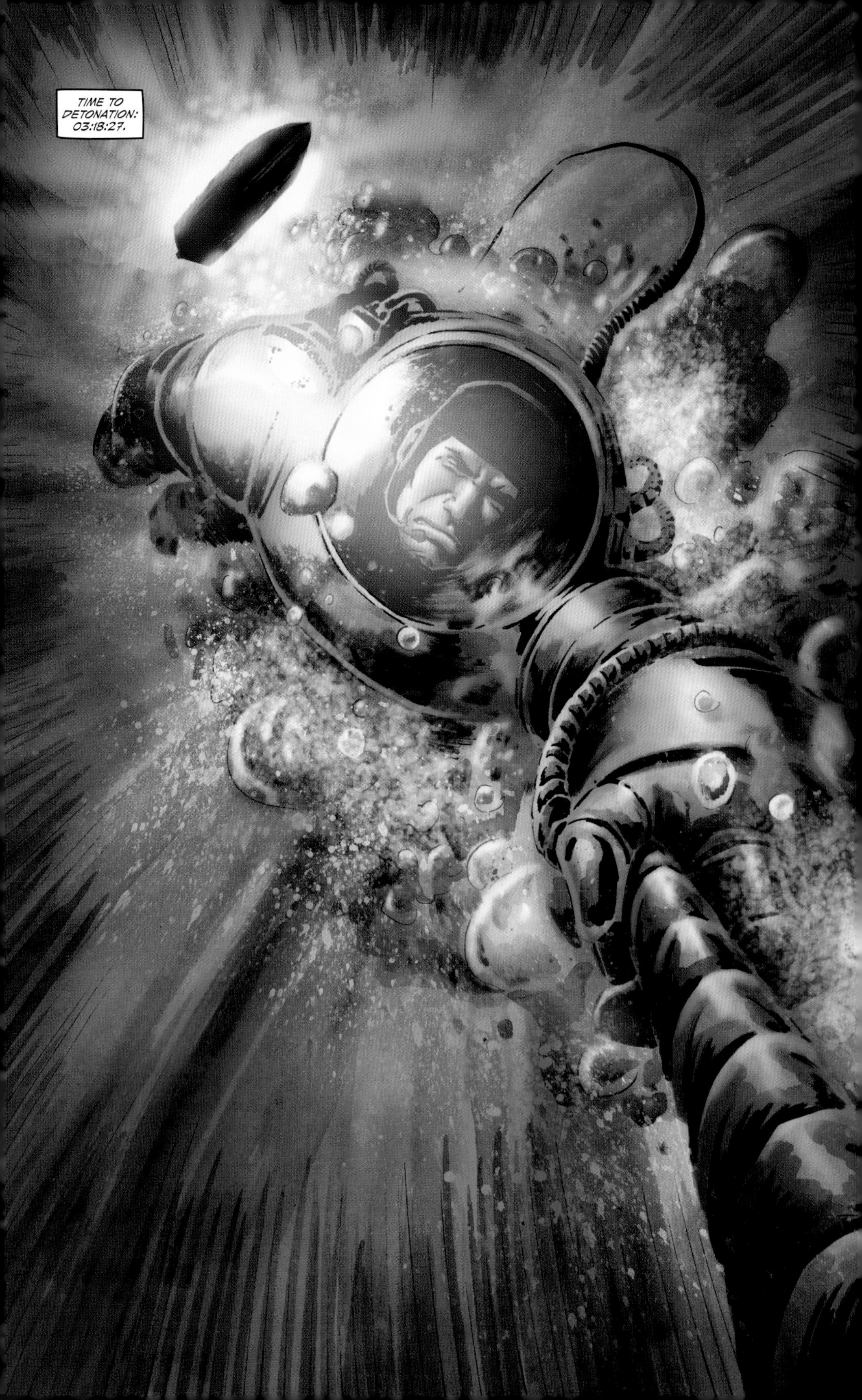
TIME TO DETONATION: 03:18:27.

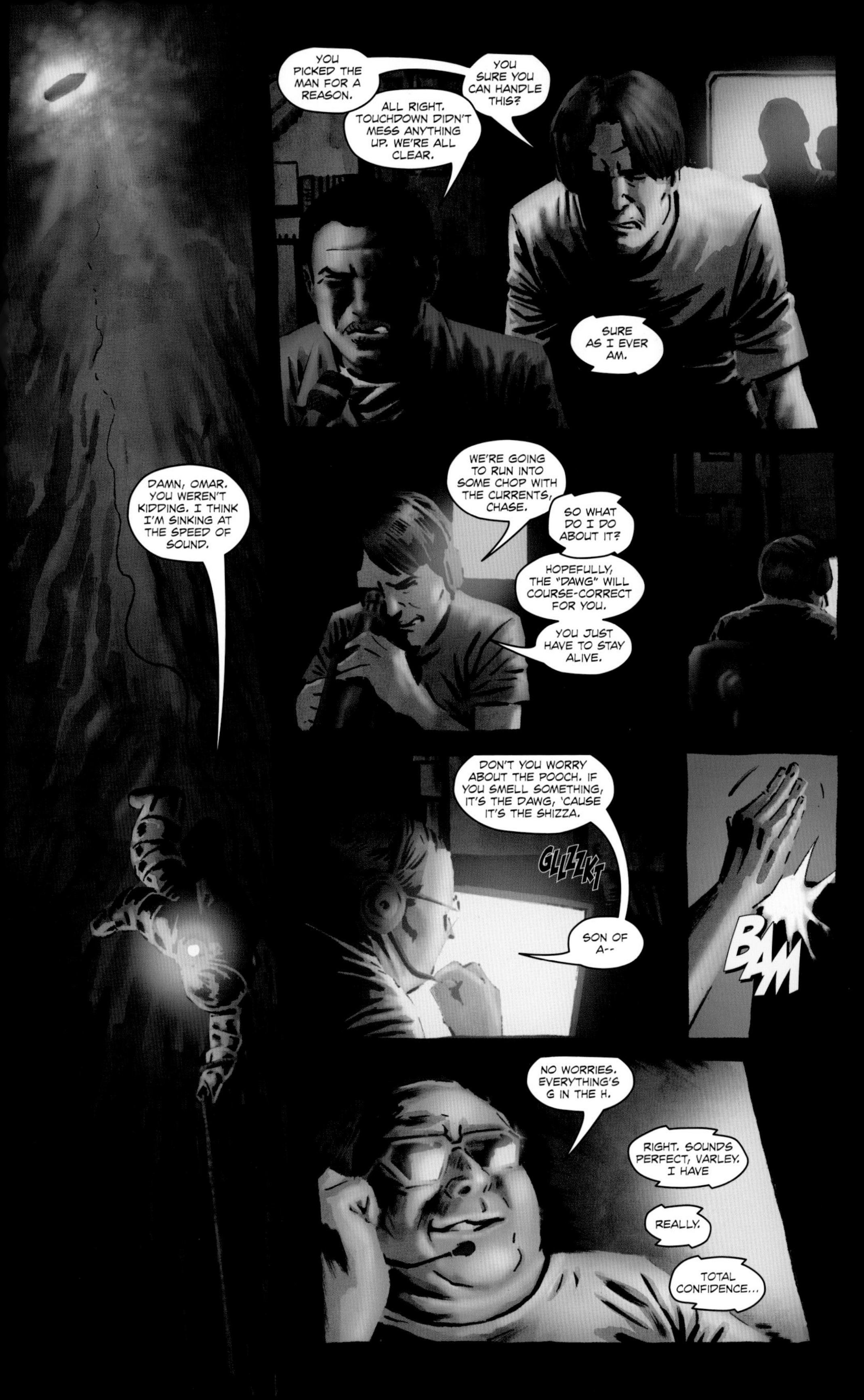
YOU PICKED THE MAN FOR A REASON.
YOU SURE YOU CAN HANDLE THIS?
ALL RIGHT. TOUCHDOWN DIDN'T MESS ANYTHING UP. WE'RE ALL CLEAR.
SURE AS I EVER AM.
DAMN, OMAR. YOU WEREN'T KIDDING. I THINK I'M SINKING AT THE SPEED OF SOUND.
WE'RE GOING TO RUN INTO SOME CHOP WITH THE CURRENTS, CHASE.
SO WHAT DO I DO ABOUT IT?
HOPEFULLY, THE "DAWG" WILL COURSE-CORRECT FOR YOU.
YOU JUST HAVE TO STAY ALIVE.
DON'T YOU WORRY ABOUT THE POOCH. IF YOU SMELL SOMETHING, IT'S THE DAWG, 'CAUSE IT'S THE SHIZZA.
GLIZZKT
SON OF A--
BAM
NO WORRIES. EVERYTHING'S G IN THE H.
RIGHT. SOUNDS PERFECT, VARLEY. I HAVE
REALLY.
TOTAL CONFIDENCE...

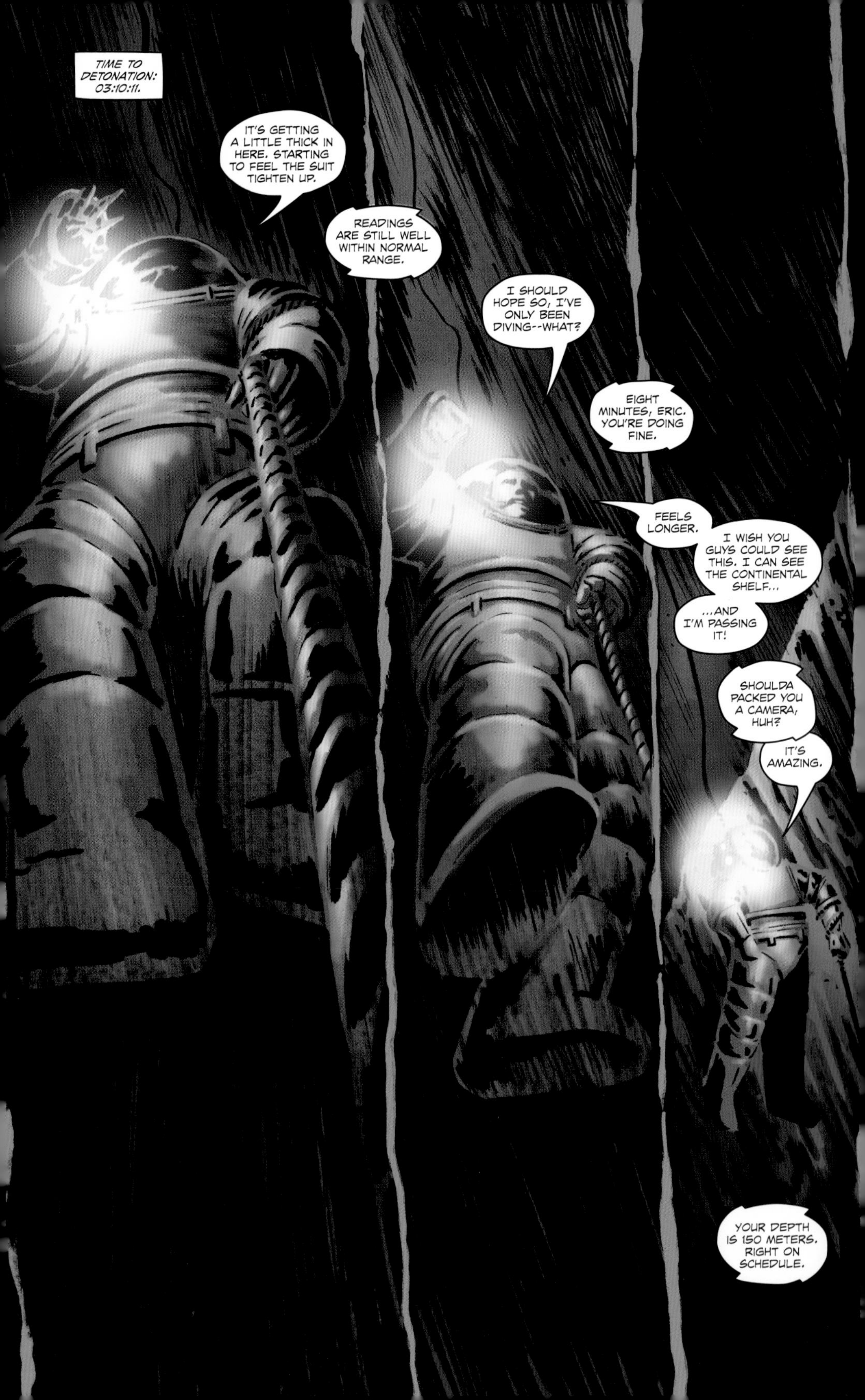
TIME TO DETONATION: 03:10:11.
IT'S GETTING A LITTLE THICK IN HERE. STARTING TO FEEL THE SUIT TIGHTEN UP.
READINGS ARE STILL WELL WITHIN NORMAL RANGE.
I SHOULD HOPE SO, I'VE ONLY BEEN DIVING--WHAT?
EIGHT MINUTES, ERIC. YOU'RE DOING FINE.
FEELS LONGER.
I WISH YOU GUYS COULD SEE THIS. I CAN SEE THE CONTINENTAL SHELF...
...AND I'M PASSING IT!
SHOULDA PACKED YOU A CAMERA, HUH?
IT'S AMAZING.
YOUR DEPTH IS 150 METERS. RIGHT ON SCHEDULE.

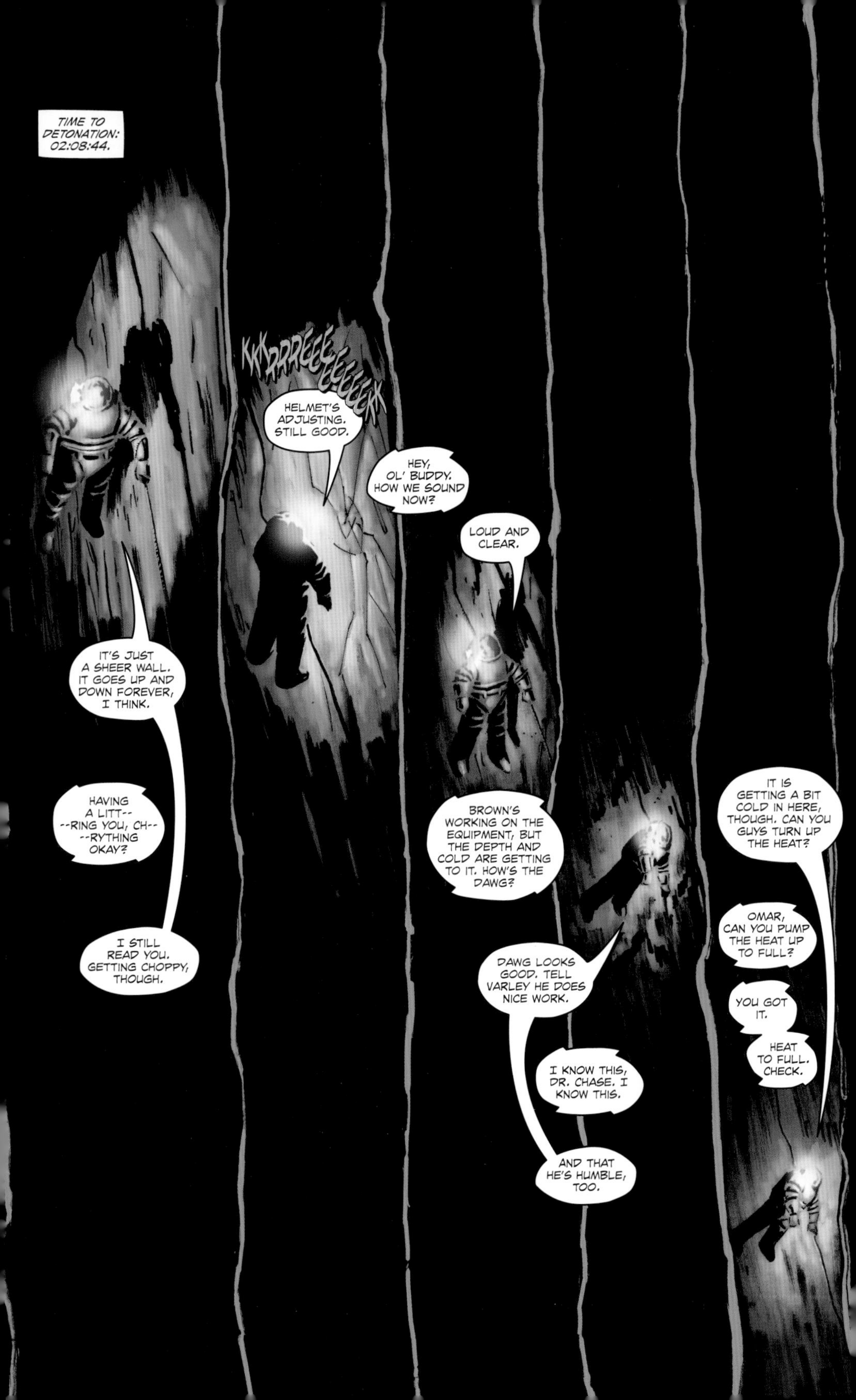
TIME TO DETONATION: 02:08:44.
KKKRRREEEEEEEEEEEEKK
HELMET'S ADJUSTING. STILL GOOD.
HEY, OL' BUDDY. HOW WE SOUND NOW?
LOUD AND CLEAR.
IT'S JUST A SHEER WALL. IT GOES UP AND DOWN FOREVER, I THINK.
HAVING A LITT-- --RING YOU, CH-- --RYTHING OKAY?
I STILL READ YOU. GETTING CHOPPY, THOUGH.
BROWN'S WORKING ON THE EQUIPMENT, BUT THE DEPTH AND COLD ARE GETTING TO IT. HOW'S THE DAWG?
DAWG LOOKS GOOD. TELL VARLEY HE DOES NICE WORK.
I KNOW THIS, DR. CHASE. I KNOW THIS.
AND THAT HE'S HUMBLE, TOO.
IT IS GETTING A BIT COLD IN HERE, THOUGH. CAN YOU GUYS TURN UP THE HEAT?
OMAR, CAN YOU PUMP THE HEAT UP TO FULL?
YOU GOT IT.
HEAT TO FULL. CHECK.

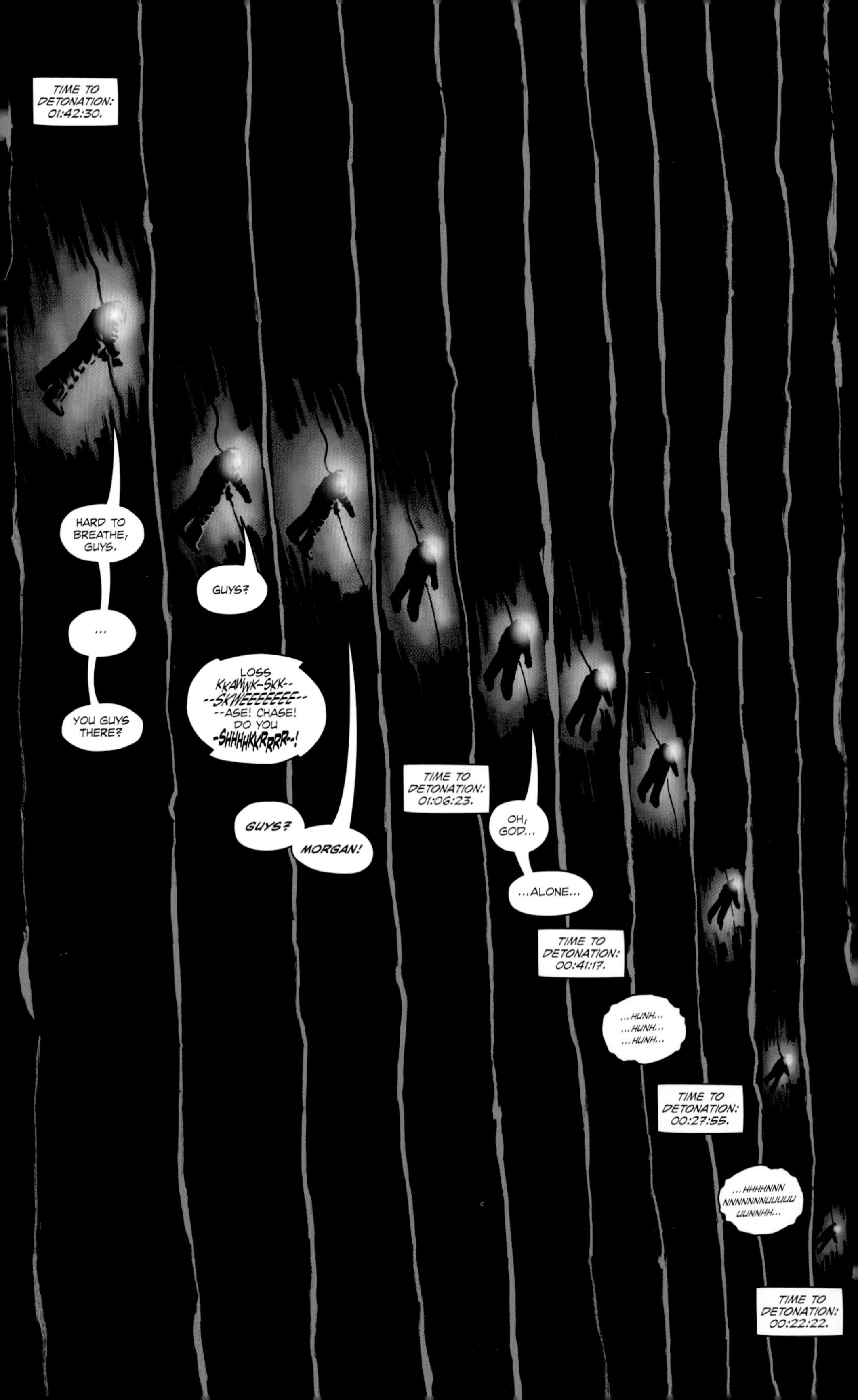
TIME TO DETONATION: 01:42:30.
HARD TO BREATHE, GUYS.
...
YOU GUYS THERE?
GUYS?
LOSS KKAWNK-SKK-- --SKWEEEEEEEE-- --ASE! CHASE! DO YOU -SHHHHKKRRRR--!
GUYS?
MORGAN!
TIME TO DETONATION: 01:06:23.
OH, GOD...
...ALONE...
TIME TO DETONATION: 00:41:17.
...HUNH... ...HUNH... ...HUNH...
TIME TO DETONATION: 00:27:55.
...HHHHNNN NNNNNNNUUUUU UUNNHH...
TIME TO DETONATION: 00:22:22.

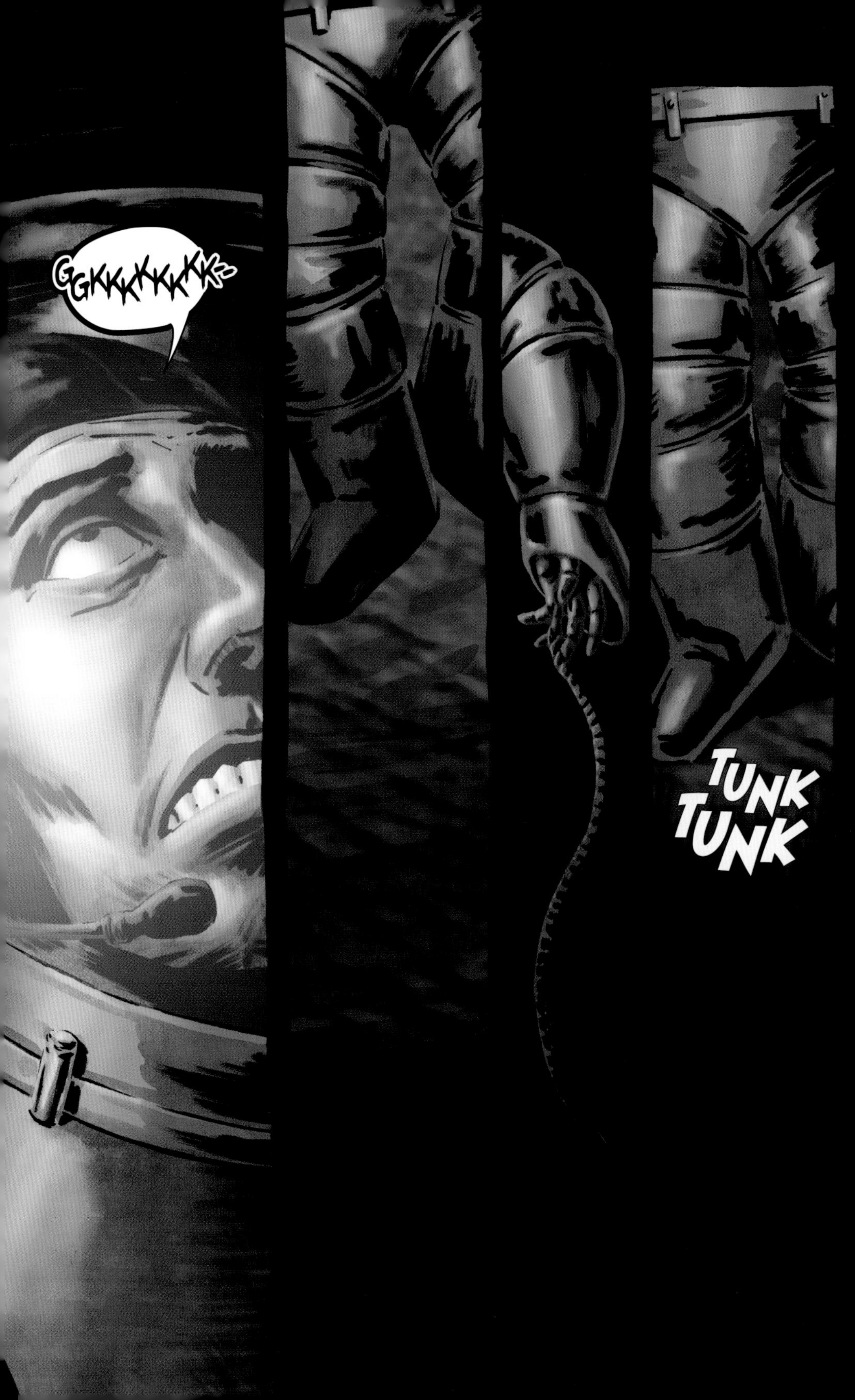
GGKKKKKKKK--
TUNK
TUNK

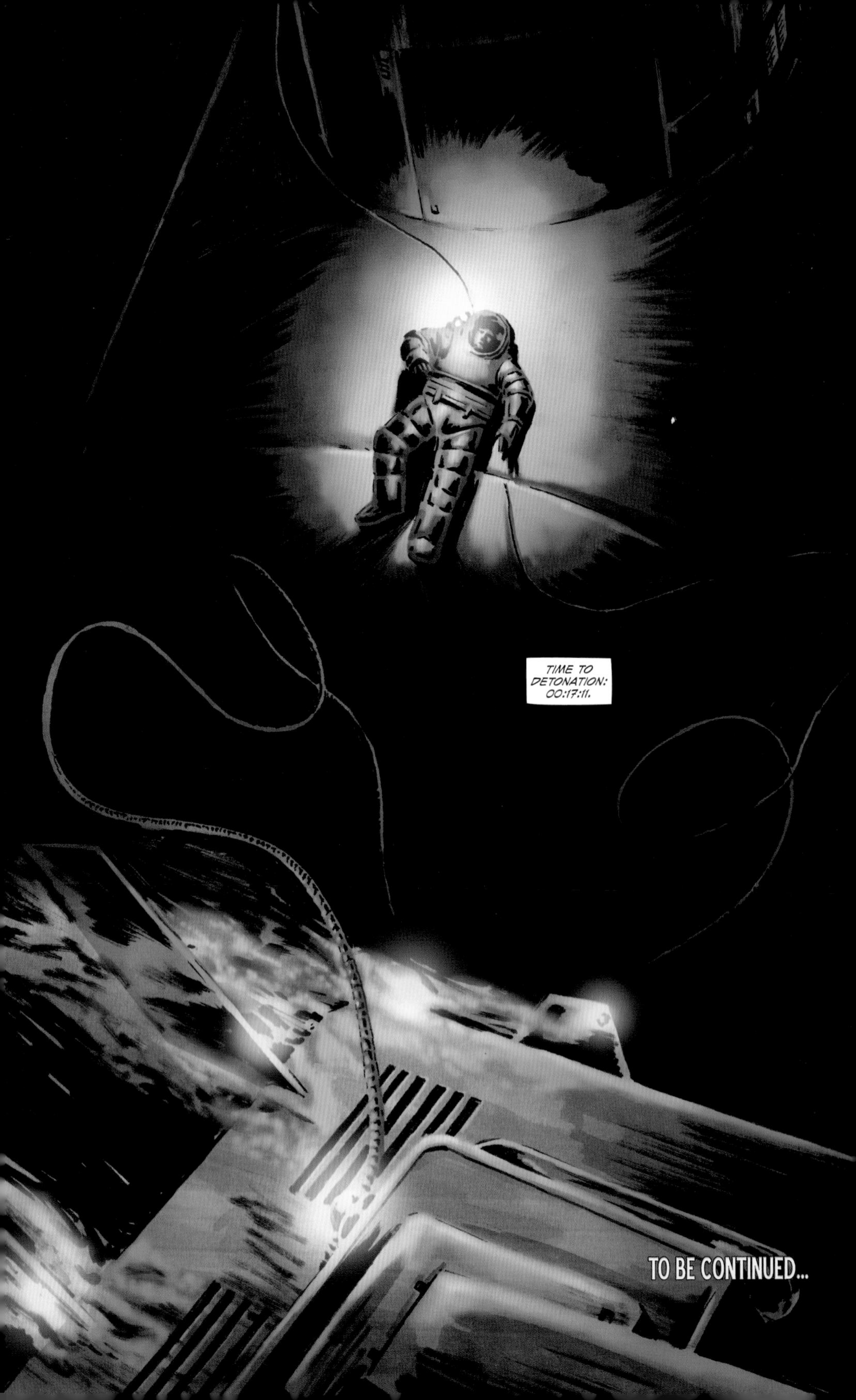
TIME TO DETONATION: 00:17:11.
TO BE CONTINUED...

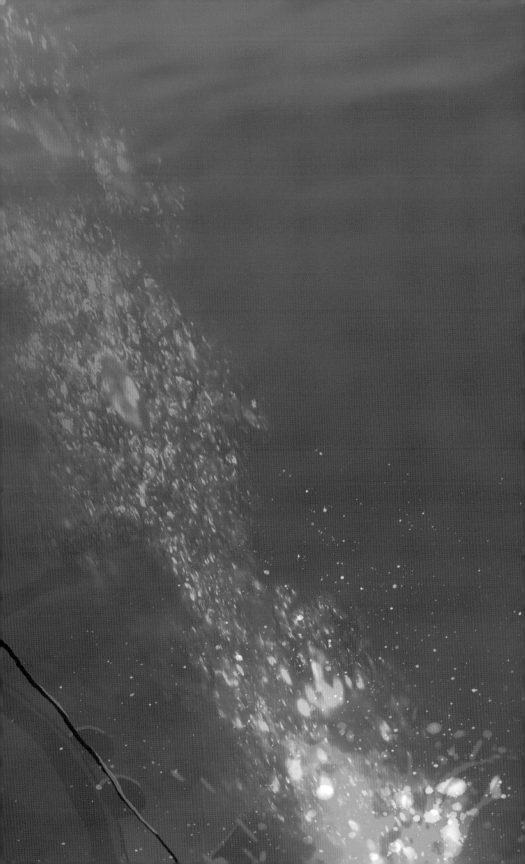

# CHAPTER 3

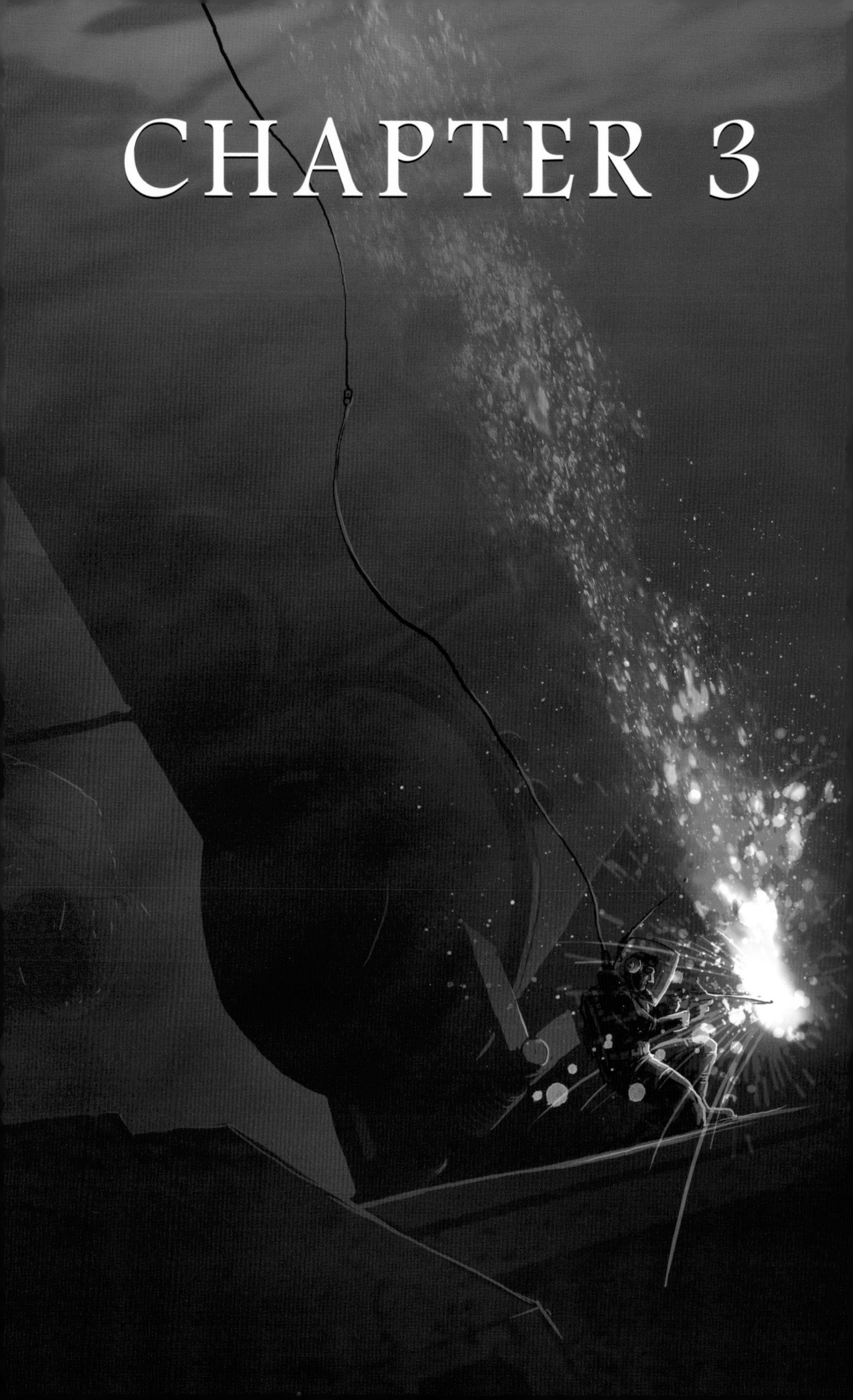

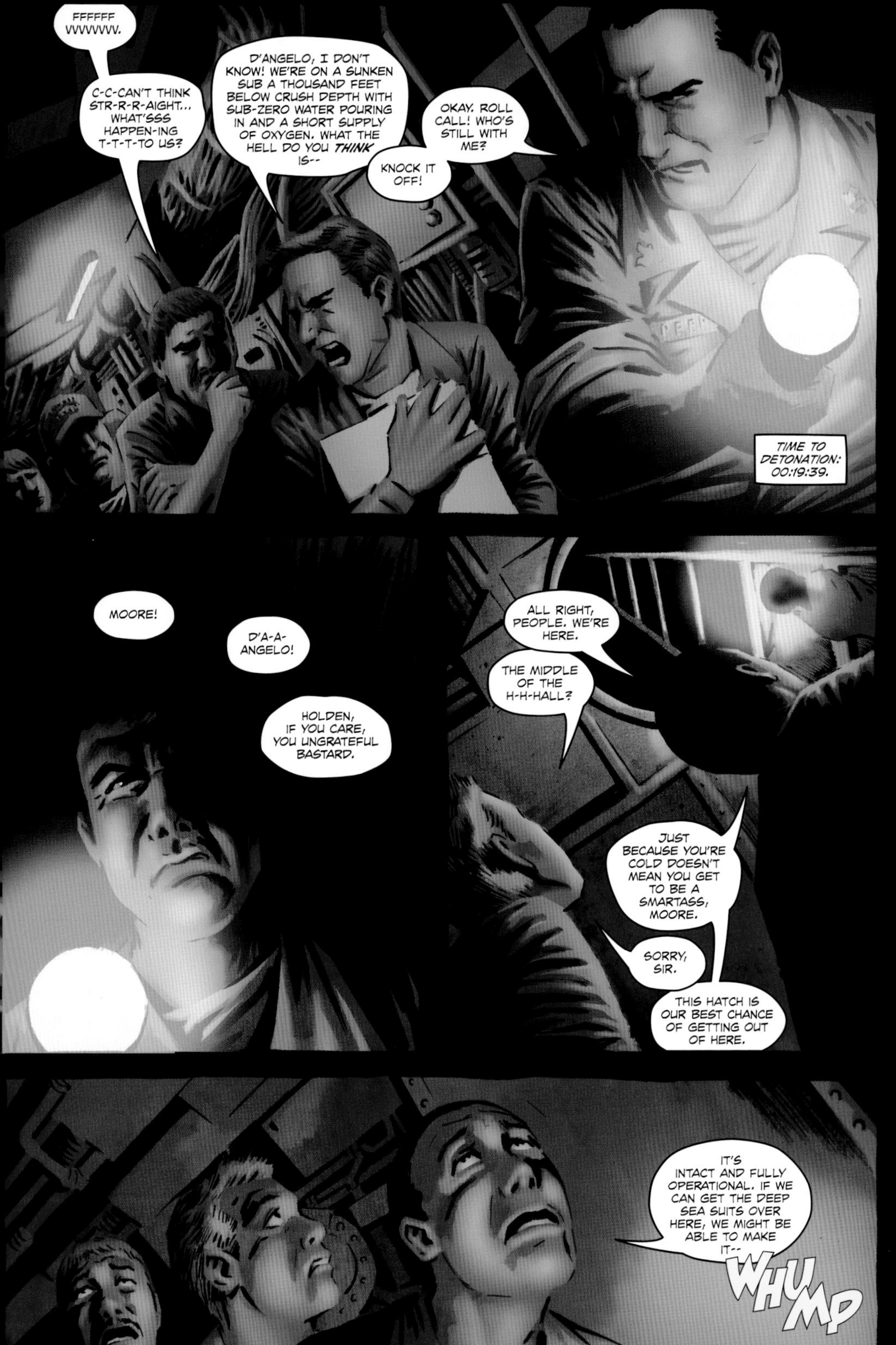
FFFFFF VVVVVVVV.
C-C-CAN'T THINK STR-R-R-AIGHT... WHAT'SSS HAPPEN-ING T-T-T-TO US?
D'ANGELO, I DON'T KNOW! WE'RE ON A SUNKEN SUB A THOUSAND FEET BELOW CRUSH DEPTH WITH SUB-ZERO WATER POURING IN AND A SHORT SUPPLY OF OXYGEN. WHAT THE HELL DO YOU *THINK* IS--
KNOCK IT OFF!
OKAY. ROLL CALL! WHO'S STILL WITH ME?
TIME TO DETONATION: 00:19:39.
MOORE!
D'A-A-ANGELO!
HOLDEN, IF YOU CARE, YOU UNGRATEFUL BASTARD.
ALL RIGHT, PEOPLE. WE'RE HERE.
THE MIDDLE OF THE H-H-HALL?
JUST BECAUSE YOU'RE COLD DOESN'T MEAN YOU GET TO BE A SMARTASS, MOORE.
SORRY, SIR.
THIS HATCH IS OUR BEST CHANCE OF GETTING OUT OF HERE.
IT'S INTACT AND FULLY OPERATIONAL. IF WE CAN GET THE DEEP SEA SUITS OVER HERE, WE MIGHT BE ABLE TO MAKE IT--
WHUMP

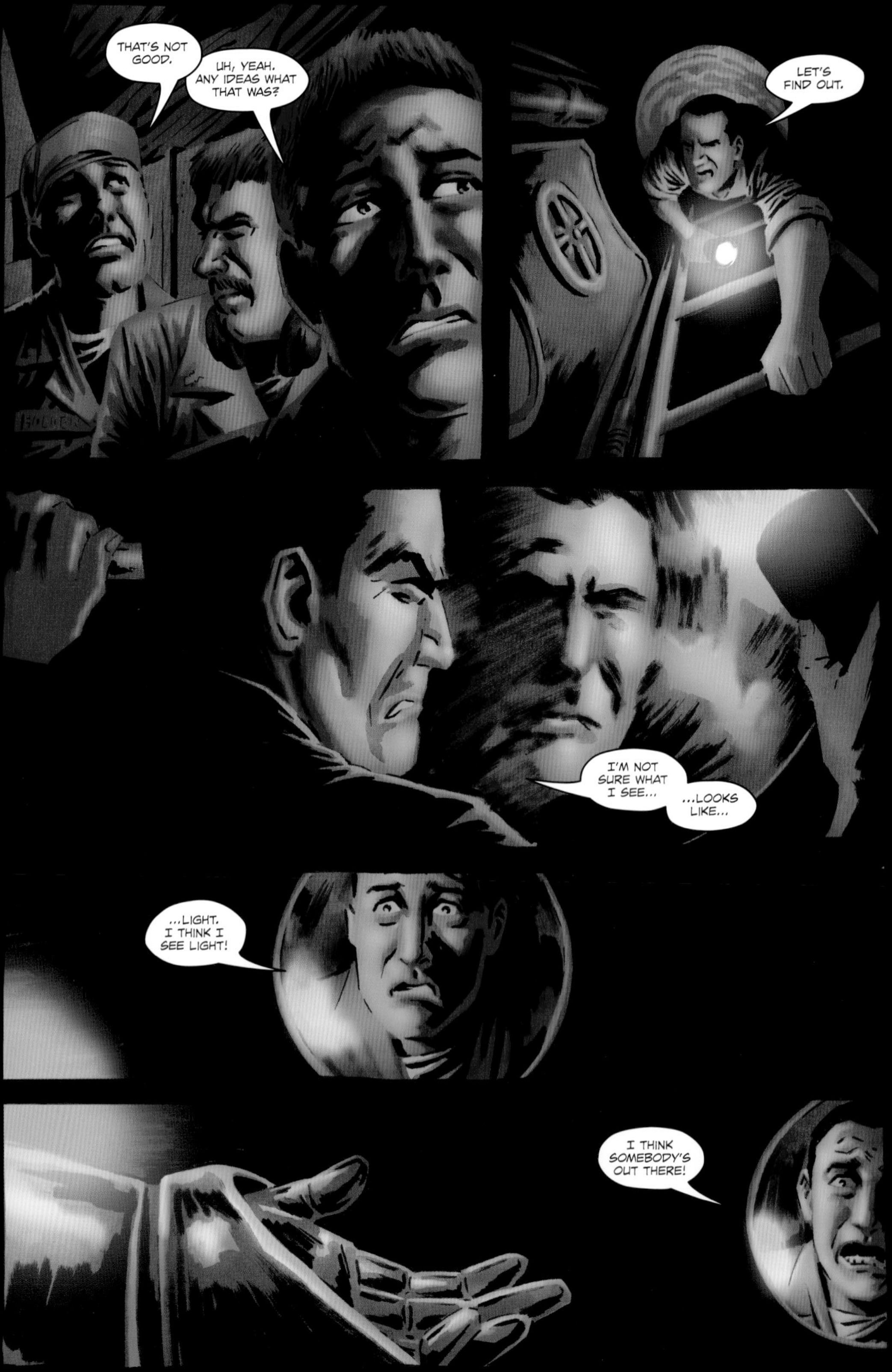
THAT'S NOT GOOD.
UH, YEAH. ANY IDEAS WHAT THAT WAS?
LET'S FIND OUT.
I'M NOT SURE WHAT I SEE...
...LOOKS LIKE...
...LIGHT. I THINK I SEE LIGHT!
I THINK SOMEBODY'S OUT THERE!

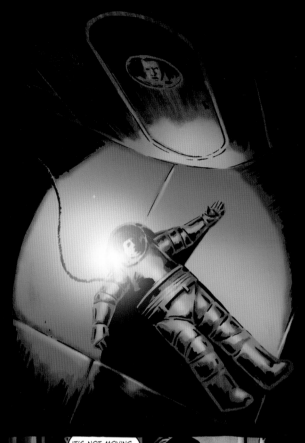

TIME TO
DETONATION:
00:17:11.

IT'S NOT MOVING.
THE LIGHT ISN'T
MOVING.

WHAT
DOES THAT
MEAN?

LET ME
THINK...

SUPPLIES. IT'S
GOT TO BE
SUPPLIES.

W-W-WHAT
K-KIND OF
SU-U-UPLIES?

ONLY ONE
WAY TO FIND
OUT...

...WE'RE
BRINGING
IT IN.

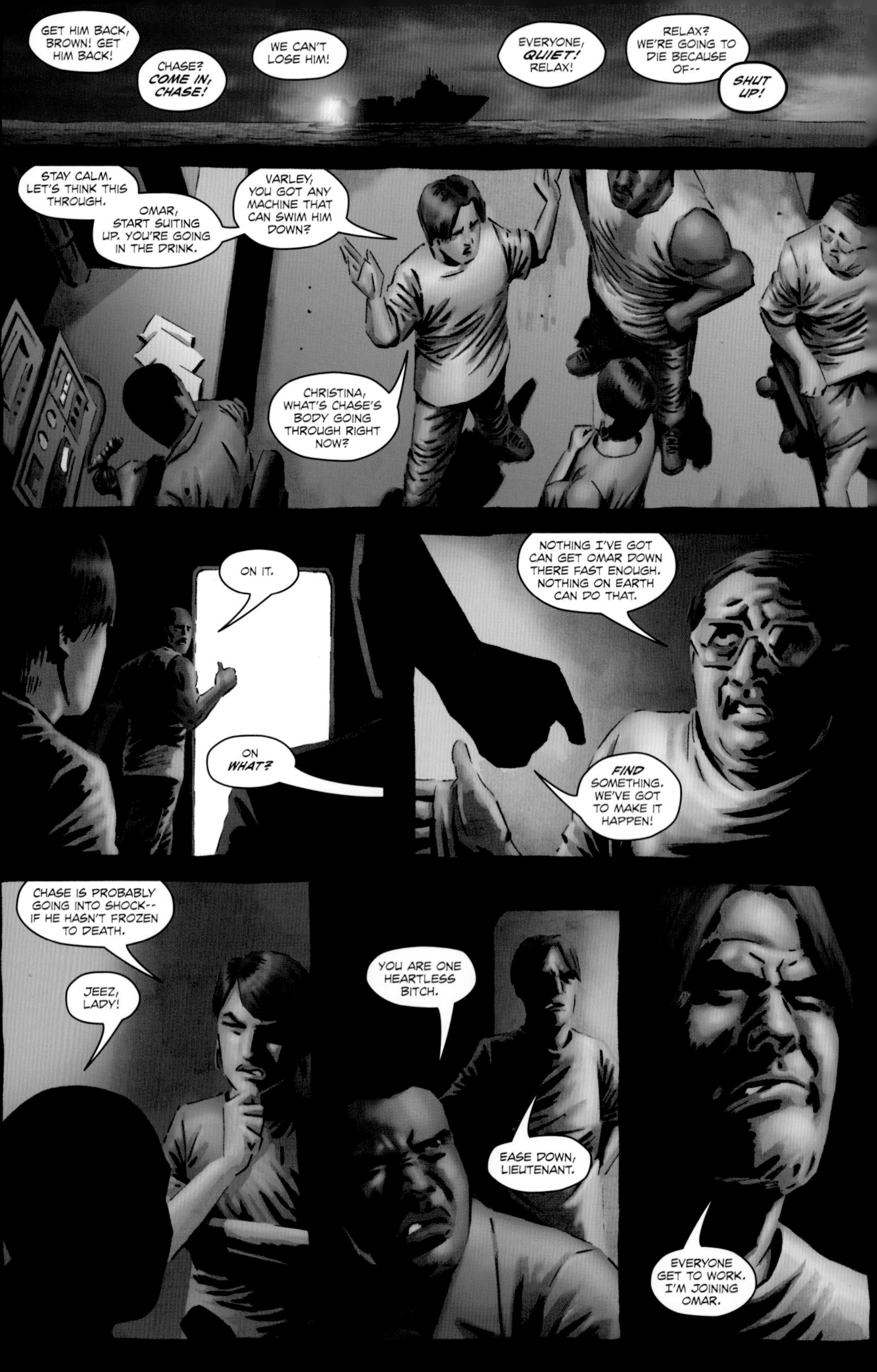
GET HIM BACK, BROWN! GET HIM BACK!
CHASE? COME IN, CHASE!
WE CAN'T LOSE HIM!
EVERYONE, QUIET! RELAX!
RELAX? WE'RE GOING TO DIE BECAUSE OF--
SHUT UP!
STAY CALM. LET'S THINK THIS THROUGH.
OMAR, START SUITING UP. YOU'RE GOING IN THE DRINK.
VARLEY, YOU GOT ANY MACHINE THAT CAN SWIM HIM DOWN?
CHRISTINA, WHAT'S CHASE'S BODY GOING THROUGH RIGHT NOW?
ON IT.
ON WHAT?
NOTHING I'VE GOT CAN GET OMAR DOWN THERE FAST ENOUGH. NOTHING ON EARTH CAN DO THAT.
FIND SOMETHING. WE'VE GOT TO MAKE IT HAPPEN!
CHASE IS PROBABLY GOING INTO SHOCK-- IF HE HASN'T FROZEN TO DEATH.
JEEZ, LADY!
YOU ARE ONE HEARTLESS BITCH.
EASE DOWN, LIEUTENANT.
EVERYONE GET TO WORK. I'M JOINING OMAR.

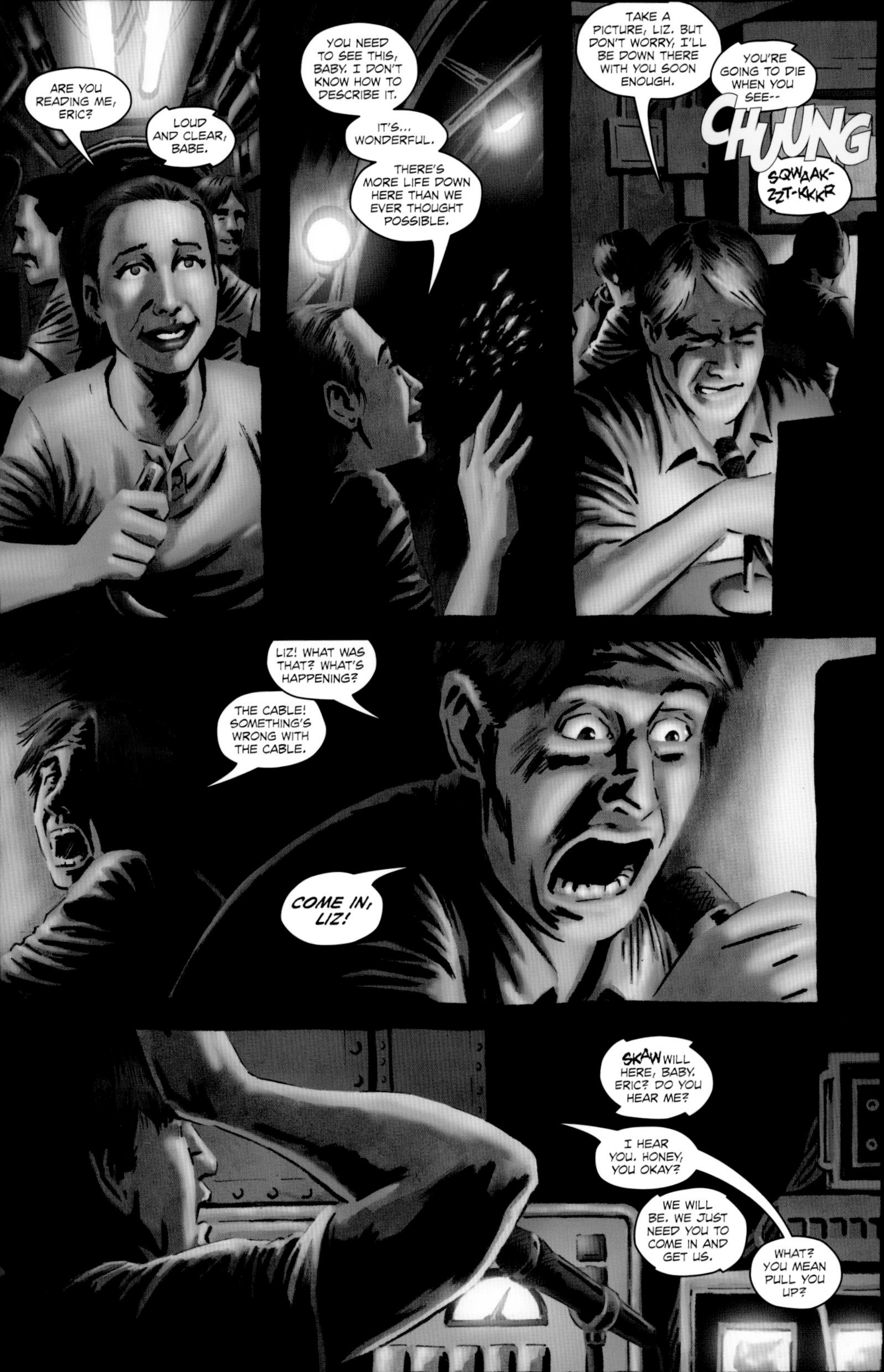
ARE YOU READING ME, ERIC?
LOUD AND CLEAR, BABE.
YOU NEED TO SEE THIS, BABY. I DON'T KNOW HOW TO DESCRIBE IT.
IT'S... WONDERFUL.
THERE'S MORE LIFE DOWN HERE THAN WE EVER THOUGHT POSSIBLE.
TAKE A PICTURE, LIZ. BUT DON'T WORRY, I'LL BE DOWN THERE WITH YOU SOON ENOUGH.
YOU'RE GOING TO DIE WHEN YOU SEE--
CHUUNG
SQWAAK-ZZT-KKKR
LIZ! WHAT WAS THAT? WHAT'S HAPPENING?
THE CABLE! SOMETHING'S WRONG WITH THE CABLE.
COME IN, LIZ!
SKAW WILL HERE, BABY. ERIC? DO YOU HEAR ME?
I HEAR YOU. HONEY, YOU OKAY?
WE WILL BE. WE JUST NEED YOU TO COME IN AND GET US.
WHAT? YOU MEAN PULL YOU UP?

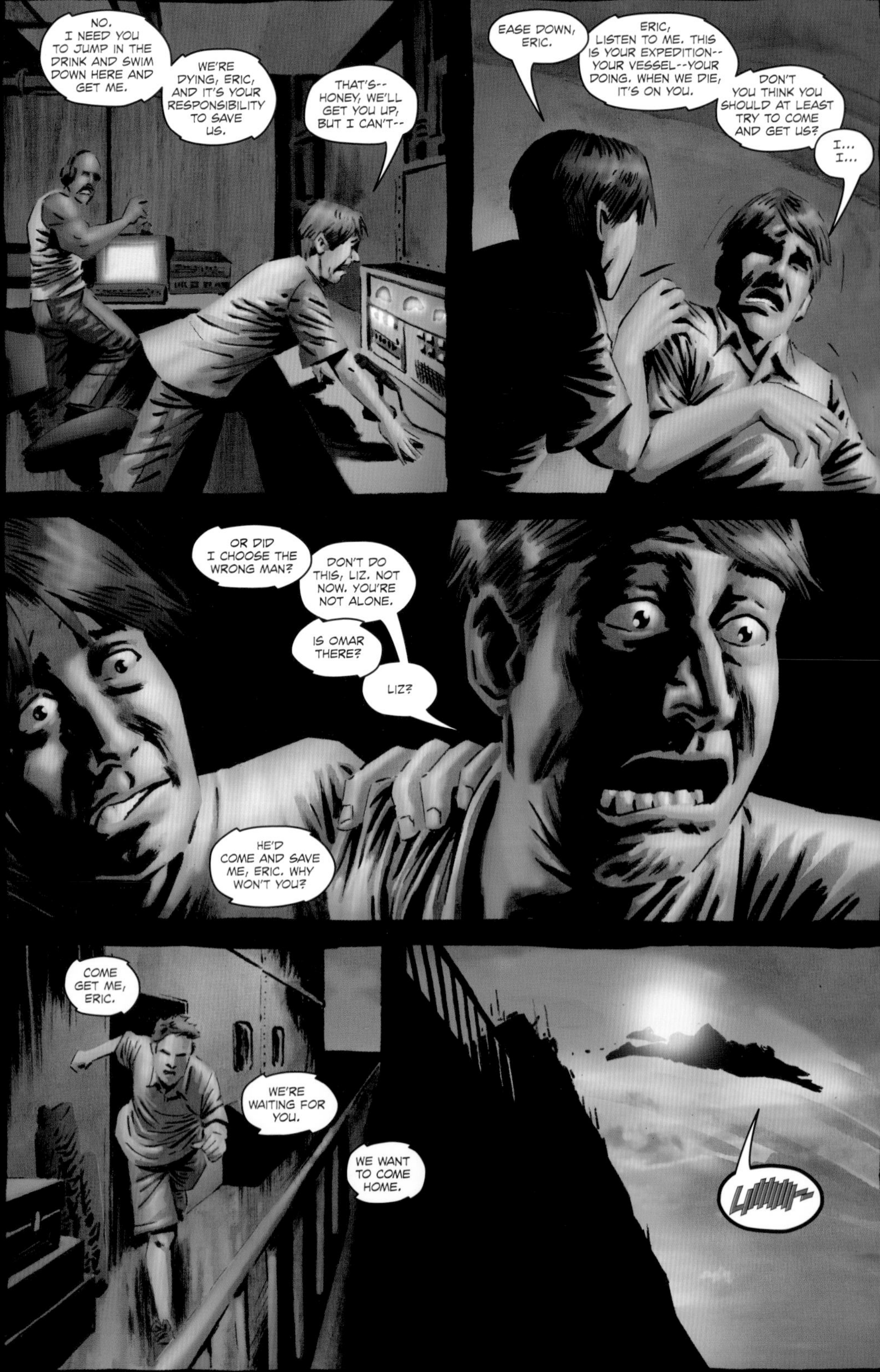

NO. I NEED YOU TO JUMP IN THE DRINK AND SWIM DOWN HERE AND GET ME.
WE'RE DYING, ERIC, AND IT'S YOUR RESPONSIBILITY TO SAVE US.
THAT'S-- HONEY, WE'LL GET YOU UP, BUT I CAN'T--
EASE DOWN, ERIC.
ERIC, LISTEN TO ME. THIS IS YOUR EXPEDITION-- YOUR VESSEL--YOUR DOING. WHEN WE DIE, IT'S ON YOU.
DON'T YOU THINK YOU SHOULD AT LEAST TRY TO COME AND GET US?
I... I...
OR DID I CHOOSE THE WRONG MAN?
DON'T DO THIS, LIZ. NOT NOW. YOU'RE NOT ALONE.
IS OMAR THERE?
LIZ?
HE'D COME AND SAVE ME, ERIC. WHY WON'T YOU?
COME GET ME, ERIC.
WE'RE WAITING FOR YOU.
WE WANT TO COME HOME.

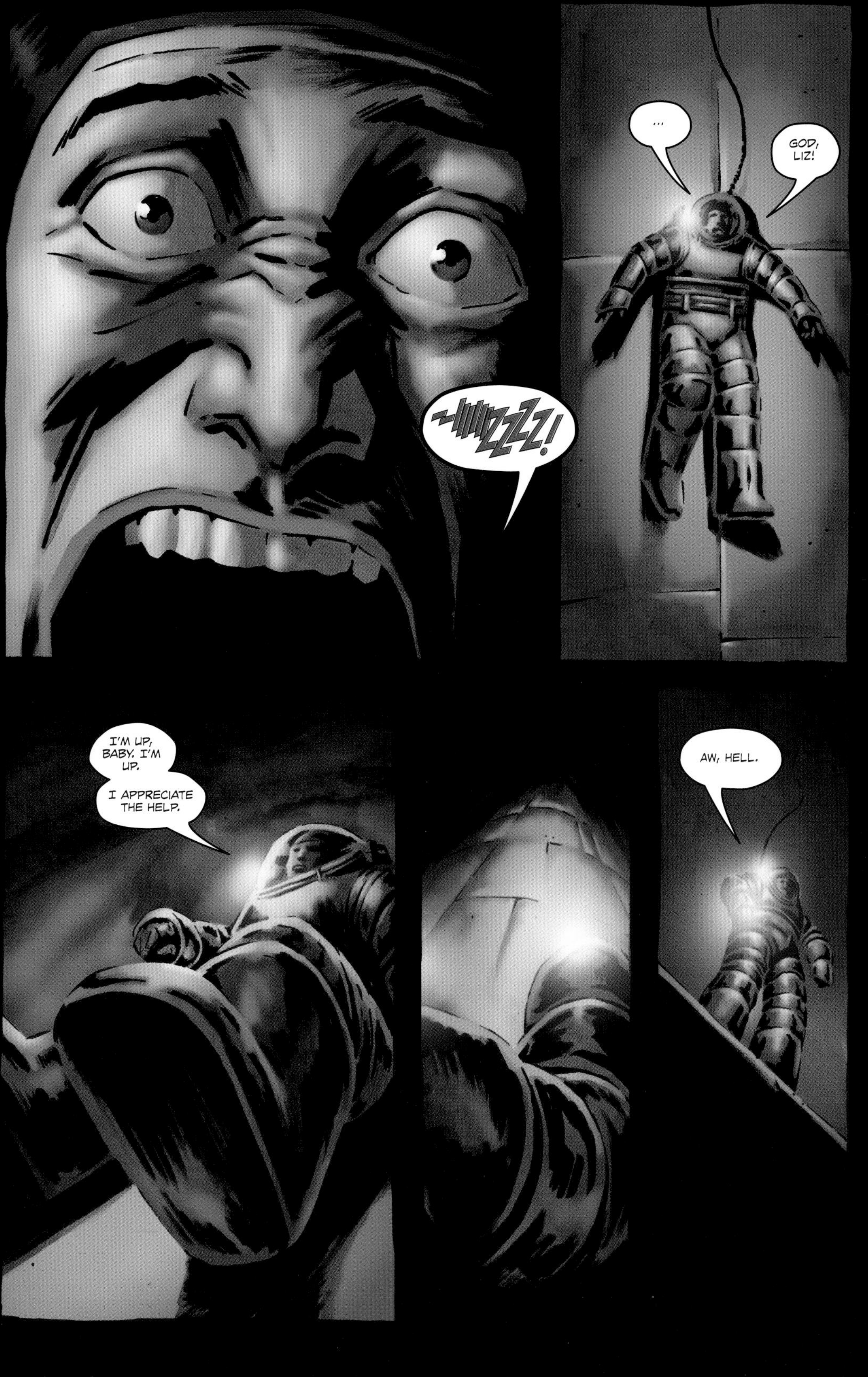

-IIIIIIZZZZ!
...
GOD, LIZ!
I'M UP, BABY. I'M UP.
I APPRECIATE THE HELP.
AW, HELL.

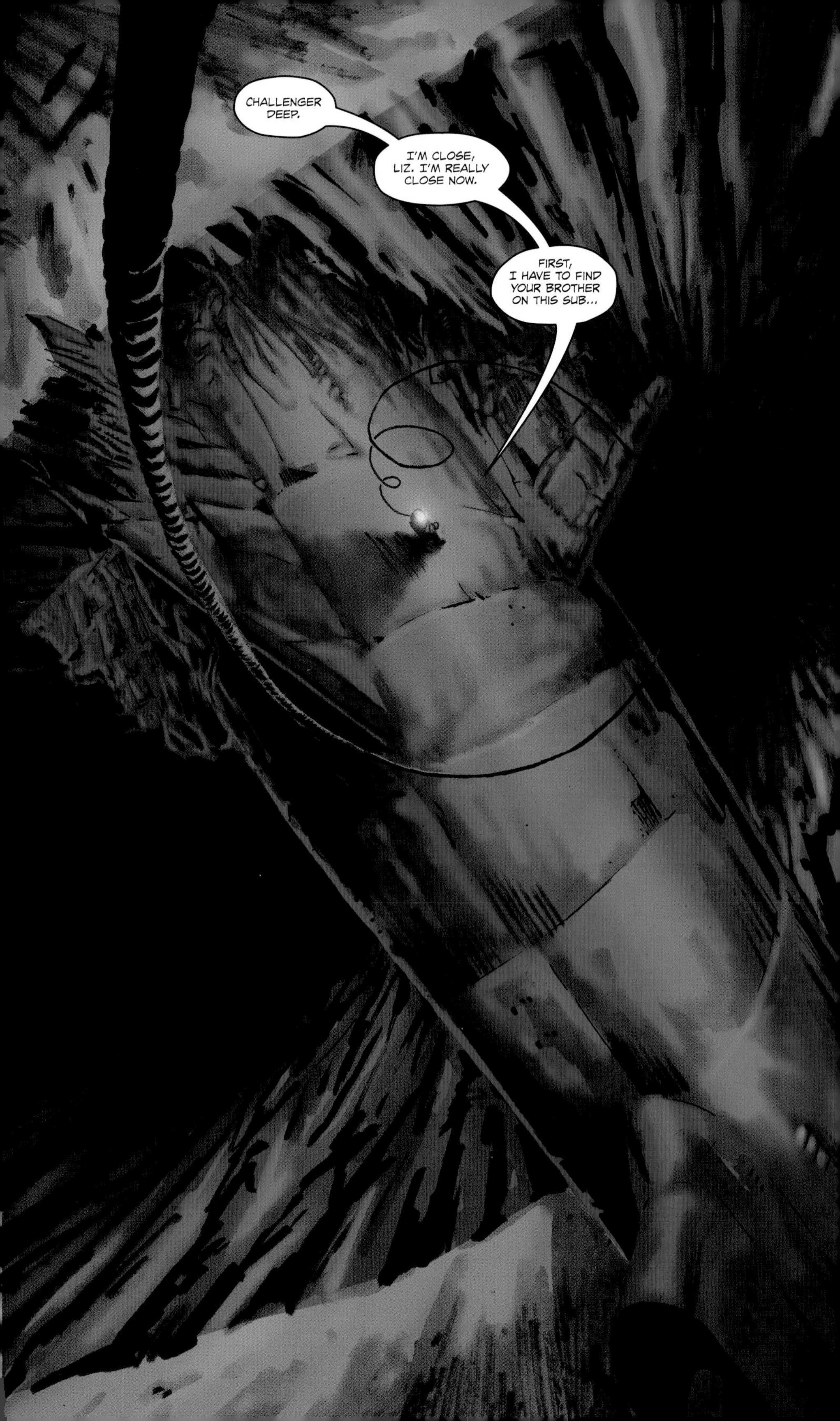
CHALLENGER DEEP.
I'M CLOSE, LIZ. I'M REALLY CLOSE NOW.
FIRST, I HAVE TO FIND YOUR BROTHER ON THIS SUB...

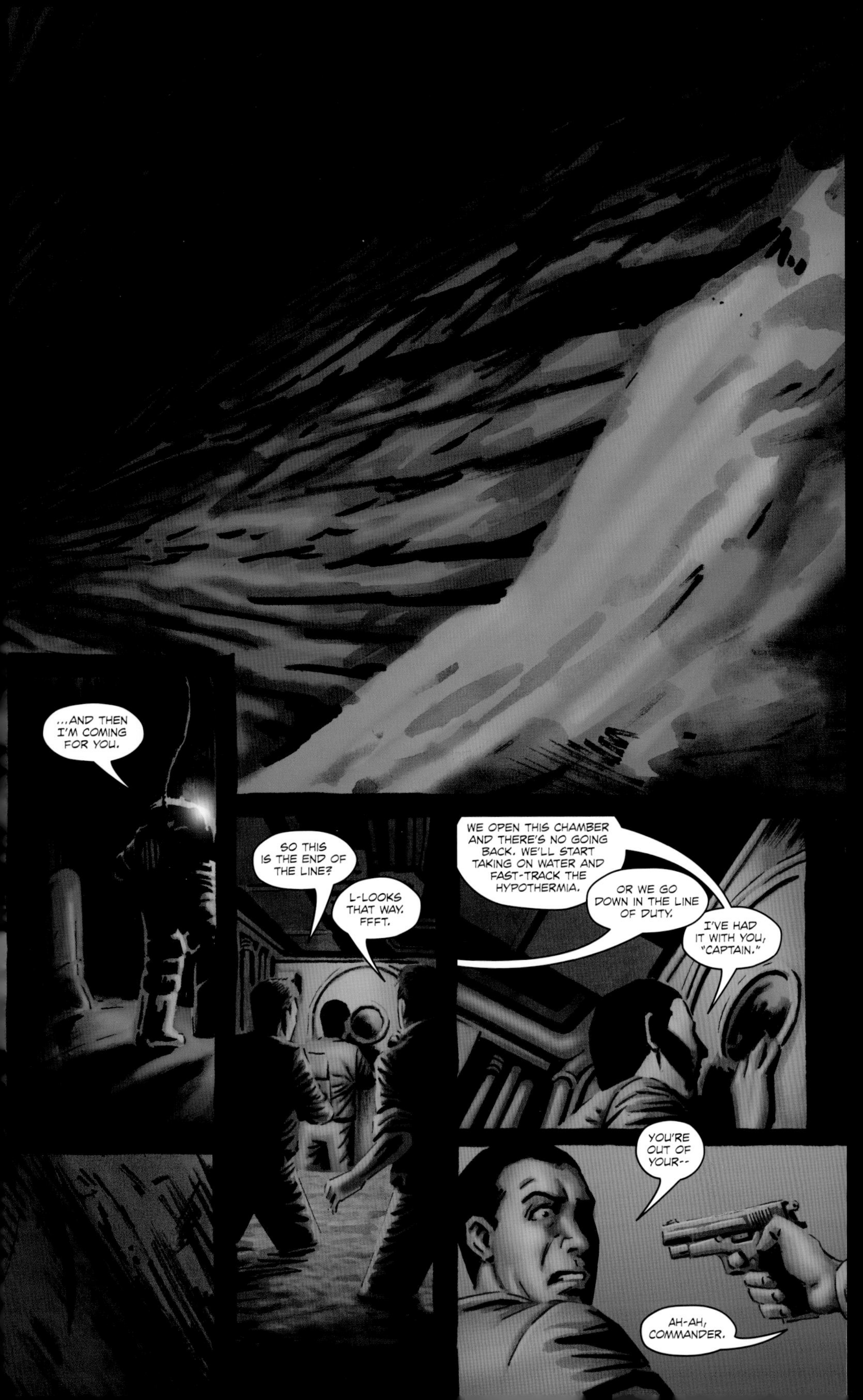
...AND THEN I'M COMING FOR YOU.
SO THIS IS THE END OF THE LINE?
L-LOOKS THAT WAY. FFFT.
WE OPEN THIS CHAMBER AND THERE'S NO GOING BACK. WE'LL START TAKING ON WATER AND FAST-TRACK THE HYPOTHERMIA.
OR WE GO DOWN IN THE LINE OF DUTY.
I'VE HAD IT WITH YOU, "CAPTAIN."
YOU'RE OUT OF YOUR--
AH-AH, COMMANDER.

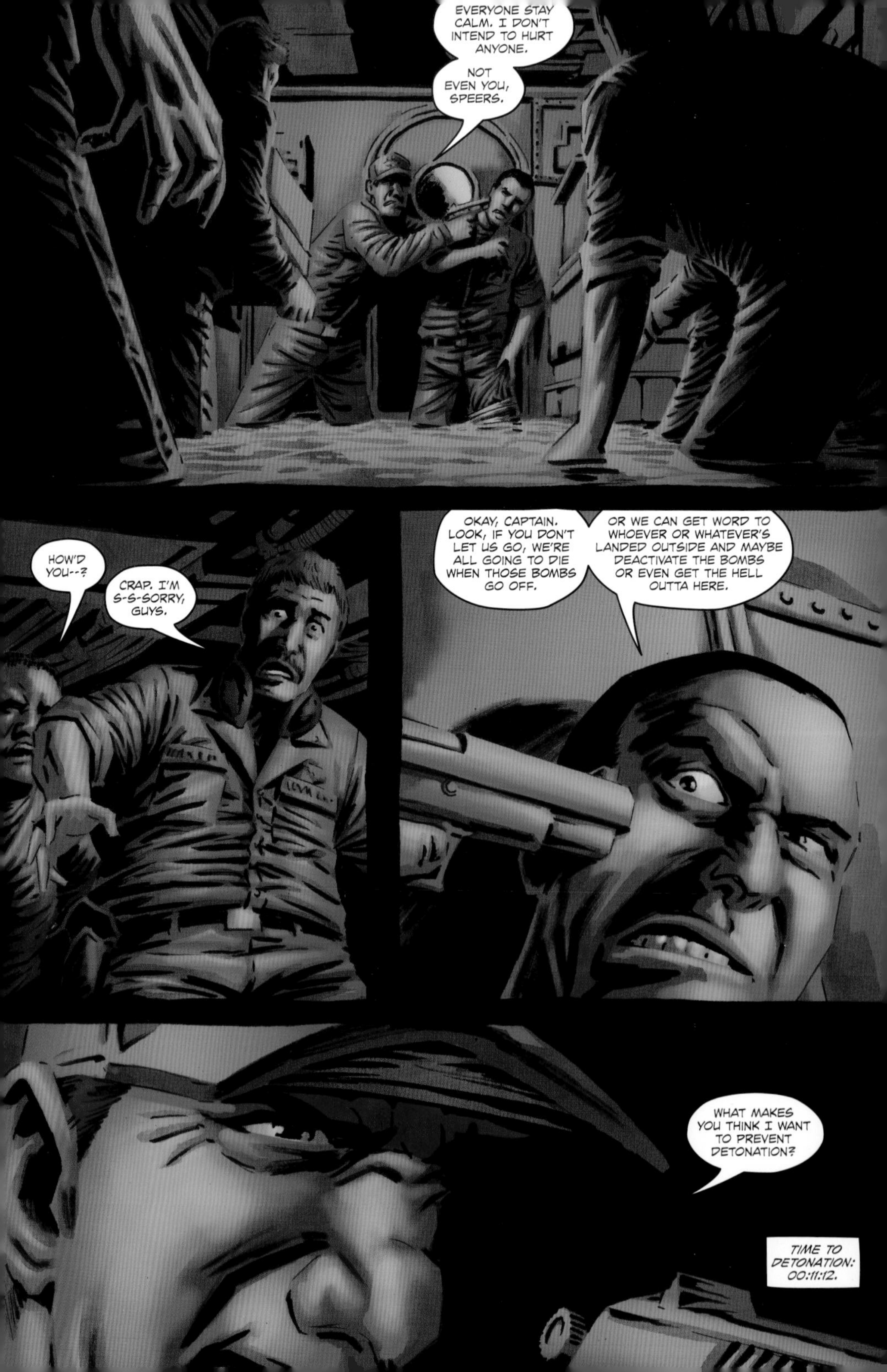
EVERYONE STAY CALM. I DON'T INTEND TO HURT ANYONE.
NOT EVEN YOU, SPEERS.
HOW'D YOU--?
CRAP. I'M S-S-SORRY, GUYS.
OKAY, CAPTAIN. LOOK, IF YOU DON'T LET US GO, WE'RE ALL GOING TO DIE WHEN THOSE BOMBS GO OFF.
OR WE CAN GET WORD TO WHOEVER OR WHATEVER'S LANDED OUTSIDE AND MAYBE DEACTIVATE THE BOMBS OR EVEN GET THE HELL OUTTA HERE.
WHAT MAKES YOU THINK I WANT TO PREVENT DETONATION?
TIME TO DETONATION: 00:11:12.

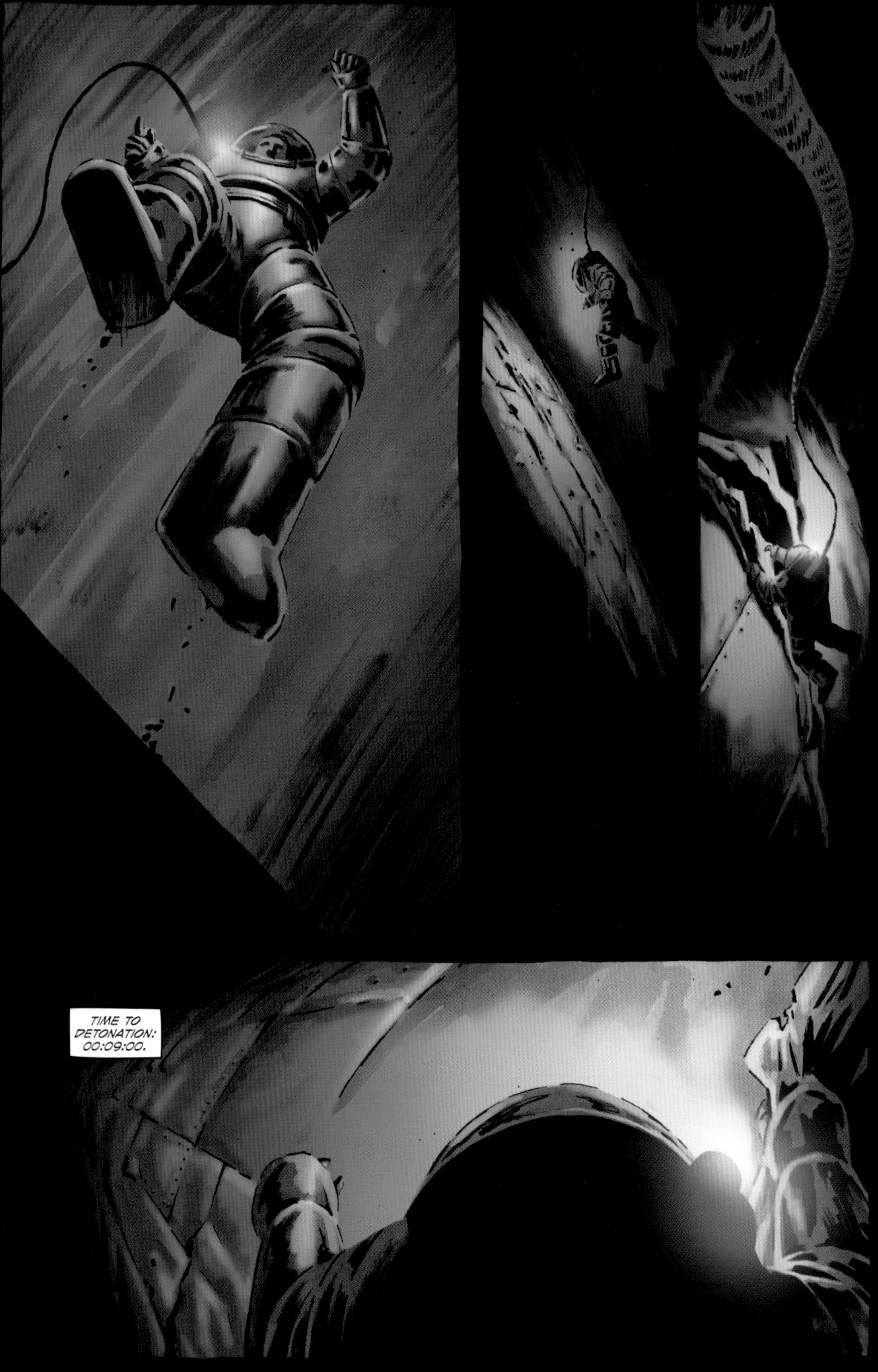
TIME TO DETONATION: 00:09:00.

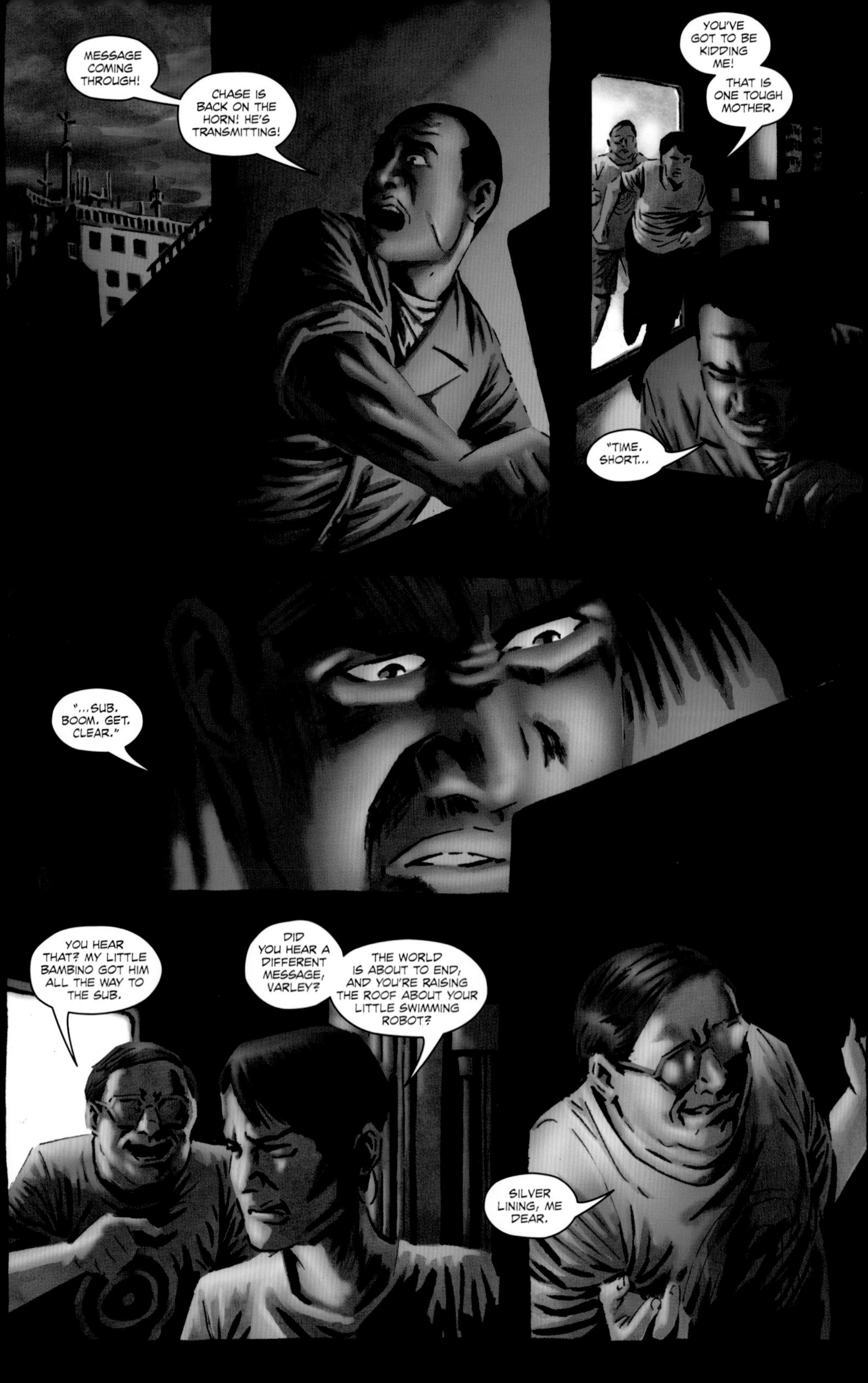
MESSAGE COMING THROUGH!
CHASE IS BACK ON THE HORN! HE'S TRANSMITTING!
YOU'VE GOT TO BE KIDDING ME!
THAT IS ONE TOUGH MOTHER.
"TIME. SHORT...
"...SUB. BOOM. GET. CLEAR."
YOU HEAR THAT? MY LITTLE BAMBINO GOT HIM ALL THE WAY TO THE SUB.
DID YOU HEAR A DIFFERENT MESSAGE, VARLEY?
THE WORLD IS ABOUT TO END, AND YOU'RE RAISING THE ROOF ABOUT YOUR LITTLE SWIMMING ROBOT?
SILVER LINING, ME DEAR.

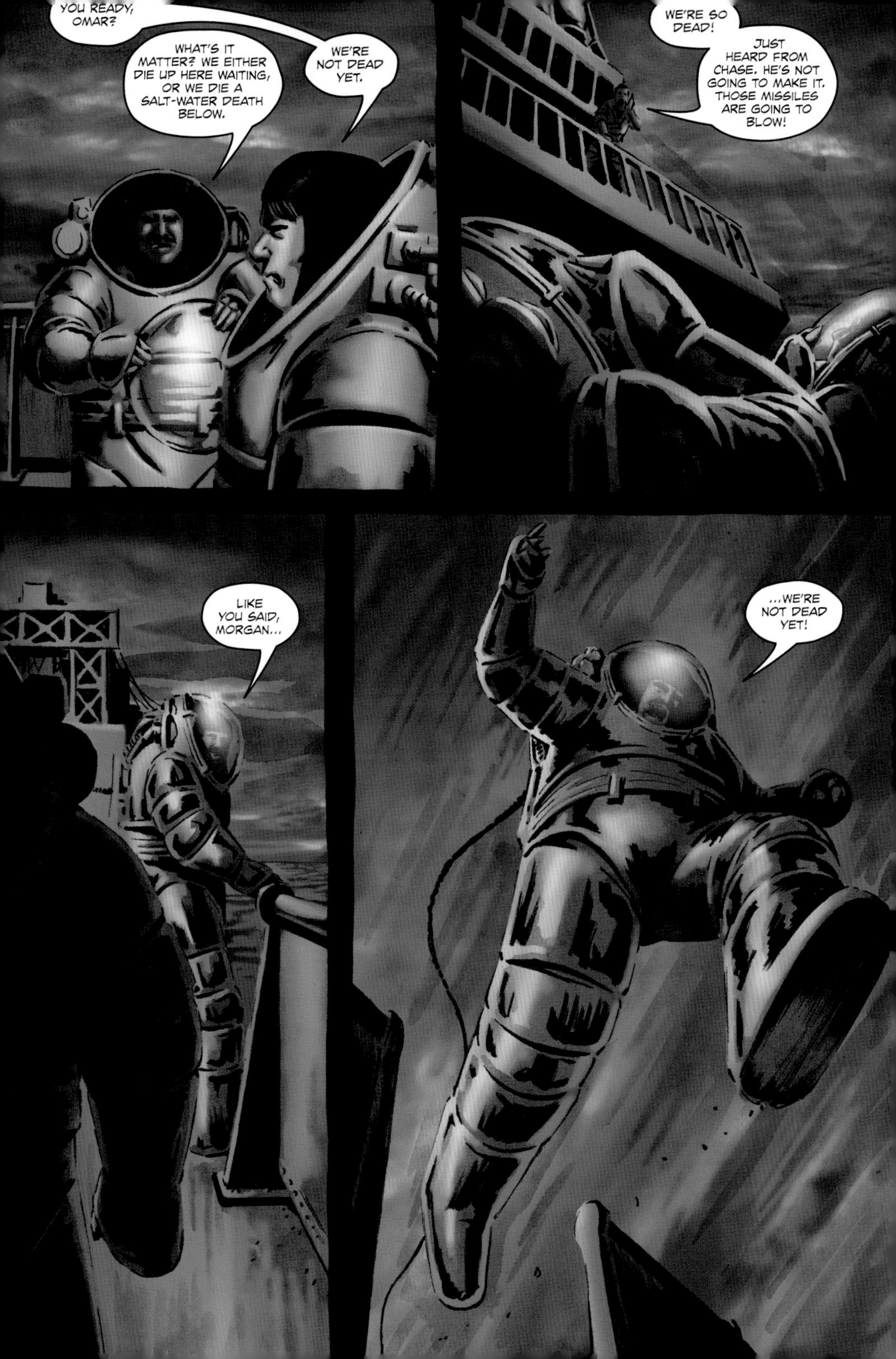
YOU READY, OMAR?
WHAT'S IT MATTER? WE EITHER DIE UP HERE WAITING, OR WE DIE A SALT-WATER DEATH BELOW.
WE'RE NOT DEAD YET.
WE'RE SO DEAD!
JUST HEARD FROM CHASE. HE'S NOT GOING TO MAKE IT. THOSE MISSILES ARE GOING TO BLOW!
LIKE YOU SAID, MORGAN...
...WE'RE NOT DEAD YET!

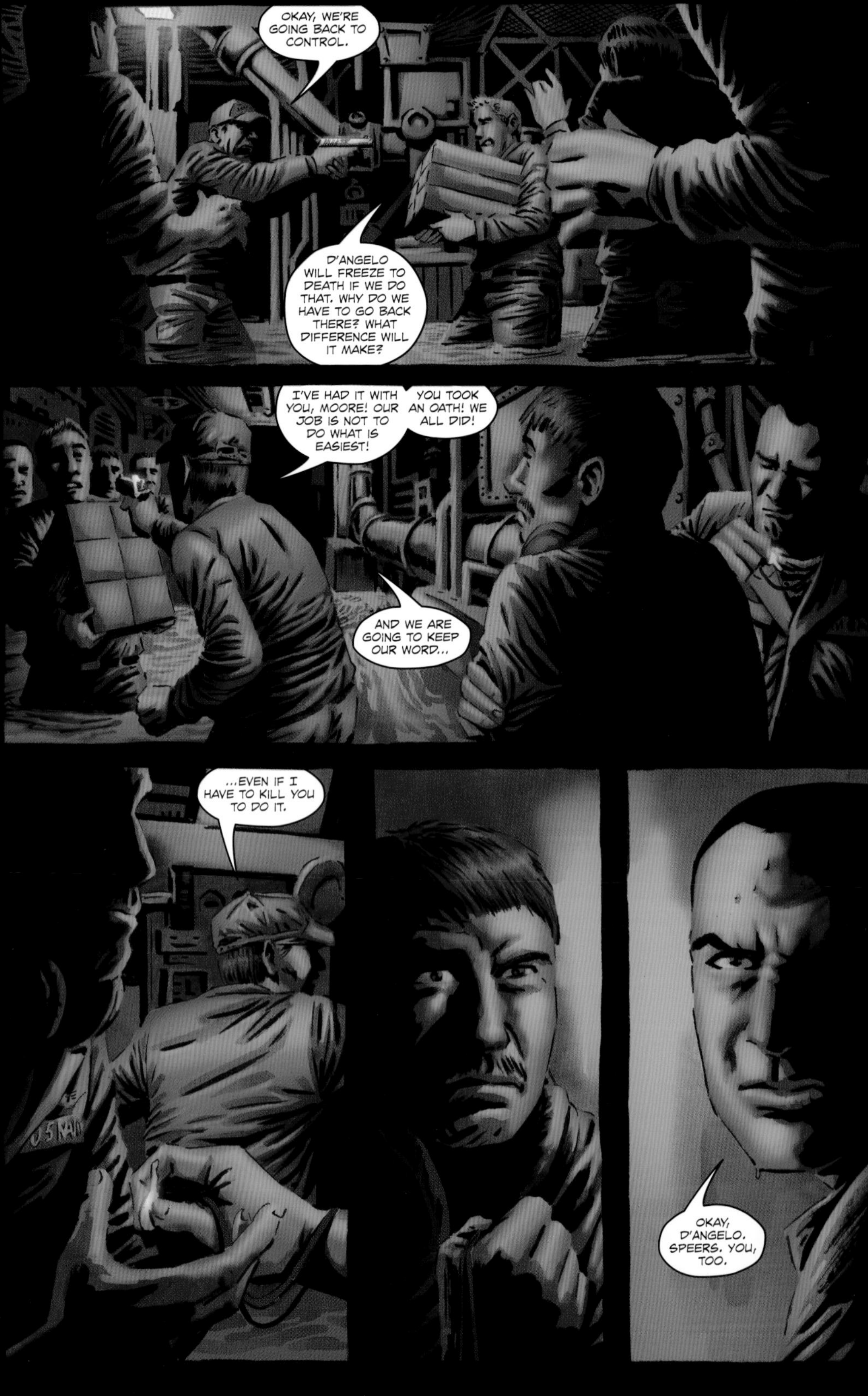
OKAY, WE'RE GOING BACK TO CONTROL.
D'ANGELO WILL FREEZE TO DEATH IF WE DO THAT. WHY DO WE HAVE TO GO BACK THERE? WHAT DIFFERENCE WILL IT MAKE?
I'VE HAD IT WITH YOU, MOORE! OUR JOB IS NOT TO DO WHAT IS EASIEST!
YOU TOOK AN OATH! WE ALL DID!
AND WE ARE GOING TO KEEP OUR WORD...
...EVEN IF I HAVE TO KILL YOU TO DO IT.
OKAY, D'ANGELO. SPEERS. YOU, TOO.

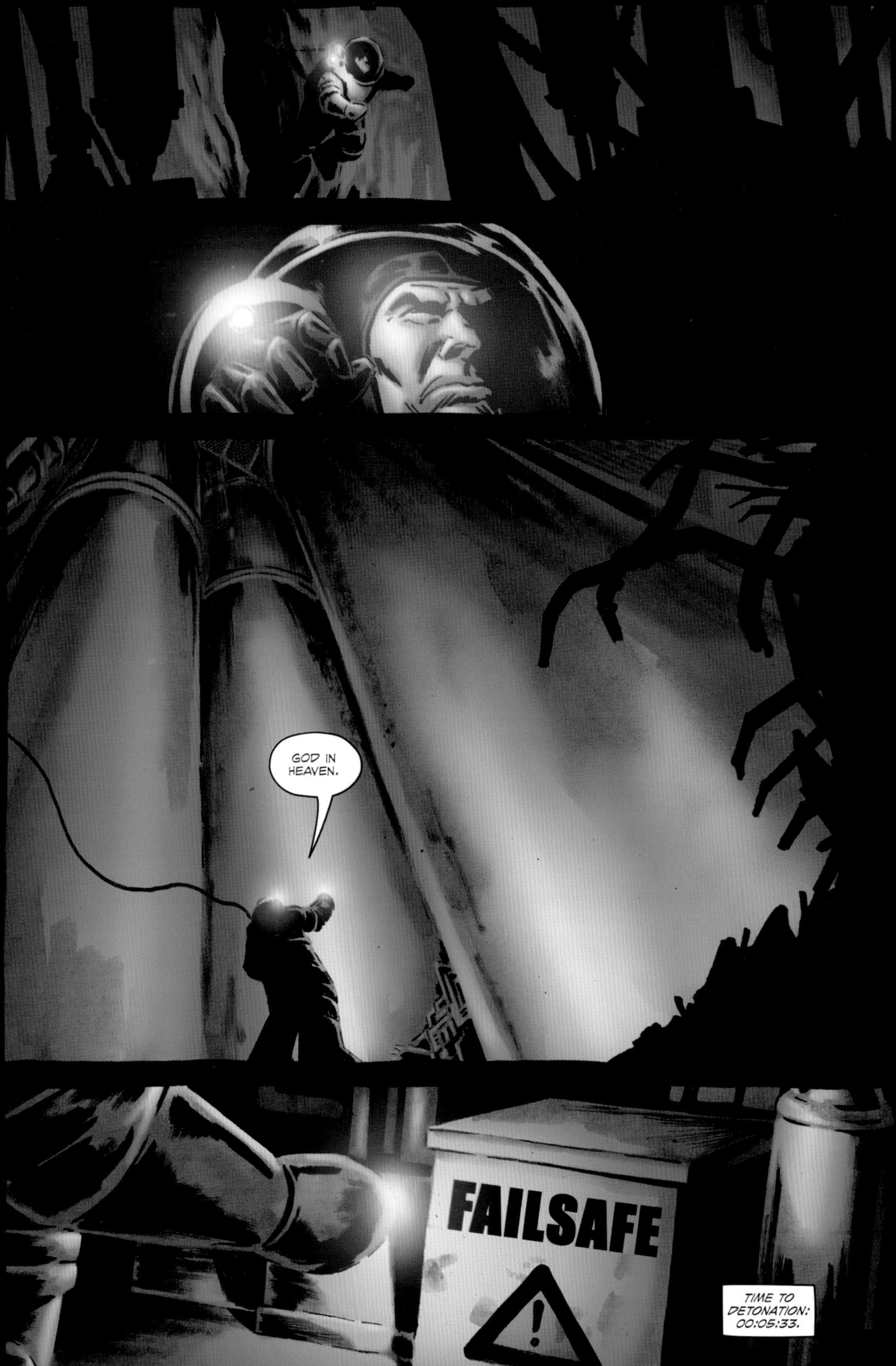
GOD IN HEAVEN.
FAILSAFE
TIME TO DETONATION: 00:05:33.

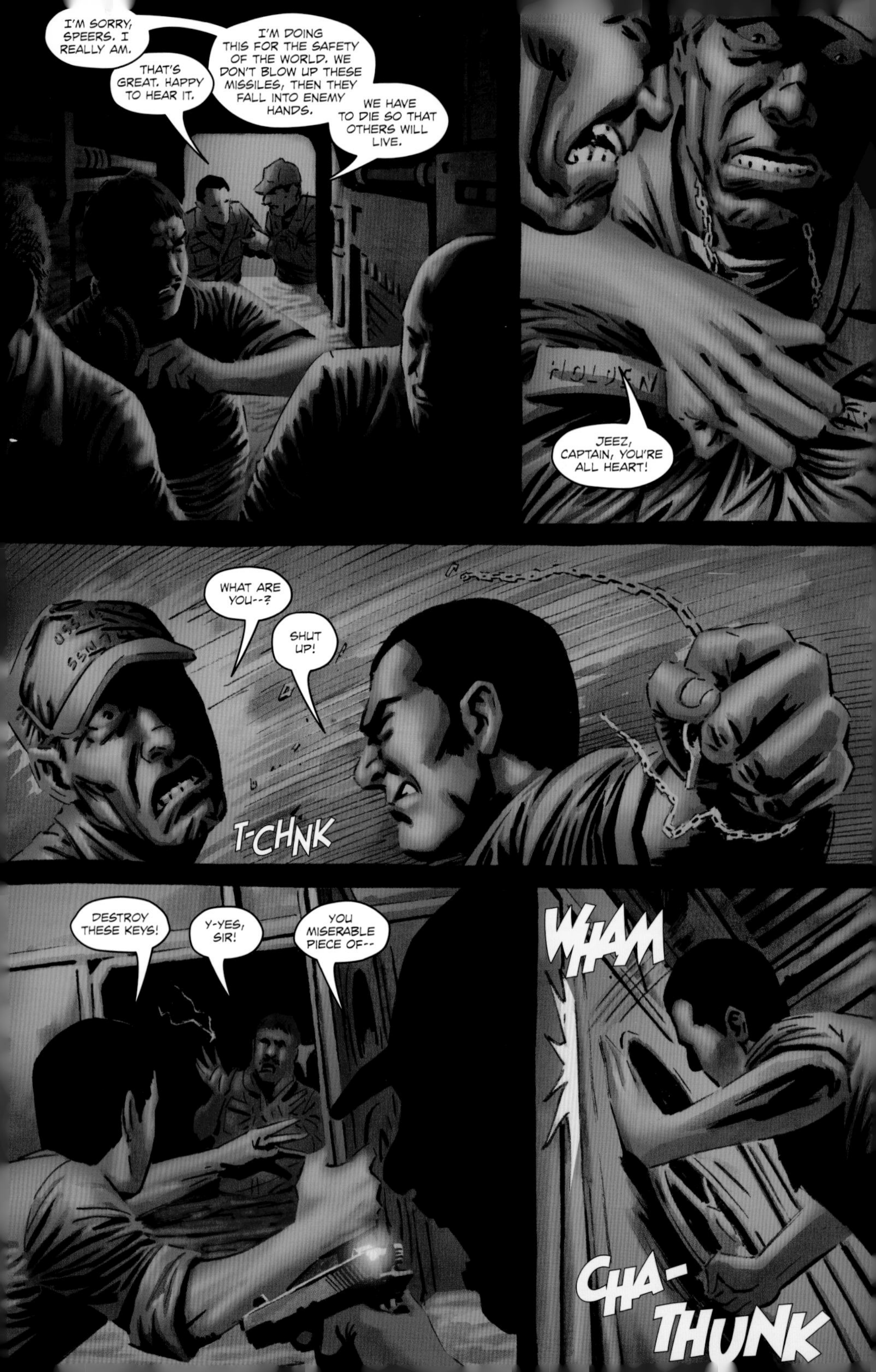
I'M SORRY, SPEERS. I REALLY AM.
THAT'S GREAT. HAPPY TO HEAR IT.
I'M DOING THIS FOR THE SAFETY OF THE WORLD. WE DON'T BLOW UP THESE MISSILES, THEN THEY FALL INTO ENEMY HANDS.
WE HAVE TO DIE SO THAT OTHERS WILL LIVE.
HOLDEN
JEEZ, CAPTAIN, YOU'RE ALL HEART!
WHAT ARE YOU--?
SHUT UP!
T-CHNK
DESTROY THESE KEYS!
Y-YES, SIR!
YOU MISERABLE PIECE OF--
WHAM
CHA-THUNK

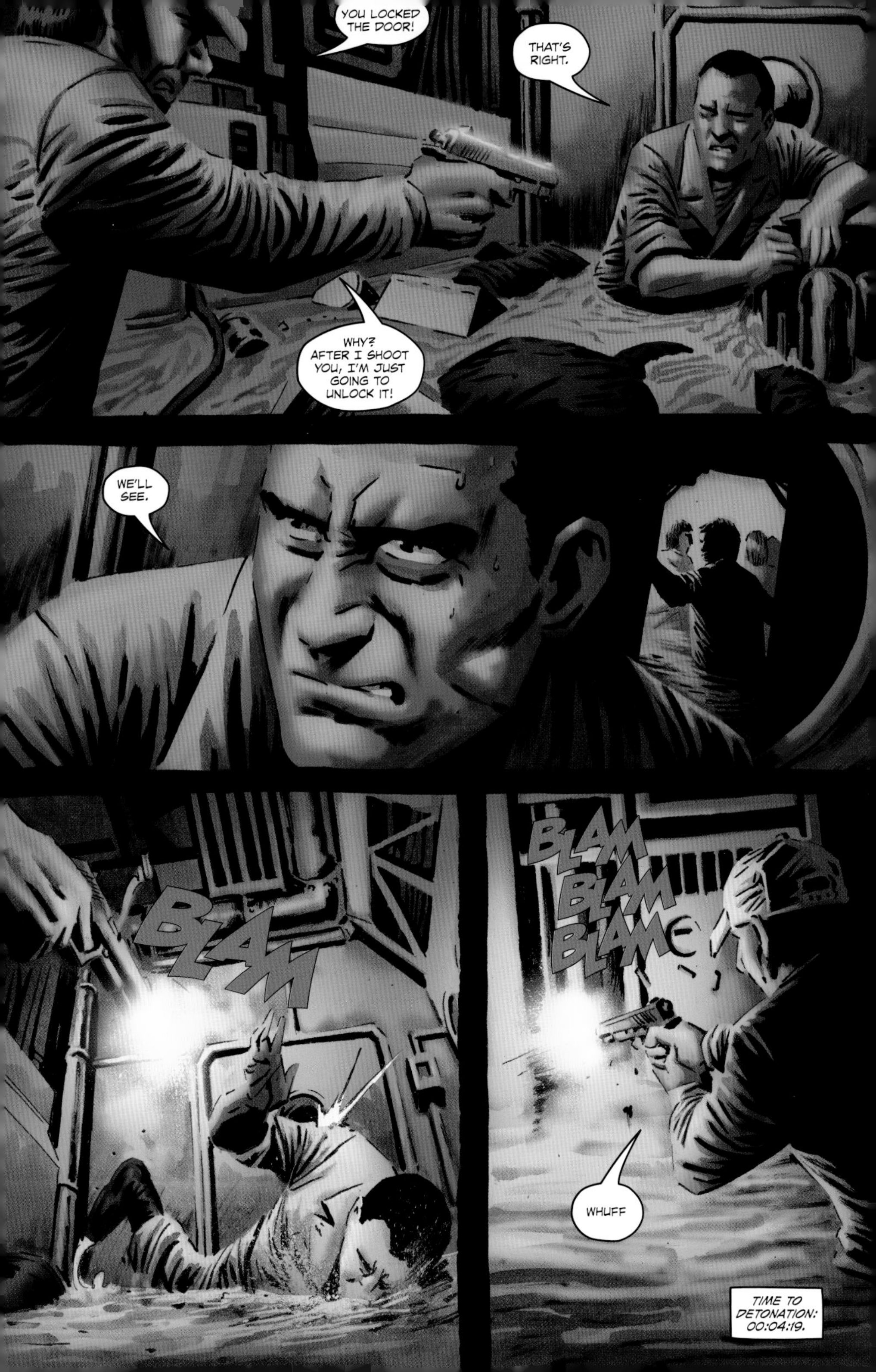
YOU LOCKED THE DOOR!
THAT'S RIGHT.
WHY? AFTER I SHOOT YOU, I'M JUST GOING TO UNLOCK IT!
WE'LL SEE.
BLAM
BLAM BLAM BLAM
WHUFF
TIME TO DETONATION: 00:04:19.

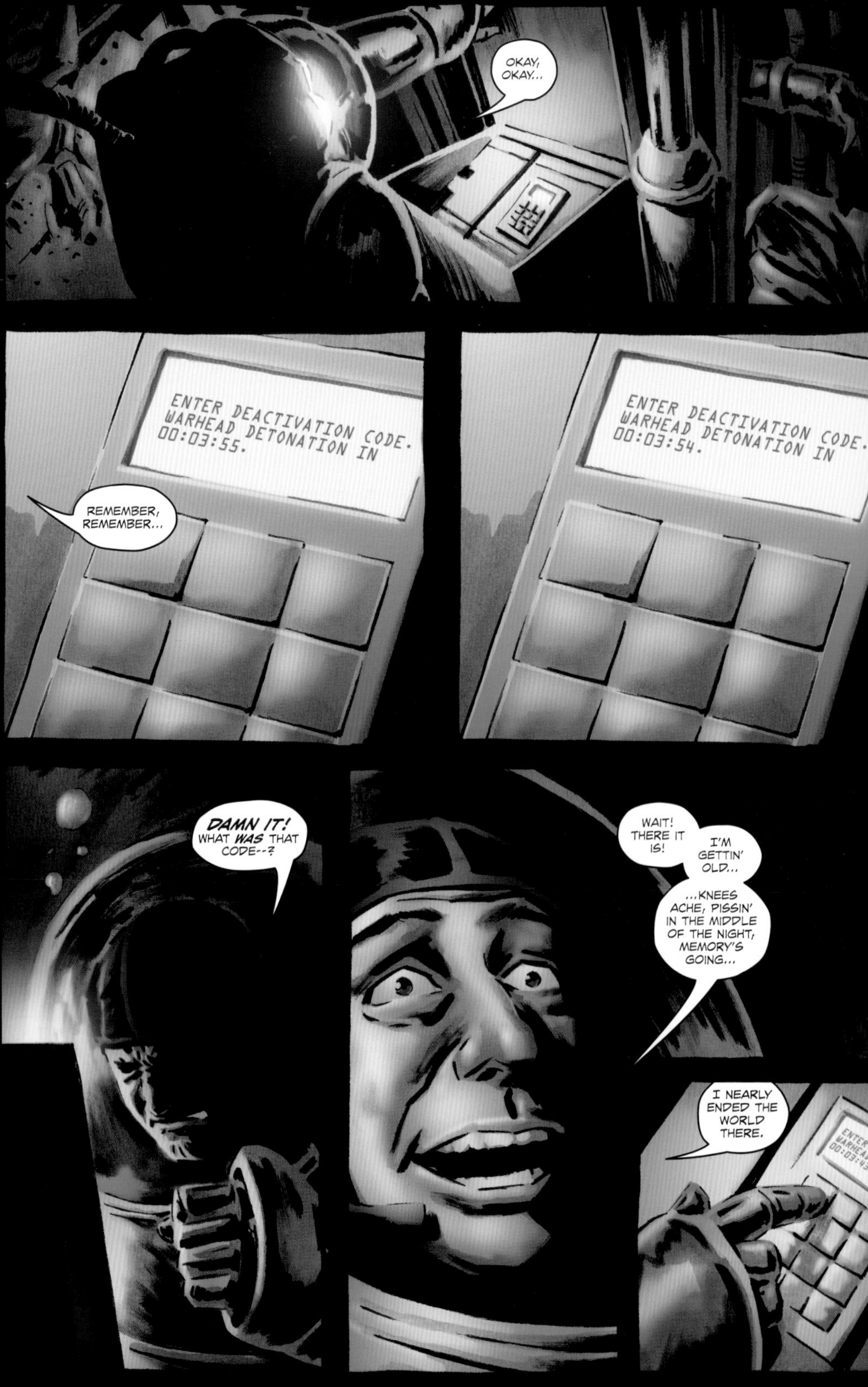
OKAY, OKAY...
ENTER DEACTIVATION CODE. WARHEAD DETONATION IN 00:03:55.
REMEMBER, REMEMBER...
ENTER DEACTIVATION CODE. WARHEAD DETONATION IN 00:03:54.
DAMN IT! WHAT WAS THAT CODE--?
WAIT! THERE IT IS!
I'M GETTIN' OLD...
...KNEES ACHE, PISSIN' IN THE MIDDLE OF THE NIGHT, MEMORY'S GOING...
I NEARLY ENDED THE WORLD THERE.

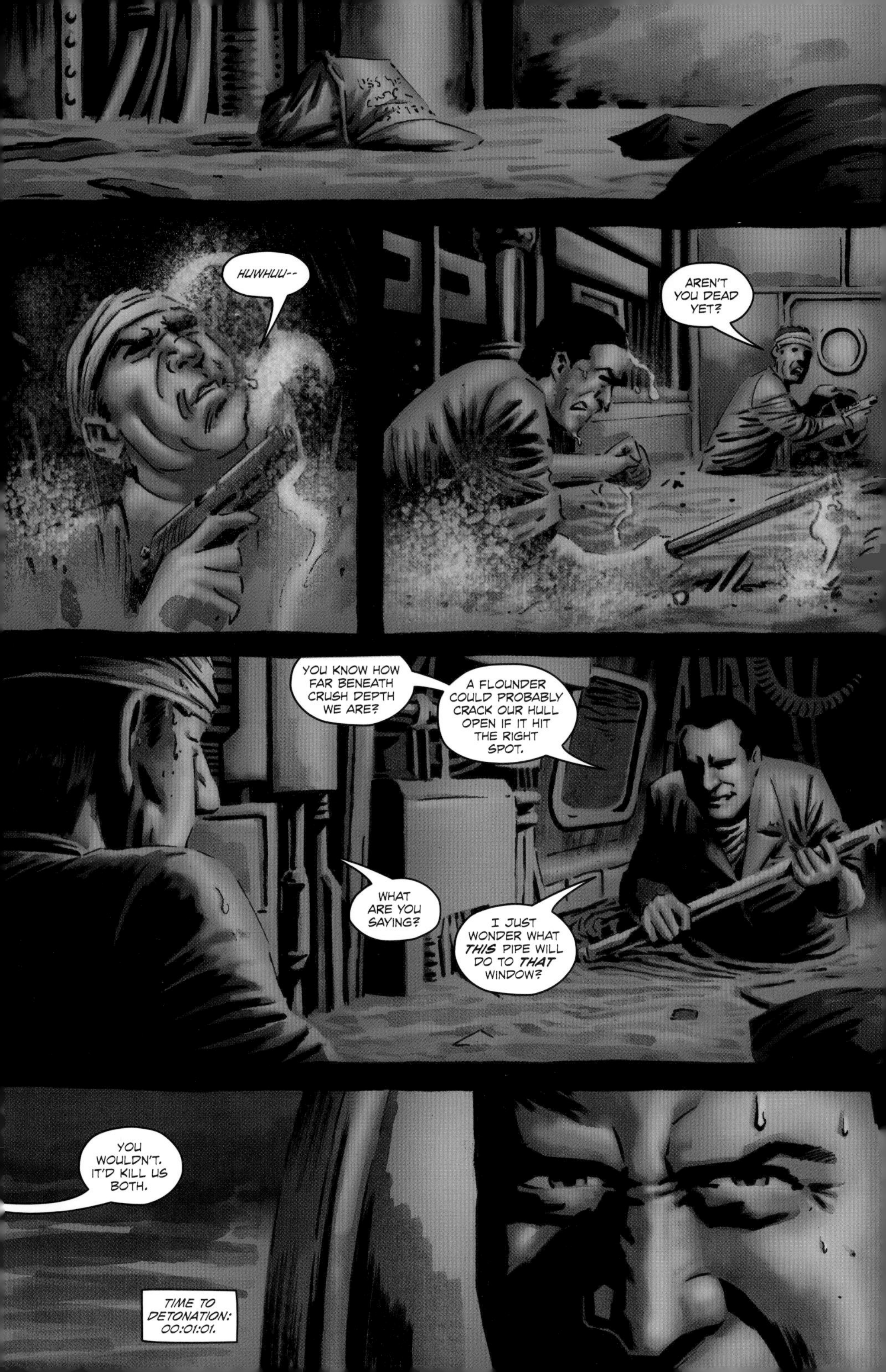

HUWHUU--
AREN'T YOU DEAD YET?
YOU KNOW HOW FAR BENEATH CRUSH DEPTH WE ARE?
A FLOUNDER COULD PROBABLY CRACK OUR HULL OPEN IF IT HIT THE RIGHT SPOT.
WHAT ARE YOU SAYING?
I JUST WONDER WHAT THIS PIPE WILL DO TO THAT WINDOW?
YOU WOULDN'T. IT'D KILL US BOTH.
TIME TO DETONATION: 00:01:01.

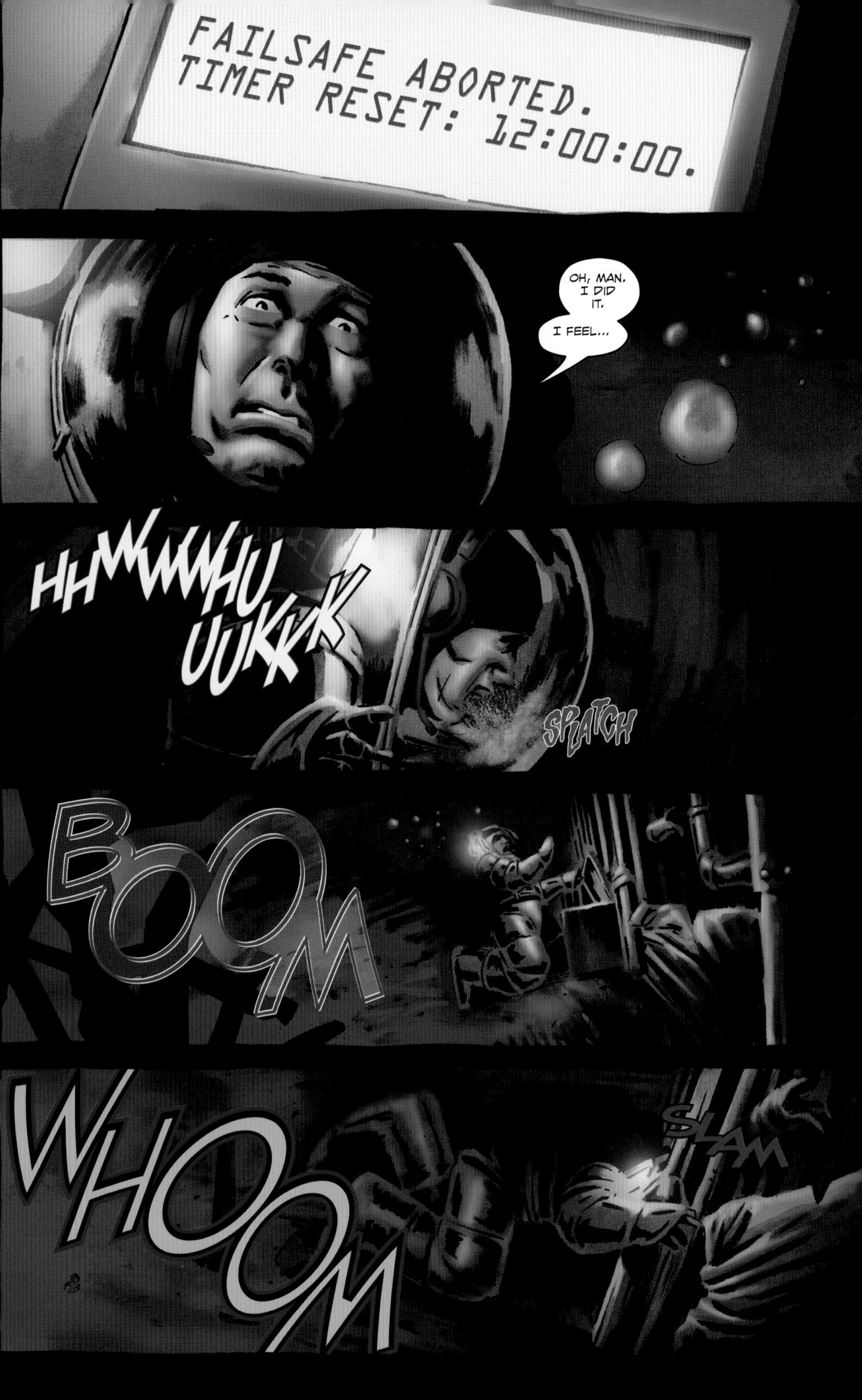
FAILSAFE ABORTED.
TIMER RESET: 12:00:00.
OH, MAN. I DID IT.
I FEEL...
HHWWWHU UUKKK
SPLATCH
BOOM
WHOOM
SLAM

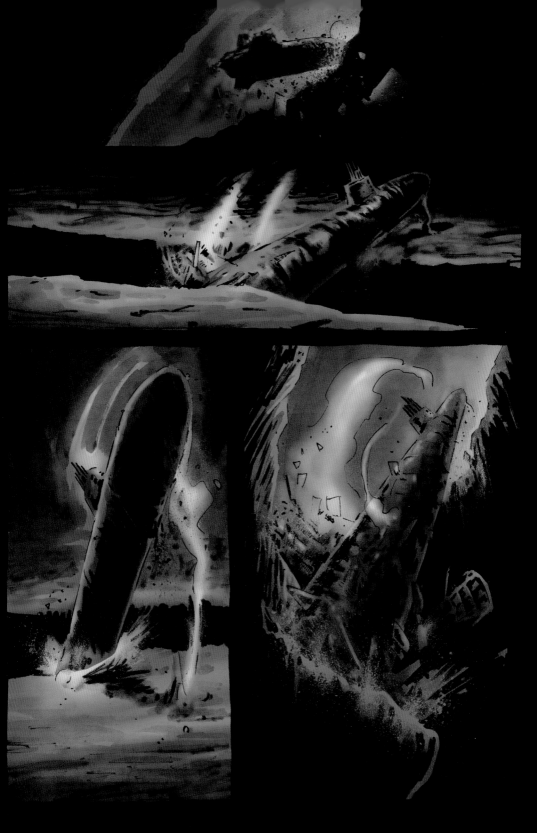

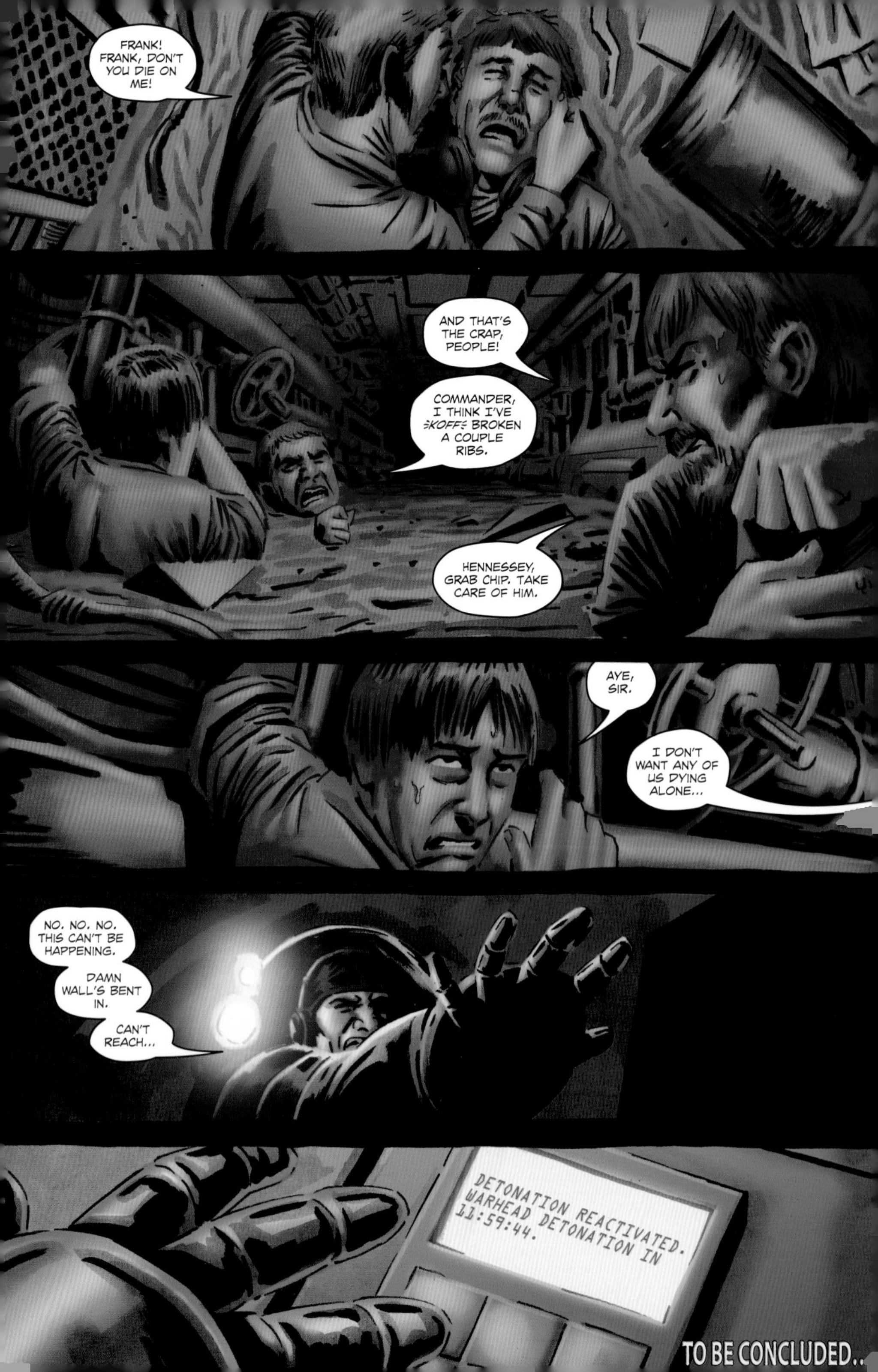
FRANK! FRANK, DON'T YOU DIE ON ME!
AND THAT'S THE CRAP, PEOPLE!
COMMANDER, I THINK I'VE *KOFF* BROKEN A COUPLE RIBS.
HENNESSEY, GRAB CHIP. TAKE CARE OF HIM.
AYE, SIR.
I DON'T WANT ANY OF US DYING ALONE...
NO. NO. NO. THIS CAN'T BE HAPPENING.
DAMN WALL'S BENT IN.
CAN'T REACH...
DETONATION REACTIVATED.
WARHEAD DETONATION IN
11:59:44.
TO BE CONCLUDED..

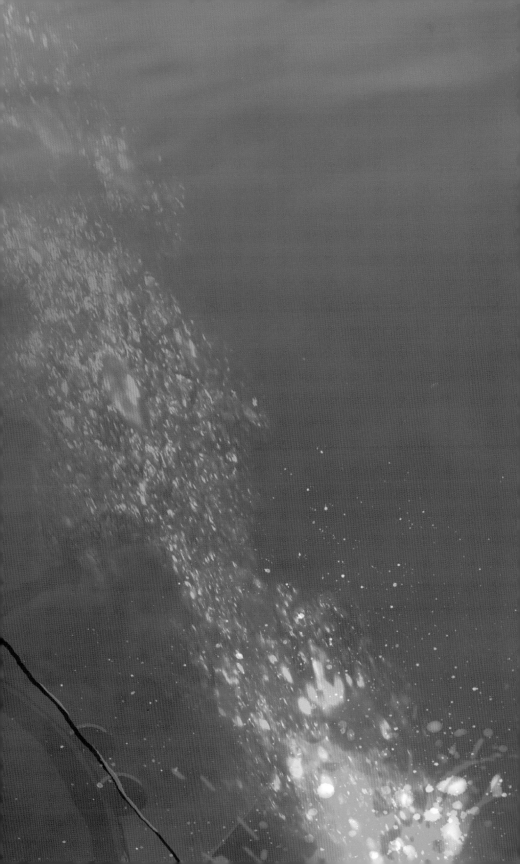

# CHAPTER 4

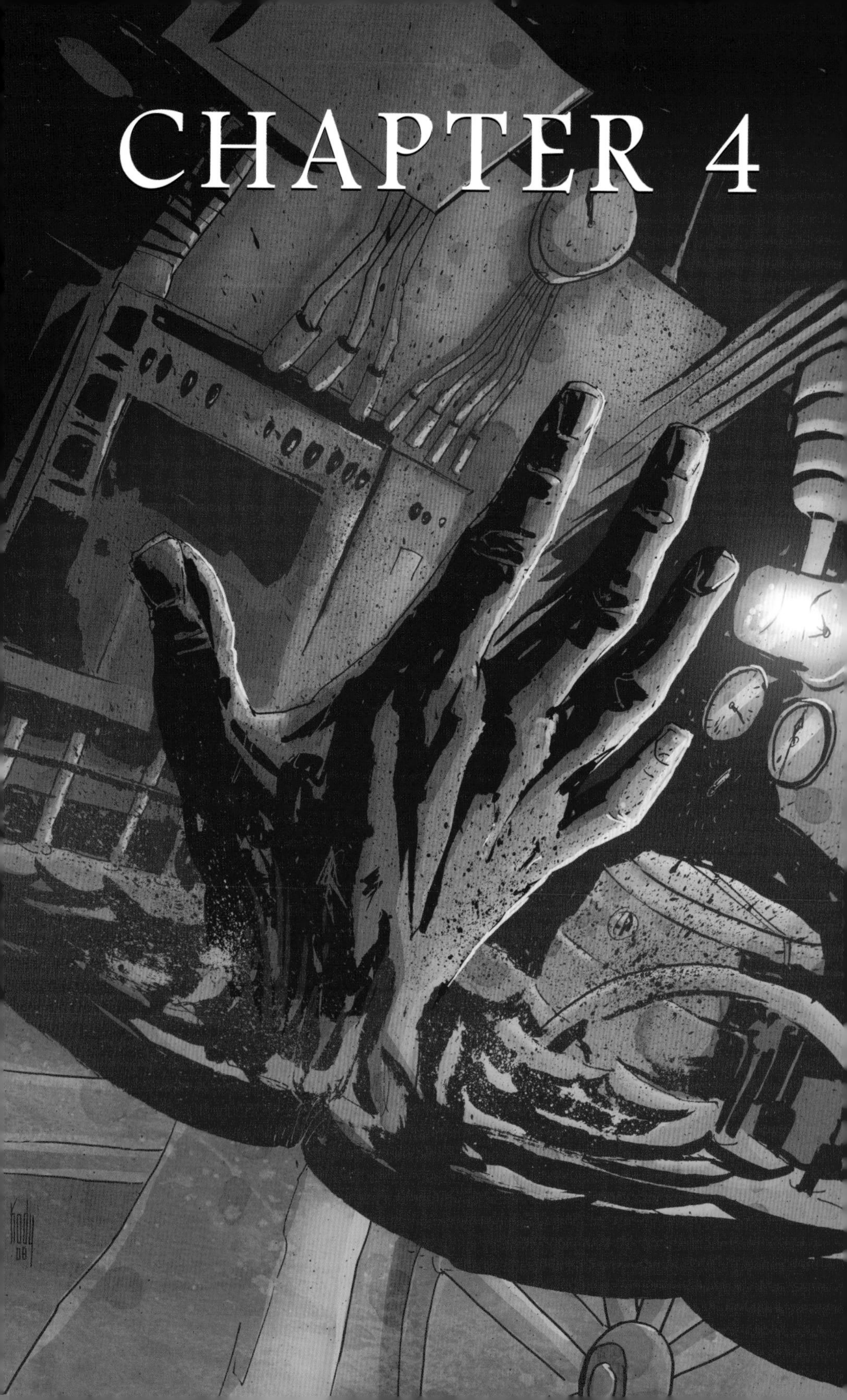

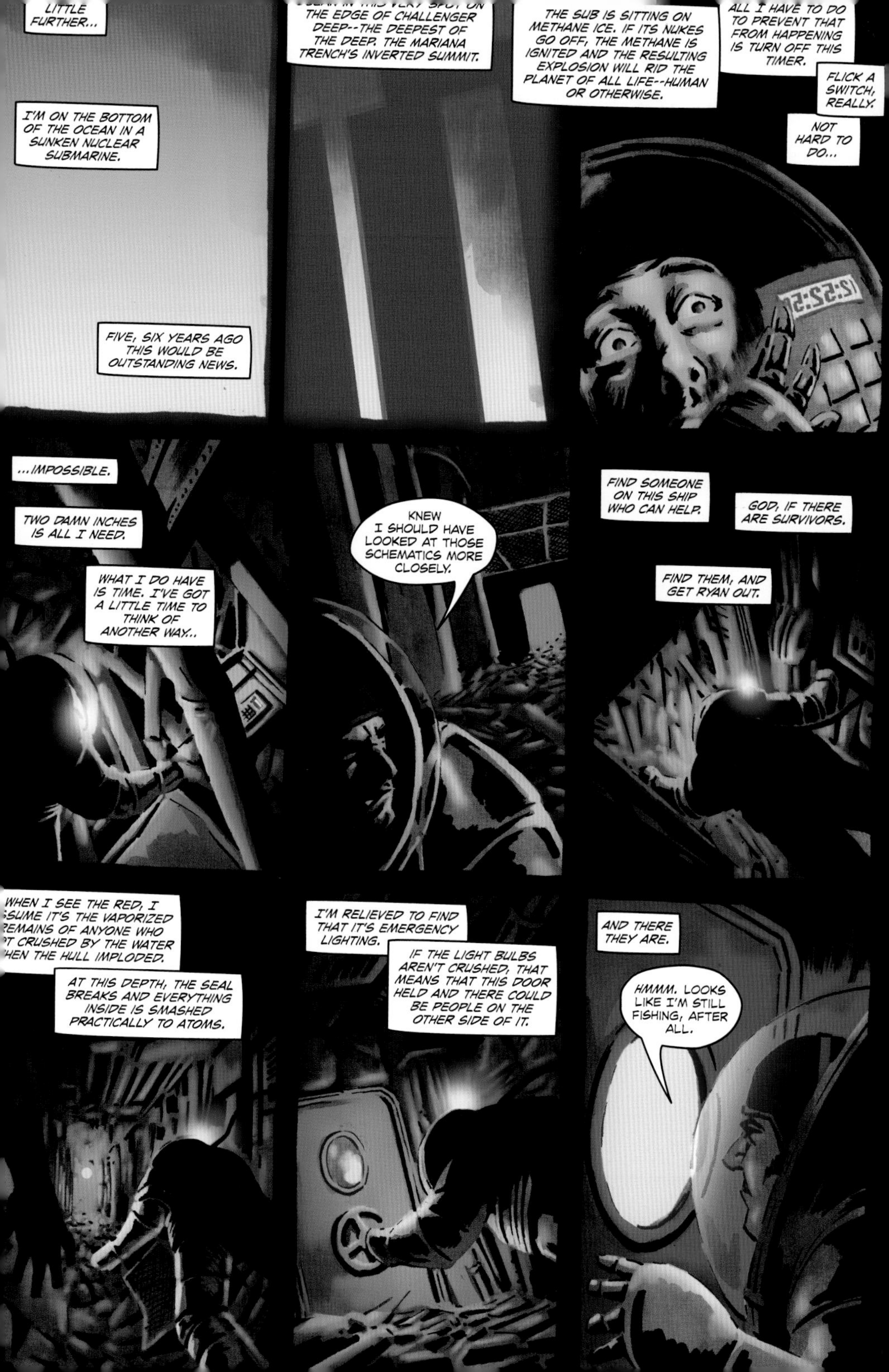

LITTLE FURTHER...
I'M ON THE BOTTOM OF THE OCEAN IN A SUNKEN NUCLEAR SUBMARINE.
FIVE, SIX YEARS AGO THIS WOULD BE OUTSTANDING NEWS.
THE EDGE OF CHALLENGER DEEP--THE DEEPEST OF THE DEEP. THE MARIANA TRENCH'S INVERTED SUMMIT.
THE SUB IS SITTING ON METHANE ICE. IF ITS NUKES GO OFF, THE METHANE IS IGNITED AND THE RESULTING EXPLOSION WILL RID THE PLANET OF ALL LIFE--HUMAN OR OTHERWISE.
ALL I HAVE TO DO TO PREVENT THAT FROM HAPPENING IS TURN OFF THIS TIMER.
FLICK A SWITCH, REALLY.
NOT HARD TO DO...
...IMPOSSIBLE.
TWO DAMN INCHES IS ALL I NEED.
WHAT I DO HAVE IS TIME. I'VE GOT A LITTLE TIME TO THINK OF ANOTHER WAY...
KNEW I SHOULD HAVE LOOKED AT THOSE SCHEMATICS MORE CLOSELY.
FIND SOMEONE ON THIS SHIP WHO CAN HELP.
GOD, IF THERE ARE SURVIVORS.
FIND THEM, AND GET RYAN OUT.
WHEN I SEE THE RED, I SSUME IT'S THE VAPORIZED REMAINS OF ANYONE WHO T CRUSHED BY THE WATER HEN THE HULL IMPLODED.
AT THIS DEPTH, THE SEAL BREAKS AND EVERYTHING INSIDE IS SMASHED PRACTICALLY TO ATOMS.
I'M RELIEVED TO FIND THAT IT'S EMERGENCY LIGHTING.
IF THE LIGHT BULBS AREN'T CRUSHED, THAT MEANS THAT THIS DOOR HELD AND THERE COULD BE PEOPLE ON THE OTHER SIDE OF IT.
AND THERE THEY ARE.
HMMM. LOOKS LIKE I'M STILL FISHING, AFTER ALL.

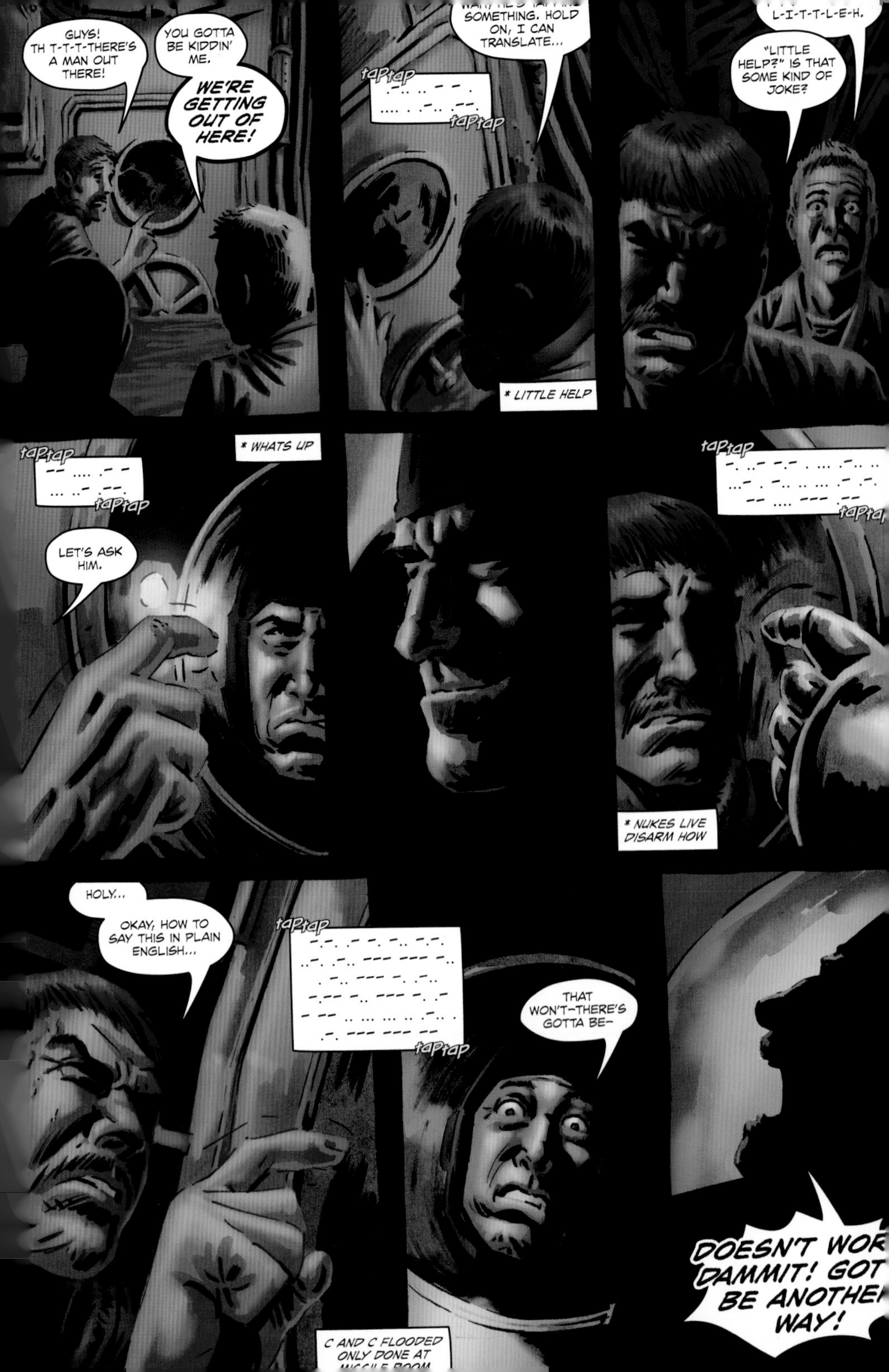
GUYS! TH T-T-T-THERE'S A MAN OUT THERE!
YOU GOTTA BE KIDDIN' ME.
WE'RE GETTING OUT OF HERE!
tap tap
tap tap
SOMETHING. HOLD ON, I CAN TRANSLATE...
* LITTLE HELP
L-I-T-T-L-E-H.
"LITTLE HELP?" IS THAT SOME KIND OF JOKE?
tap tap
tap tap
* WHATS UP
LET'S ASK HIM.
tap tap
tap tap
* NUKES LIVE DISARM HOW
HOLY...
OKAY, HOW TO SAY THIS IN PLAIN ENGLISH...
tap tap
tap tap
THAT WON'T–THERE'S GOTTA BE–
C AND C FLOODED ONLY DONE AT
DOESN'T WOR DAMMIT! GOT BE ANOTHE WAY!

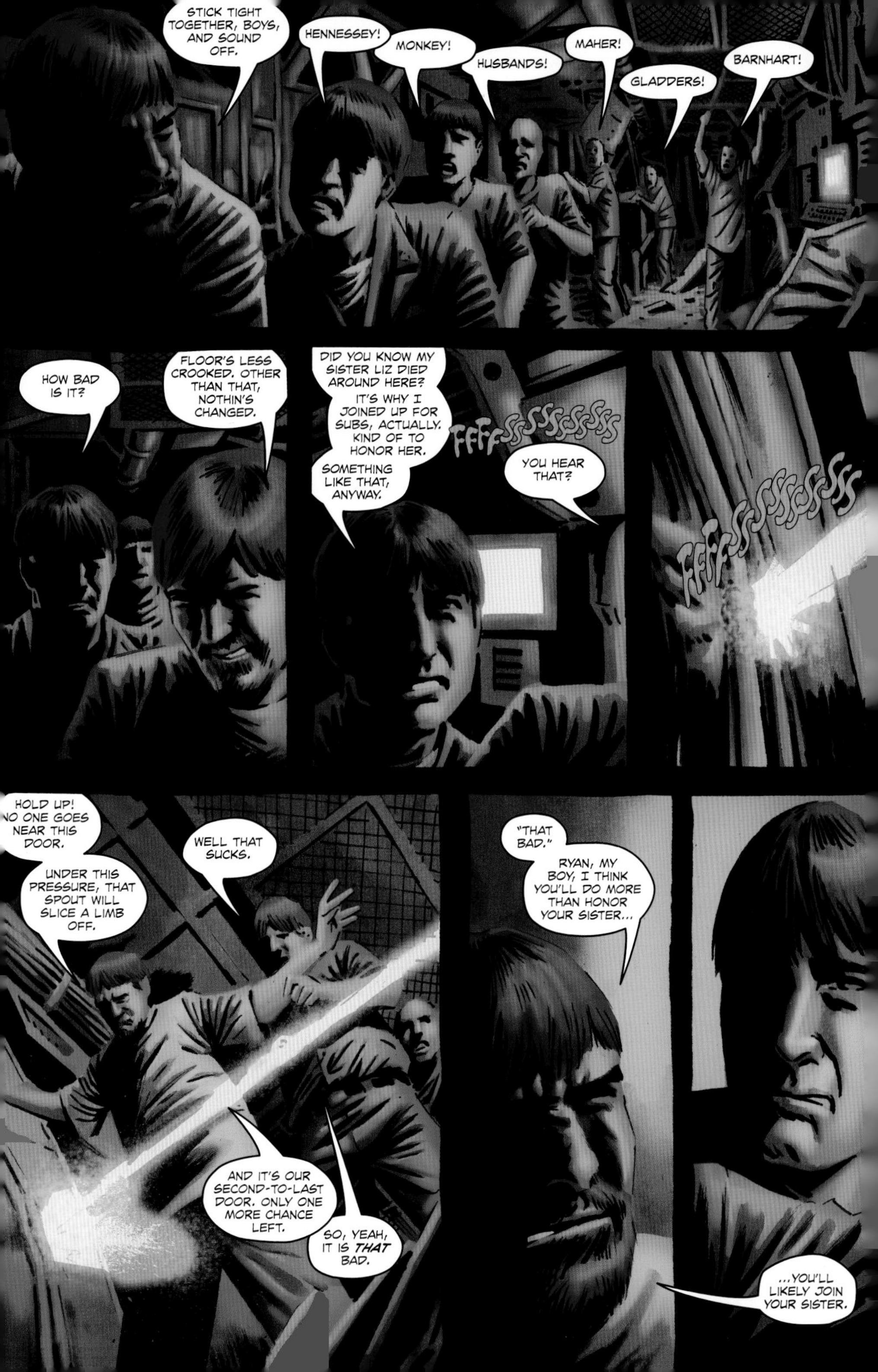
STICK TIGHT TOGETHER, BOYS, AND SOUND OFF.
HENNESSEY!
MONKEY!
HUSBANDS!
MAHER!
GLADDERS!
BARNHART!
HOW BAD IS IT?
FLOOR'S LESS CROOKED. OTHER THAN THAT, NOTHIN'S CHANGED.
DID YOU KNOW MY SISTER LIZ DIED AROUND HERE?
IT'S WHY I JOINED UP FOR SUBS, ACTUALLY. KIND OF TO HONOR HER.
SOMETHING LIKE THAT, ANYWAY.
FFFFSSSSSSSSSSS
YOU HEAR THAT?
FFFFSSSSSSSSSSSS
HOLD UP! NO ONE GOES NEAR THIS DOOR.
UNDER THIS PRESSURE, THAT SPOUT WILL SLICE A LIMB OFF.
WELL THAT SUCKS.
AND IT'S OUR SECOND-TO-LAST DOOR. ONLY ONE MORE CHANCE LEFT.
SO, YEAH, IT IS *THAT* BAD.
"THAT BAD."
RYAN, MY BOY, I THINK YOU'LL DO MORE THAN HONOR YOUR SISTER...
...YOU'LL LIKELY JOIN YOUR SISTER.

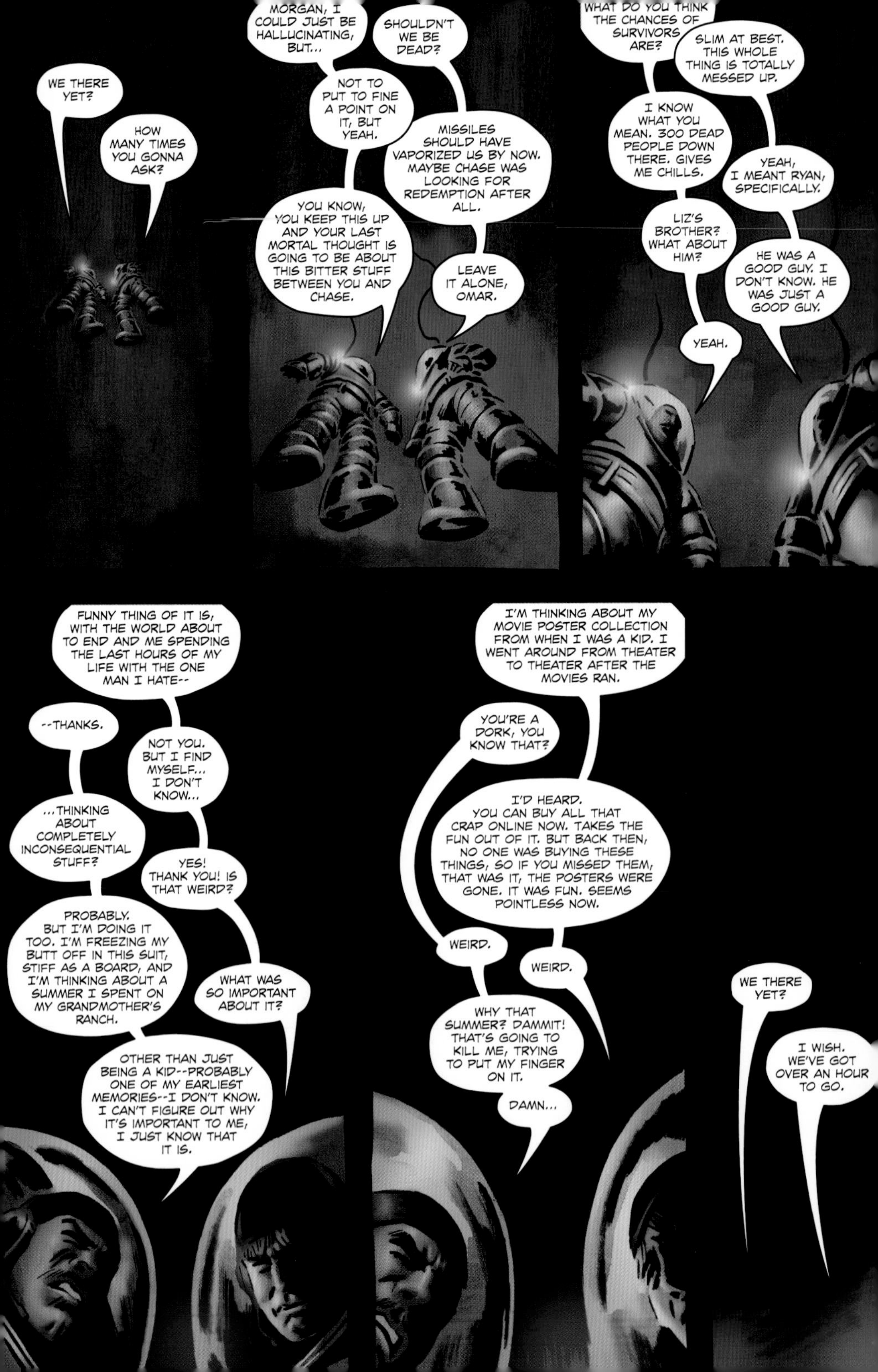
WE THERE YET?
HOW MANY TIMES YOU GONNA ASK?
MORGAN, I COULD JUST BE HALLUCINATING, BUT...
SHOULDN'T WE BE DEAD?
NOT TO PUT TO FINE A POINT ON IT, BUT YEAH.
MISSILES SHOULD HAVE VAPORIZED US BY NOW. MAYBE CHASE WAS LOOKING FOR REDEMPTION AFTER ALL.
YOU KNOW, YOU KEEP THIS UP AND YOUR LAST MORTAL THOUGHT IS GOING TO BE ABOUT THIS BITTER STUFF BETWEEN YOU AND CHASE.
LEAVE IT ALONE, OMAR.
WHAT DO YOU THINK THE CHANCES OF SURVIVORS ARE?
SLIM AT BEST. THIS WHOLE THING IS TOTALLY MESSED UP.
I KNOW WHAT YOU MEAN. 300 DEAD PEOPLE DOWN THERE. GIVES ME CHILLS.
YEAH, I MEANT RYAN, SPECIFICALLY.
LIZ'S BROTHER? WHAT ABOUT HIM?
HE WAS A GOOD GUY. I DON'T KNOW. HE WAS JUST A GOOD GUY.
YEAH.
FUNNY THING OF IT IS, WITH THE WORLD ABOUT TO END AND ME SPENDING THE LAST HOURS OF MY LIFE WITH THE ONE MAN I HATE--
--THANKS.
NOT YOU. BUT I FIND MYSELF... I DON'T KNOW...
...THINKING ABOUT COMPLETELY INCONSEQUENTIAL STUFF?
YES! THANK YOU! IS THAT WEIRD?
PROBABLY. BUT I'M DOING IT TOO. I'M FREEZING MY BUTT OFF IN THIS SUIT, STIFF AS A BOARD, AND I'M THINKING ABOUT A SUMMER I SPENT ON MY GRANDMOTHER'S RANCH.
WHAT WAS SO IMPORTANT ABOUT IT?
OTHER THAN JUST BEING A KID--PROBABLY ONE OF MY EARLIEST MEMORIES--I DON'T KNOW. I CAN'T FIGURE OUT WHY IT'S IMPORTANT TO ME, I JUST KNOW THAT IT IS.
I'M THINKING ABOUT MY MOVIE POSTER COLLECTION FROM WHEN I WAS A KID. I WENT AROUND FROM THEATER TO THEATER AFTER THE MOVIES RAN.
YOU'RE A DORK, YOU KNOW THAT?
I'D HEARD. YOU CAN BUY ALL THAT CRAP ONLINE NOW. TAKES THE FUN OUT OF IT. BUT BACK THEN, NO ONE WAS BUYING THESE THINGS, SO IF YOU MISSED THEM, THAT WAS IT, THE POSTERS WERE GONE. IT WAS FUN. SEEMS POINTLESS NOW.
WEIRD.
WEIRD.
WHY THAT SUMMER? DAMMIT! THAT'S GOING TO KILL ME, TRYING TO PUT MY FINGER ON IT.
DAMN...
WE THERE YET?
I WISH. WE'VE GOT OVER AN HOUR TO GO.

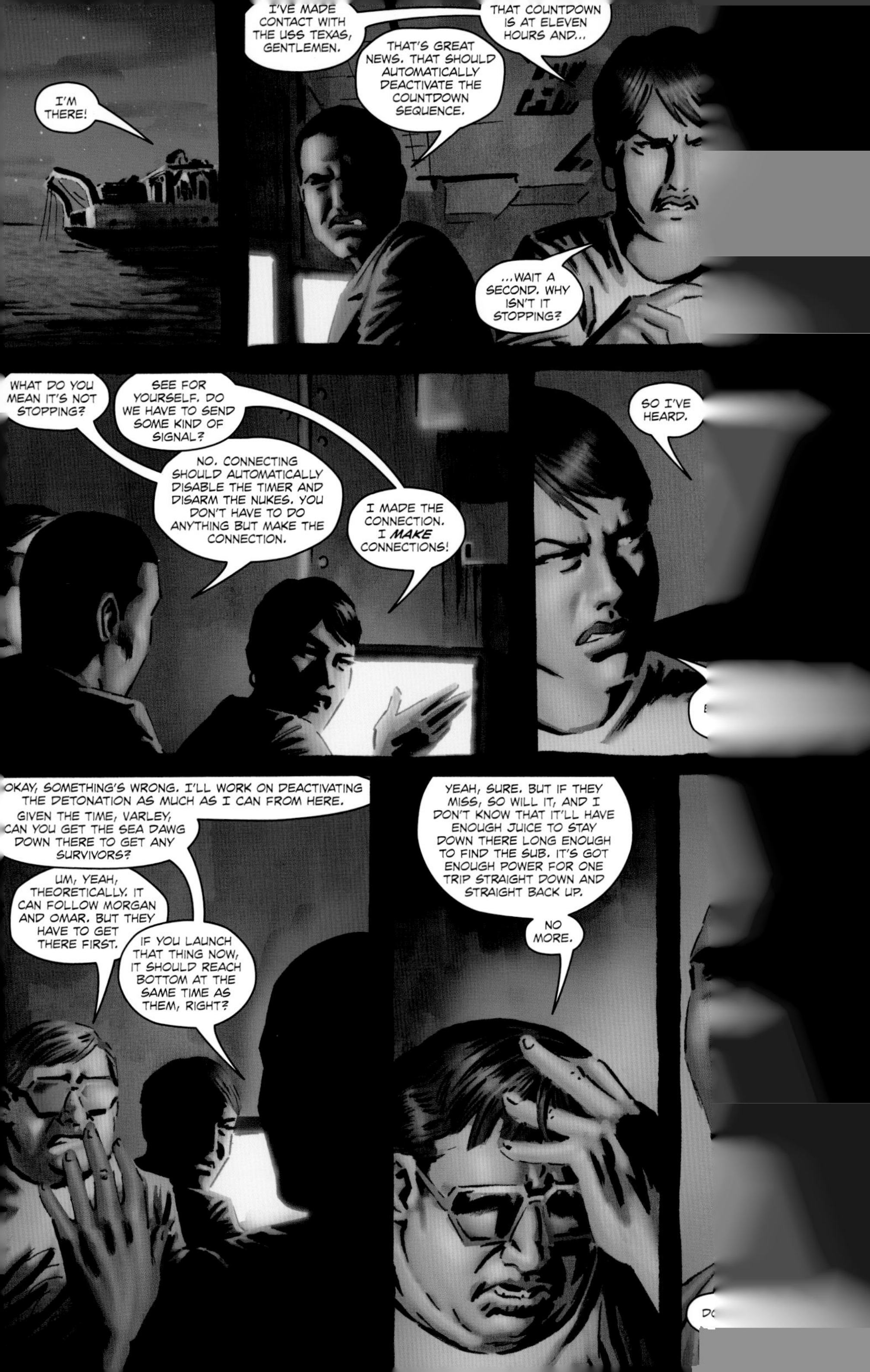
I'M THERE!
I'VE MADE CONTACT WITH THE USS TEXAS, GENTLEMEN.
THAT COUNTDOWN IS AT ELEVEN HOURS AND...
THAT'S GREAT NEWS. THAT SHOULD AUTOMATICALLY DEACTIVATE THE COUNTDOWN SEQUENCE.
...WAIT A SECOND. WHY ISN'T IT STOPPING?
WHAT DO YOU MEAN IT'S NOT STOPPING?
SEE FOR YOURSELF. DO WE HAVE TO SEND SOME KIND OF SIGNAL?
NO. CONNECTING SHOULD AUTOMATICALLY DISABLE THE TIMER AND DISARM THE NUKES. YOU DON'T HAVE TO DO ANYTHING BUT MAKE THE CONNECTION.
I MADE THE CONNECTION. I *MAKE* CONNECTIONS!
SO I'VE HEARD.
OKAY, SOMETHING'S WRONG. I'LL WORK ON DEACTIVATING THE DETONATION AS MUCH AS I CAN FROM HERE.
GIVEN THE TIME, VARLEY, CAN YOU GET THE SEA DAWG DOWN THERE TO GET ANY SURVIVORS?
UM, YEAH, THEORETICALLY. IT CAN FOLLOW MORGAN AND OMAR. BUT THEY HAVE TO GET THERE FIRST.
IF YOU LAUNCH THAT THING NOW, IT SHOULD REACH BOTTOM AT THE SAME TIME AS THEM, RIGHT?
YEAH, SURE. BUT IF THEY MISS, SO WILL IT, AND I DON'T KNOW THAT IT'LL HAVE ENOUGH JUICE TO STAY DOWN THERE LONG ENOUGH TO FIND THE SUB. IT'S GOT ENOUGH POWER FOR ONE TRIP STRAIGHT DOWN AND STRAIGHT BACK UP.
NO MORE.

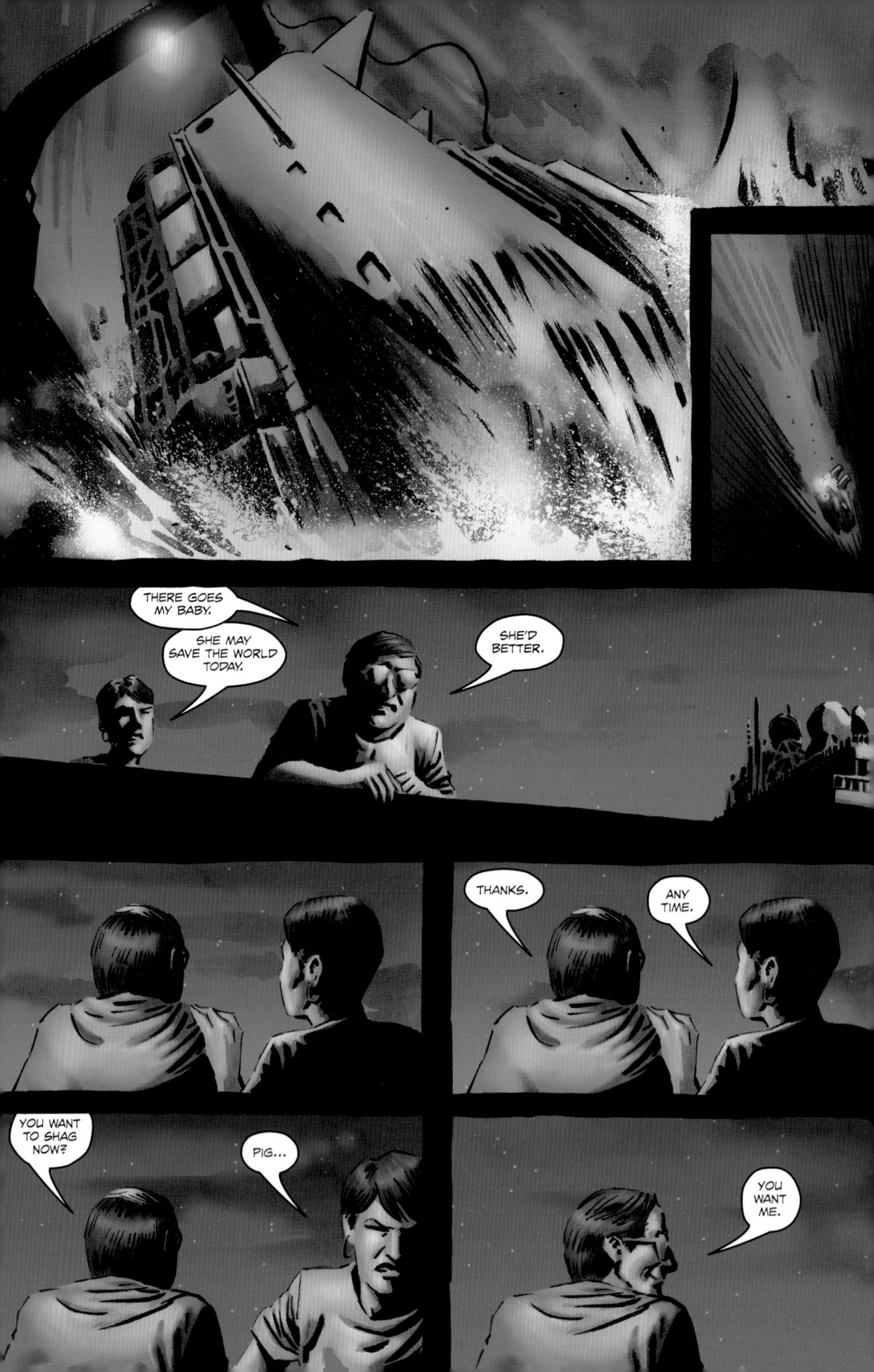
THERE GOES MY BABY.
SHE MAY SAVE THE WORLD TODAY.
SHE'D BETTER.
THANKS.
ANY TIME.
YOU WANT TO SHAG NOW?
PIG...
YOU WANT ME.

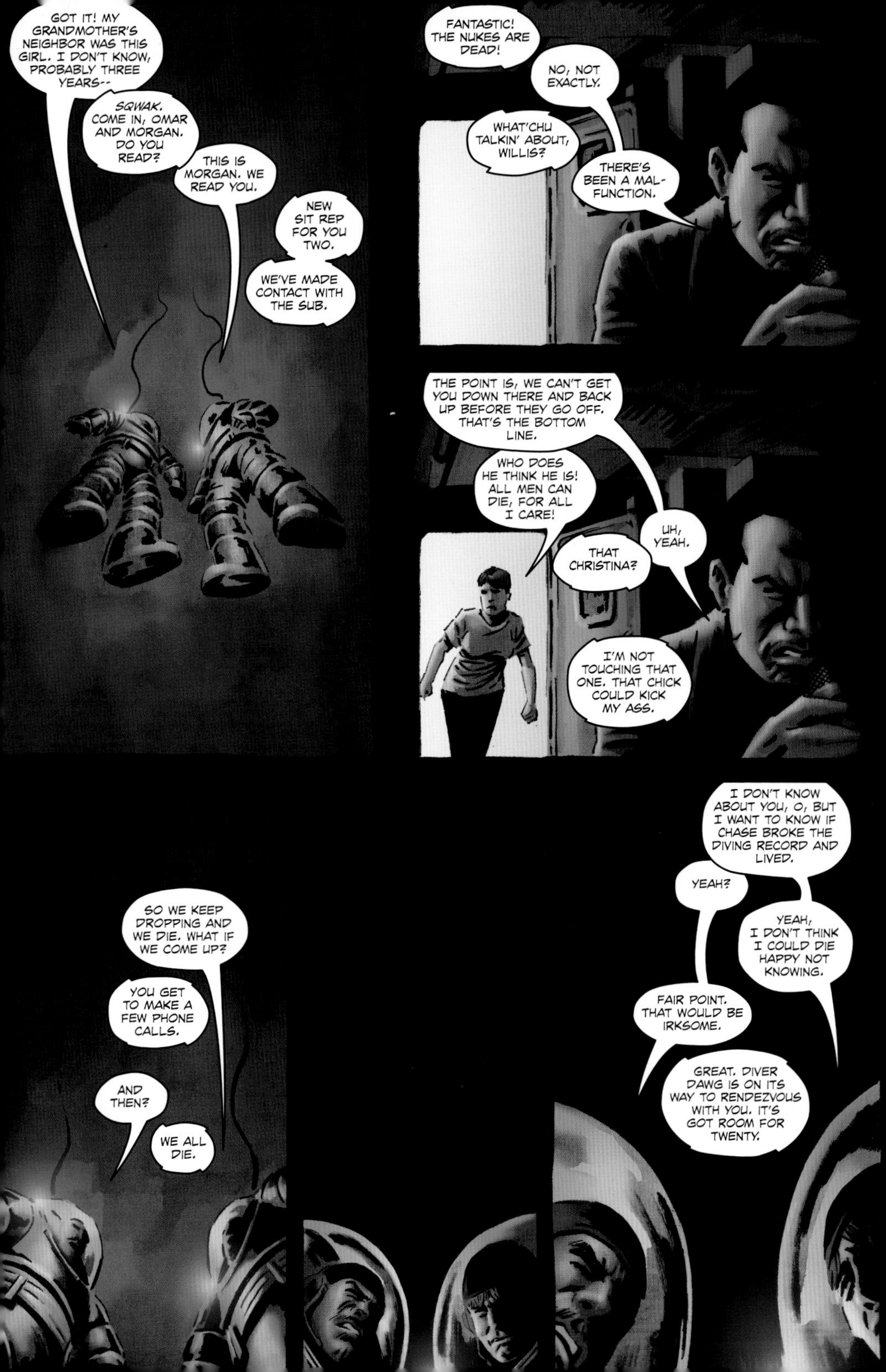
GOT IT! MY GRANDMOTHER'S NEIGHBOR WAS THIS GIRL. I DON'T KNOW, PROBABLY THREE YEARS--
SQWAK. COME IN, OMAR AND MORGAN. DO YOU READ?
THIS IS MORGAN. WE READ YOU.
NEW SIT REP FOR YOU TWO.
WE'VE MADE CONTACT WITH THE SUB.
FANTASTIC! THE NUKES ARE DEAD!
NO, NOT EXACTLY.
WHAT'CHU TALKIN' ABOUT, WILLIS?
THERE'S BEEN A MAL-FUNCTION.
THE POINT IS, WE CAN'T GET YOU DOWN THERE AND BACK UP BEFORE THEY GO OFF. THAT'S THE BOTTOM LINE.
WHO DOES HE THINK HE IS! ALL MEN CAN DIE, FOR ALL I CARE!
THAT CHRISTINA?
UH, YEAH.
I'M NOT TOUCHING THAT ONE. THAT CHICK COULD KICK MY ASS.
SO WE KEEP DROPPING AND WE DIE. WHAT IF WE COME UP?
YOU GET TO MAKE A FEW PHONE CALLS.
AND THEN?
WE ALL DIE.
I DON'T KNOW ABOUT YOU, O, BUT I WANT TO KNOW IF CHASE BROKE THE DIVING RECORD AND LIVED.
YEAH?
YEAH, I DON'T THINK I COULD DIE HAPPY NOT KNOWING.
FAIR POINT. THAT WOULD BE IRKSOME.
GREAT. DIVER DAWG IS ON ITS WAY TO RENDEZVOUS WITH YOU. IT'S GOT ROOM FOR TWENTY.

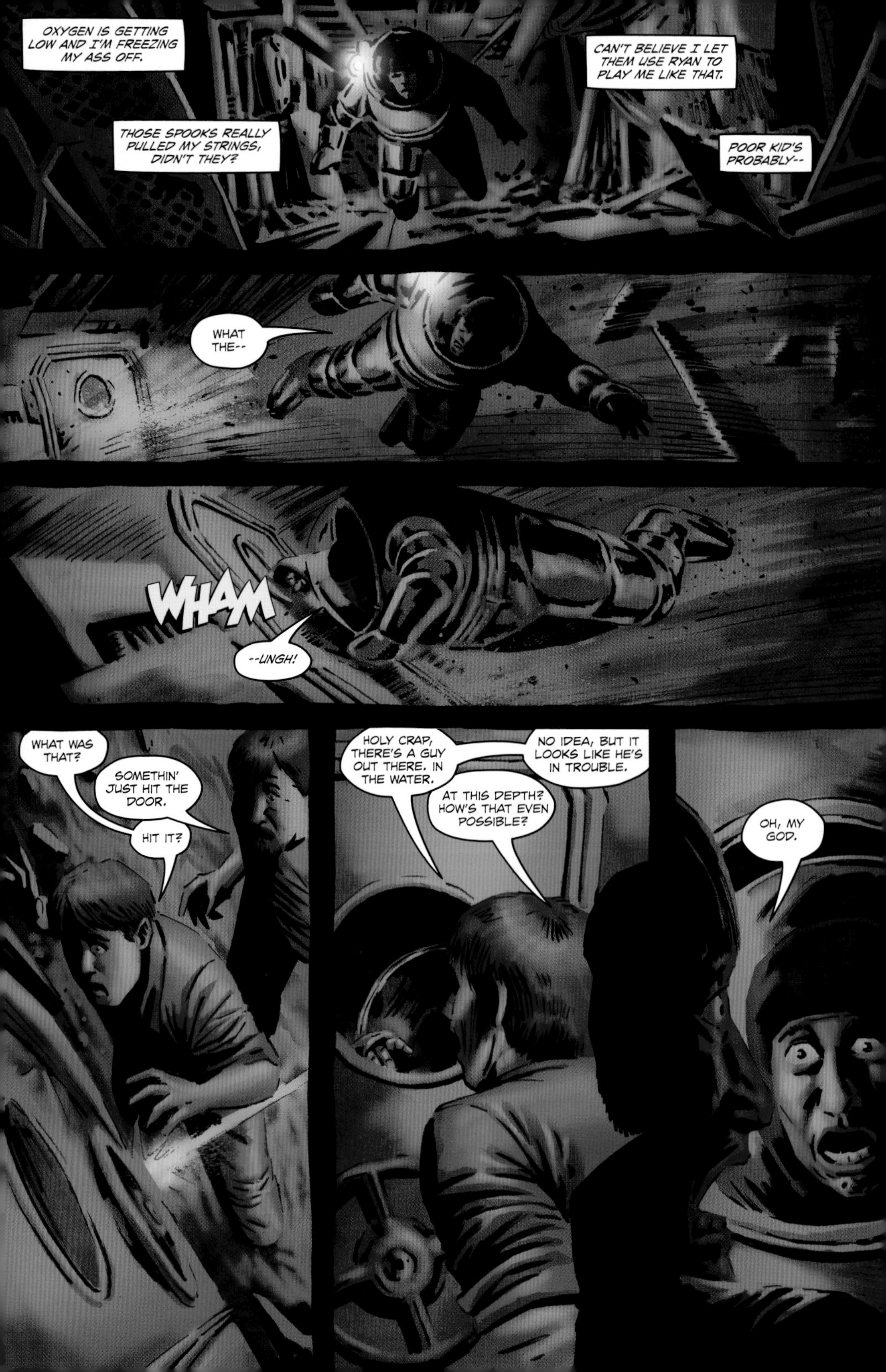
OXYGEN IS GETTING LOW AND I'M FREEZING MY ASS OFF.
THOSE SPOOKS REALLY PULLED MY STRINGS, DIDN'T THEY?
CAN'T BELIEVE I LET THEM USE RYAN TO PLAY ME LIKE THAT.
POOR KID'S PROBABLY--
WHAT THE--
WHAM
--UNGH!
WHAT WAS THAT?
SOMETHIN' JUST HIT THE DOOR.
HIT IT?
HOLY CRAP, THERE'S A GUY OUT THERE. IN THE WATER.
NO IDEA, BUT IT LOOKS LIKE HE'S IN TROUBLE.
AT THIS DEPTH? HOW'S THAT EVEN POSSIBLE?
OH, MY GOD.

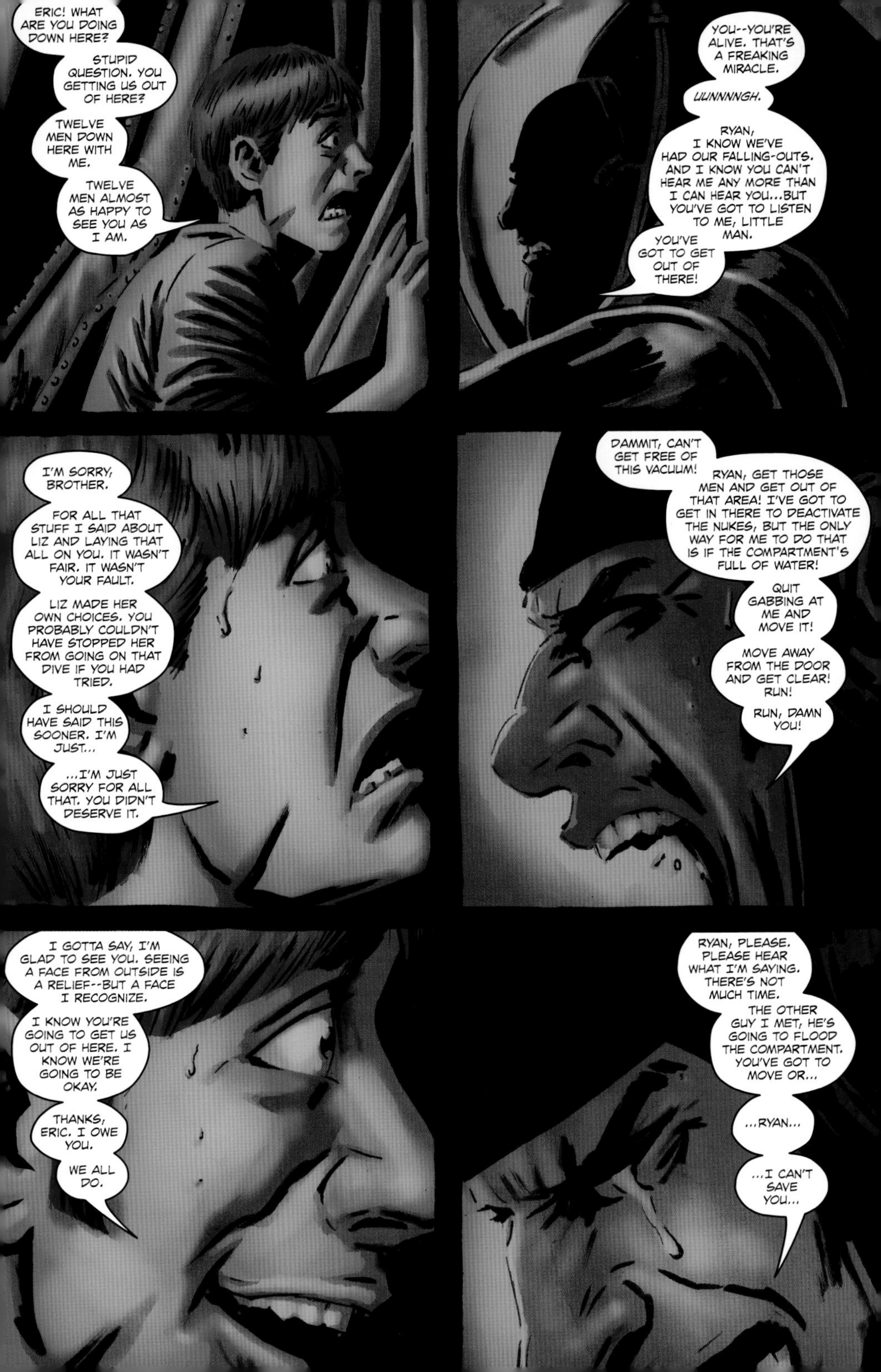
ERIC! WHAT ARE YOU DOING DOWN HERE?
STUPID QUESTION. YOU GETTING US OUT OF HERE?
TWELVE MEN DOWN HERE WITH ME.
TWELVE MEN ALMOST AS HAPPY TO SEE YOU AS I AM.
YOU--YOU'RE ALIVE. THAT'S A FREAKING MIRACLE.
UUNNNNGH.
RYAN, I KNOW WE'VE HAD OUR FALLING-OUTS. AND I KNOW YOU CAN'T HEAR ME ANY MORE THAN I CAN HEAR YOU...BUT YOU'VE GOT TO LISTEN TO ME, LITTLE MAN.
YOU'VE GOT TO GET OUT OF THERE!
I'M SORRY, BROTHER.
FOR ALL THAT STUFF I SAID ABOUT LIZ AND LAYING THAT ALL ON YOU. IT WASN'T FAIR. IT WASN'T YOUR FAULT.
LIZ MADE HER OWN CHOICES. YOU PROBABLY COULDN'T HAVE STOPPED HER FROM GOING ON THAT DIVE IF YOU HAD TRIED.
I SHOULD HAVE SAID THIS SOONER. I'M JUST...
...I'M JUST SORRY FOR ALL THAT. YOU DIDN'T DESERVE IT.
DAMMIT, CAN'T GET FREE OF THIS VACUUM!
RYAN, GET THOSE MEN AND GET OUT OF THAT AREA! I'VE GOT TO GET IN THERE TO DEACTIVATE THE NUKES, BUT THE ONLY WAY FOR ME TO DO THAT IS IF THE COMPARTMENT'S FULL OF WATER!
QUIT GABBING AT ME AND MOVE IT!
MOVE AWAY FROM THE DOOR AND GET CLEAR! RUN!
RUN, DAMN YOU!
I GOTTA SAY, I'M GLAD TO SEE YOU. SEEING A FACE FROM OUTSIDE IS A RELIEF--BUT A FACE I RECOGNIZE.
I KNOW YOU'RE GOING TO GET US OUT OF HERE. I KNOW WE'RE GOING TO BE OKAY.
THANKS, ERIC. I OWE YOU.
WE ALL DO.
RYAN, PLEASE. PLEASE HEAR WHAT I'M SAYING. THERE'S NOT MUCH TIME.
THE OTHER GUY I MET, HE'S GOING TO FLOOD THE COMPARTMENT. YOU'VE GOT TO MOVE OR...
...RYAN...
...I CAN'T SAVE YOU...

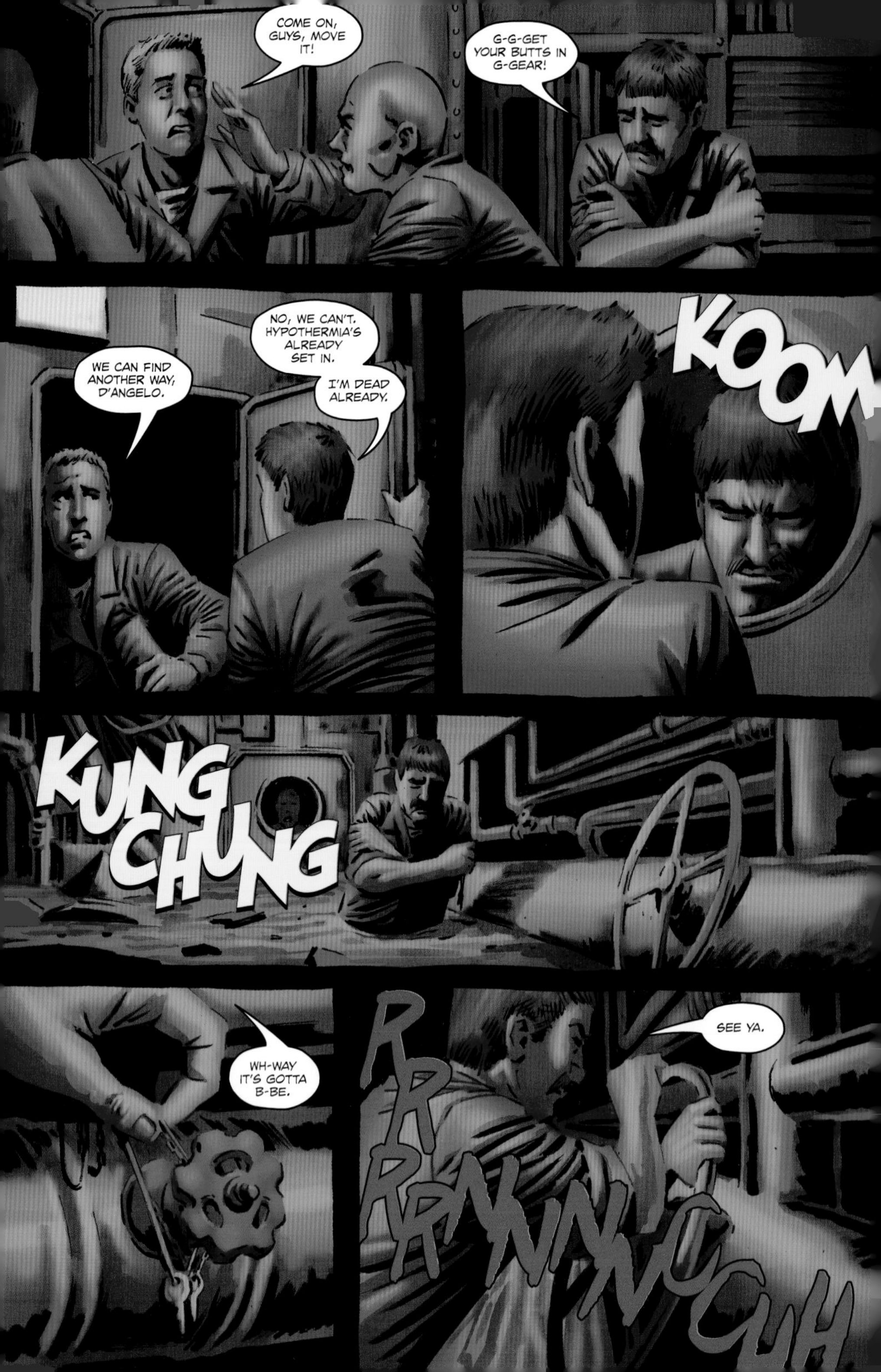
COME ON, GUYS, MOVE IT!
G-G-GET YOUR BUTTS IN G-GEAR!
WE CAN FIND ANOTHER WAY, D'ANGELO.
NO, WE CAN'T. HYPOTHERMIA'S ALREADY SET IN.
I'M DEAD ALREADY.
KOOM
KUNG CHUNG
WH-WAY IT'S GOTTA B-BE.
RRRRNNNCCHH
SEE YA.

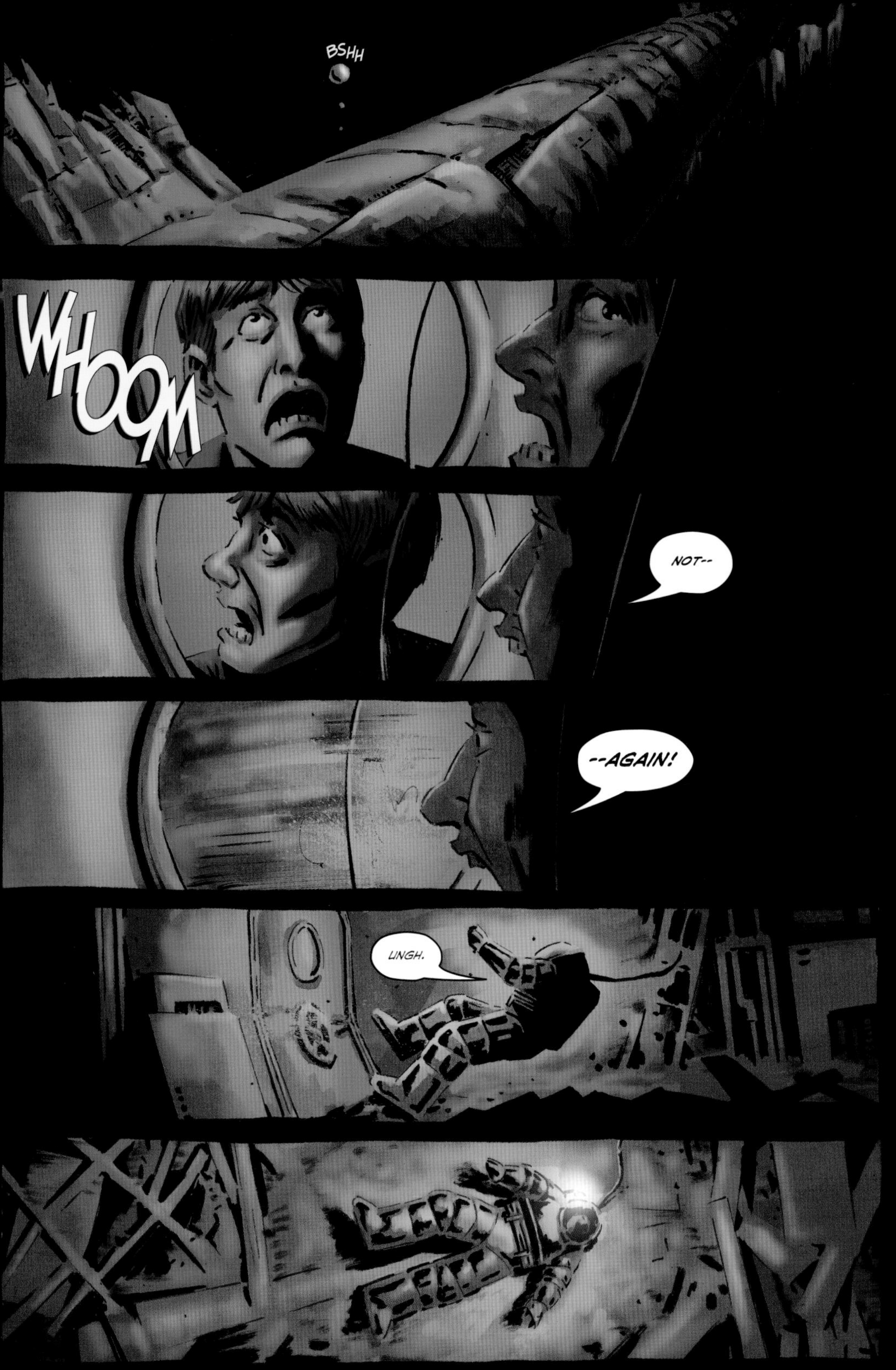
BSHH
WHOOM
NOT--
--AGAIN!
UNGH.

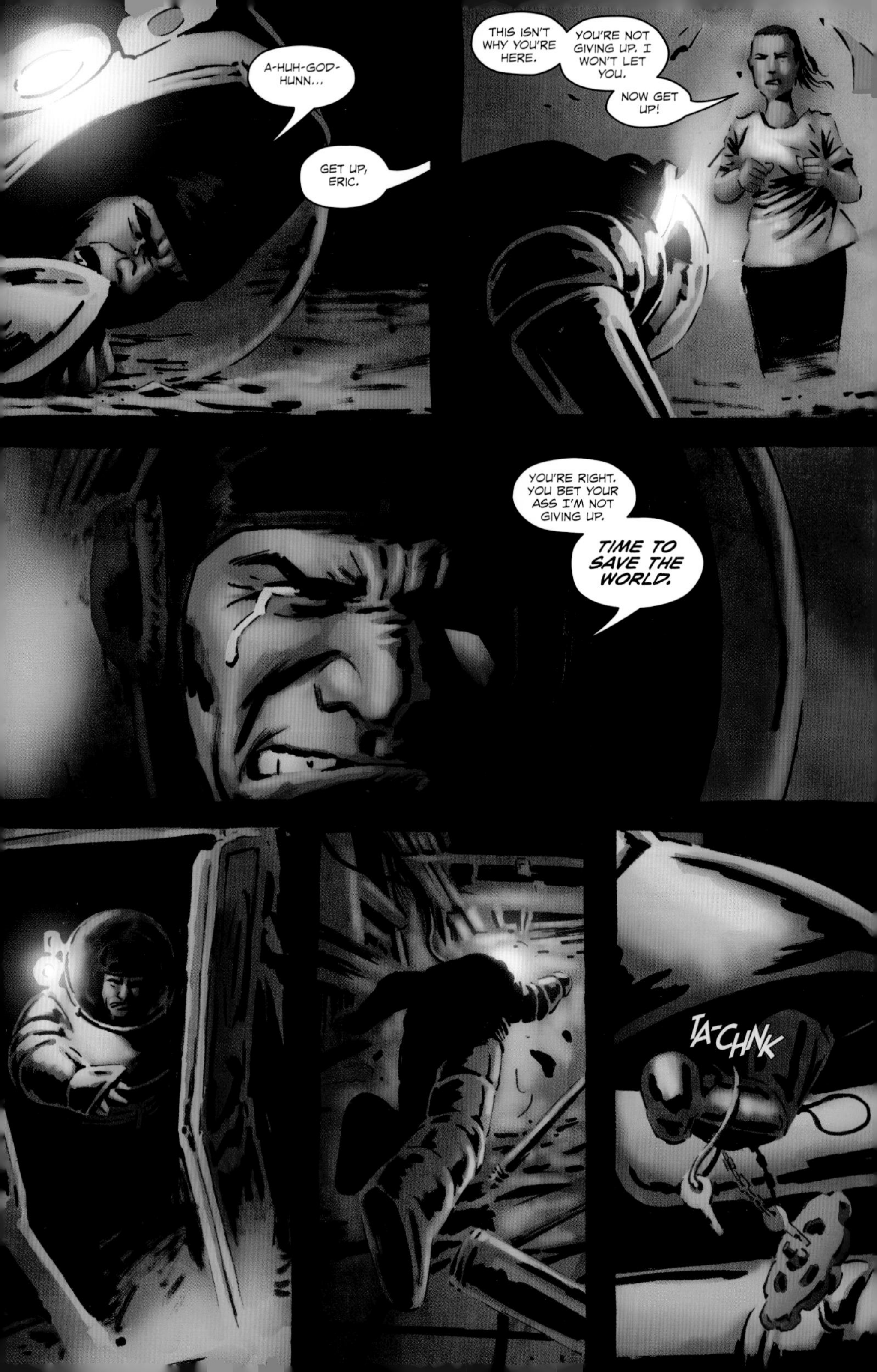
A-HUH-GOD-HUNN...
GET UP, ERIC.
THIS ISN'T WHY YOU'RE HERE.
YOU'RE NOT GIVING UP. I WON'T LET YOU.
NOW GET UP!
YOU'RE RIGHT. YOU BET YOUR ASS I'M NOT GIVING UP.
TIME TO SAVE THE WORLD.
TA-CHNK

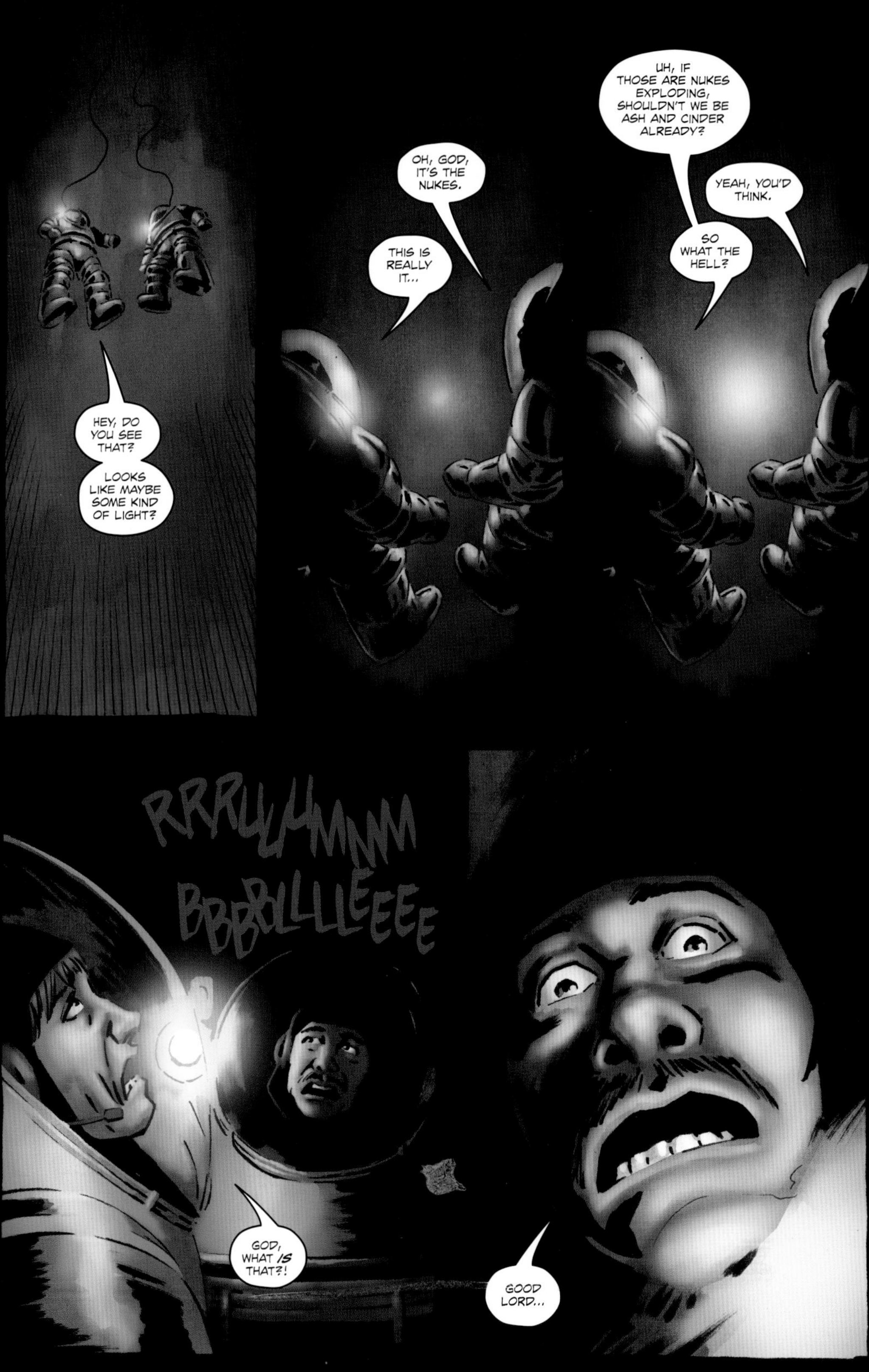

HEY, DO YOU SEE THAT?
LOOKS LIKE MAYBE SOME KIND OF LIGHT?
OH, GOD, IT'S THE NUKES.
THIS IS REALLY IT...
UH, IF THOSE ARE NUKES EXPLODING, SHOULDN'T WE BE ASH AND CINDER ALREADY?
YEAH, YOU'D THINK.
SO WHAT THE HELL?
RRRUUUMMM
BBBBOLLLLLEEEE
GOD, WHAT *IS* THAT?!
GOOD LORD...

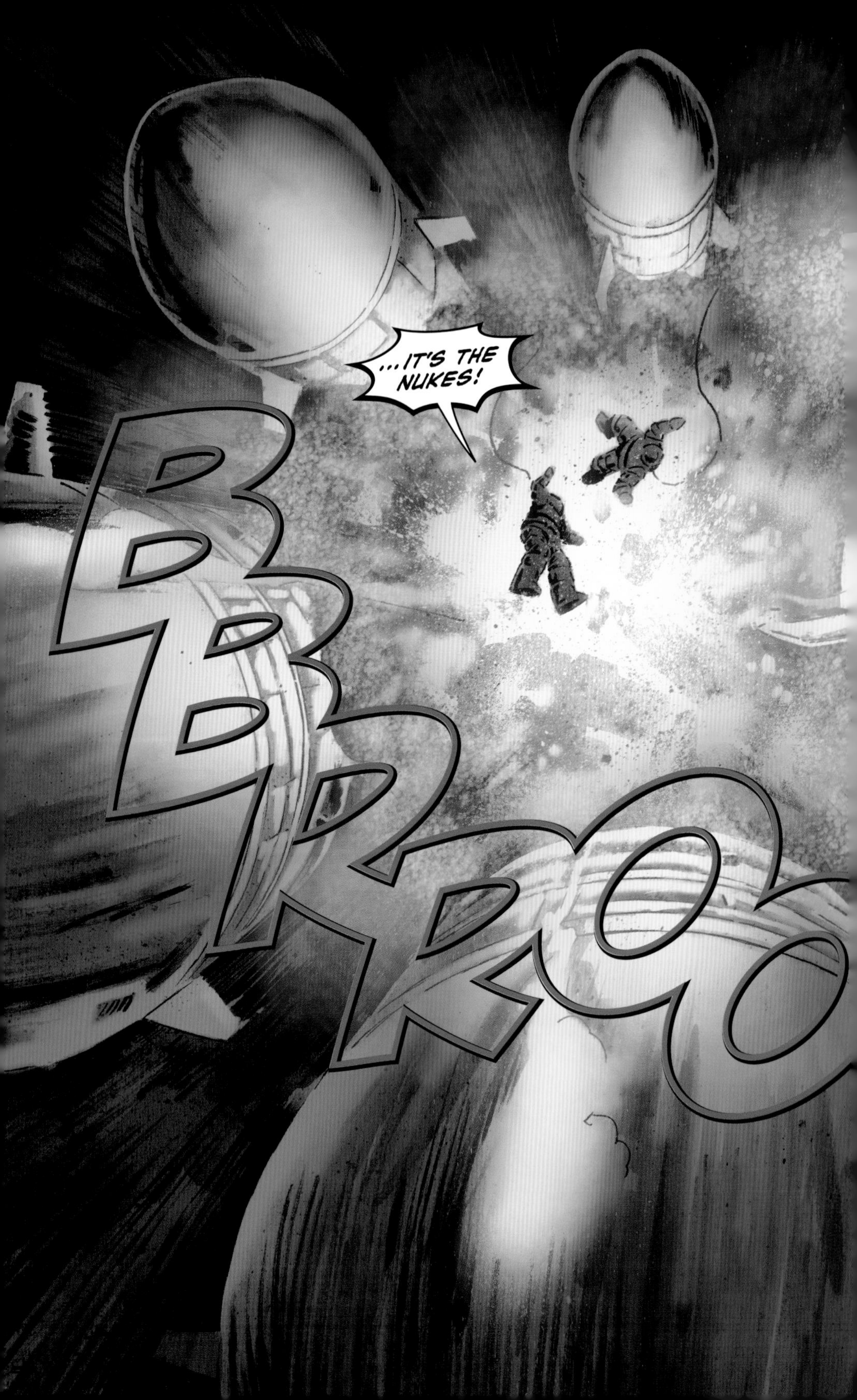
...IT'S THE NUKES!
BBBRROO

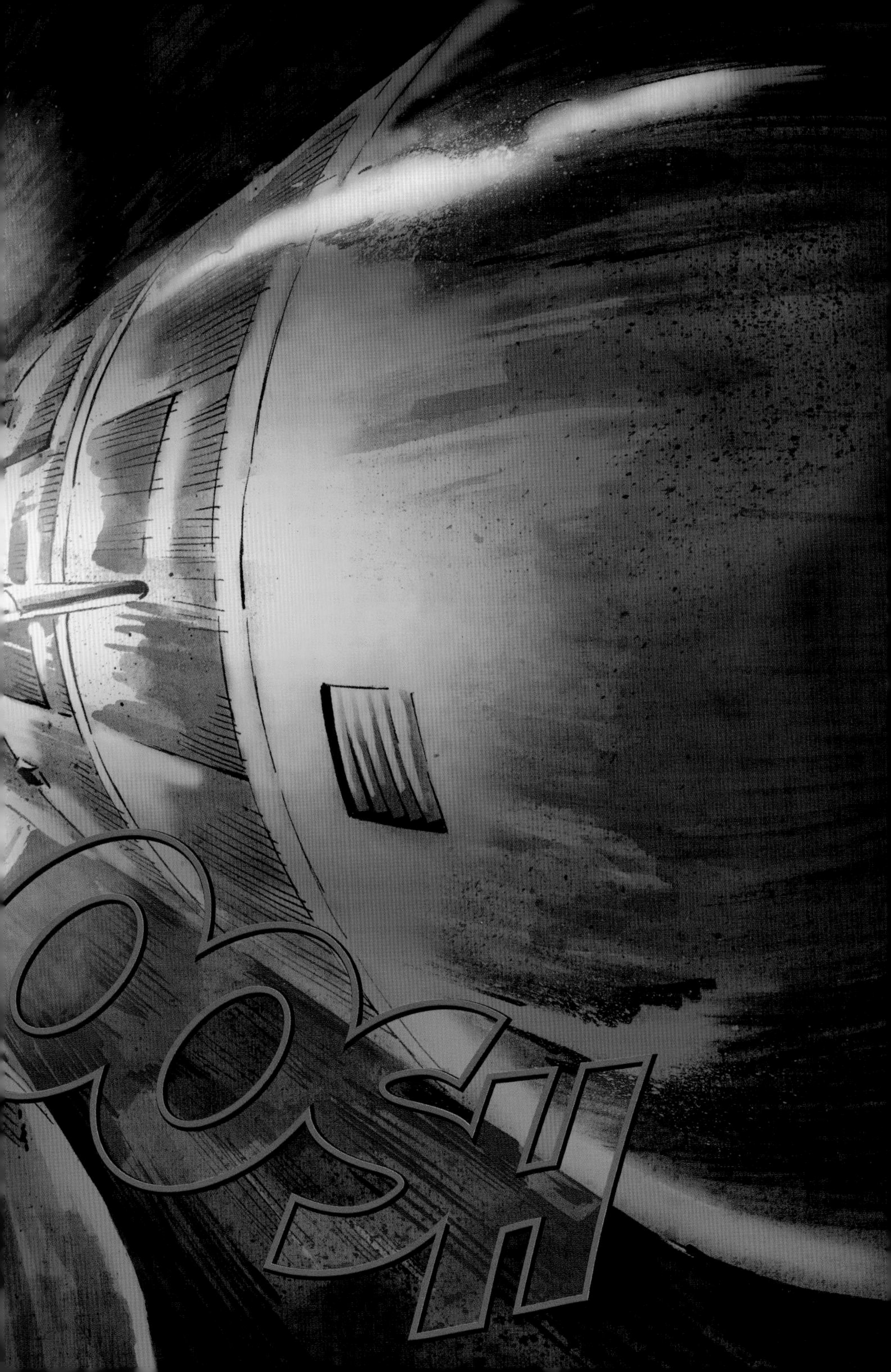
OOSH

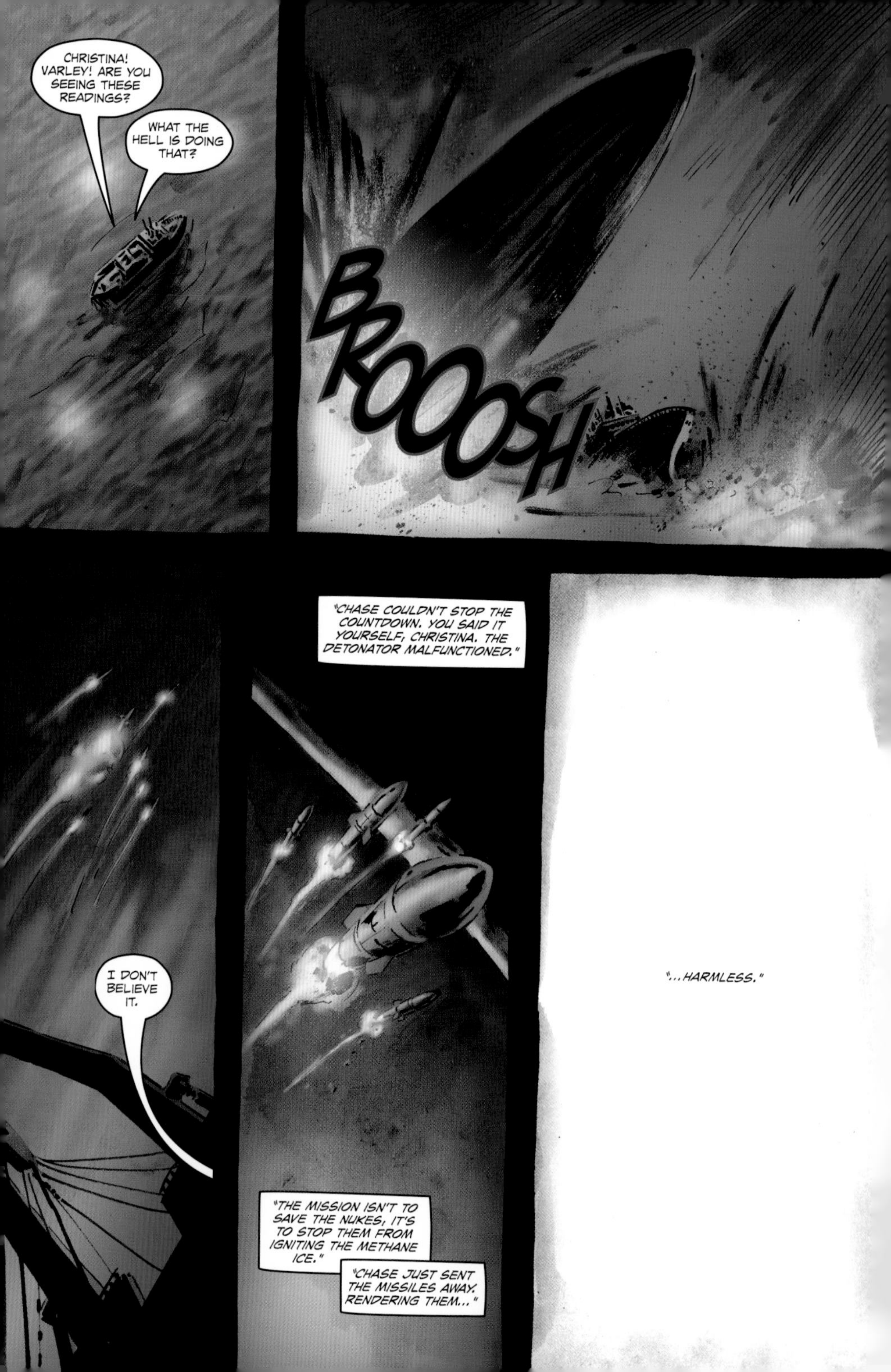
CHRISTINA! VARLEY! ARE YOU SEEING THESE READINGS?
WHAT THE HELL IS DOING THAT?
BROOOSH
"CHASE COULDN'T STOP THE COUNTDOWN. YOU SAID IT YOURSELF, CHRISTINA. THE DETONATOR MALFUNCTIONED."
I DON'T BELIEVE IT.
"THE MISSION ISN'T TO SAVE THE NUKES, IT'S TO STOP THEM FROM IGNITING THE METHANE ICE."
"CHASE JUST SENT THE MISSILES AWAY. RENDERING THEM..."
"...HARMLESS."

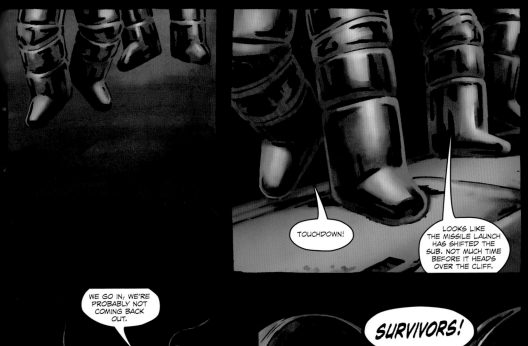

TOUCHDOWN!

LOOKS LIKE THE MISSILE LAUNCH HAS SHIFTED THE SUB. NOT MUCH TIME BEFORE IT HEADS OVER THE CLIFF.

WE GO IN, WE'RE PROBABLY NOT COMING BACK OUT.

BANG BANG BANG

SURVIVORS!

I'M CALLING IN THE SEA DAWG. SHOULD BE HERE ANY SECOND.

I'M ON THE SURVIVORS.

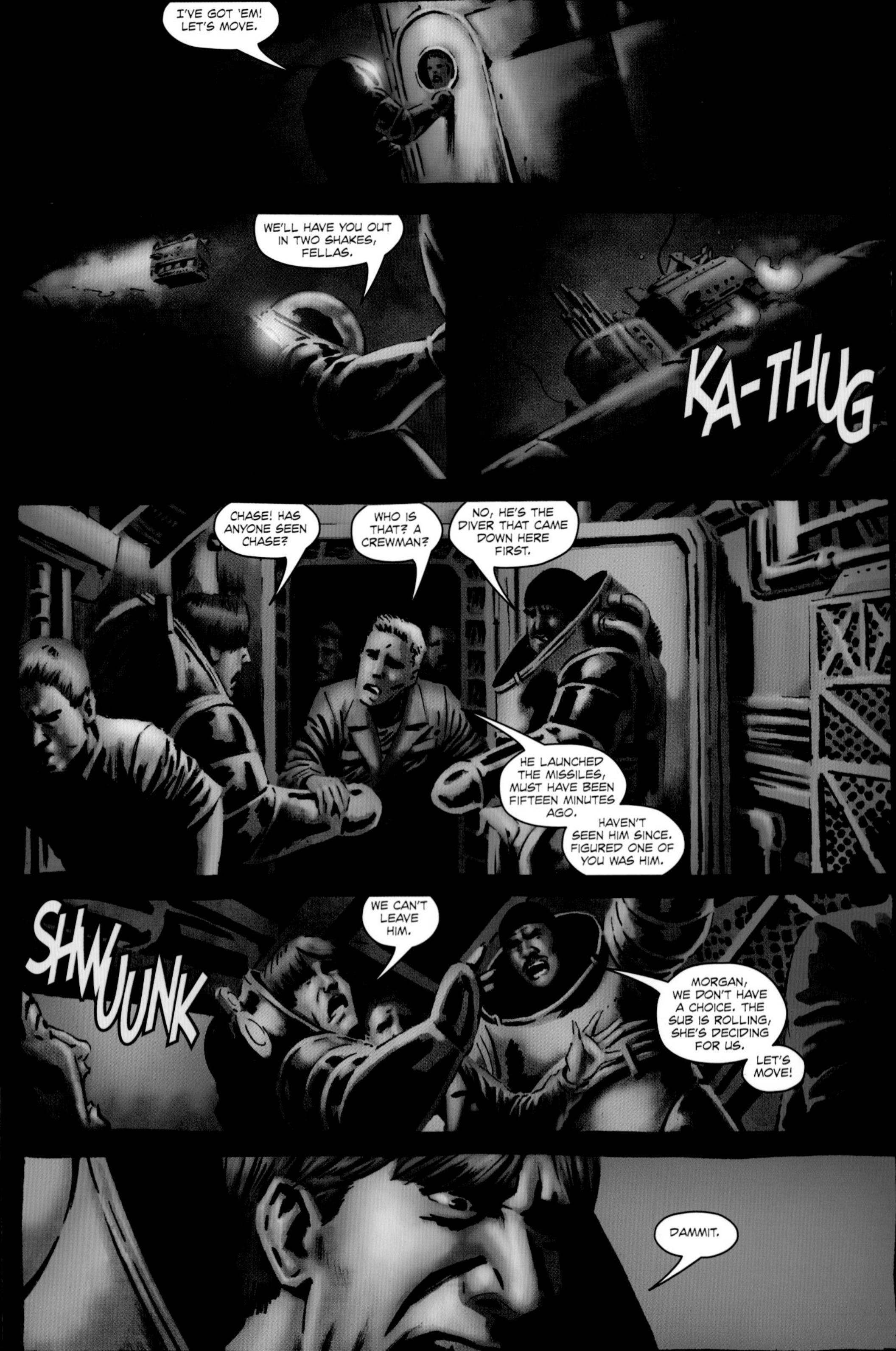
I'VE GOT 'EM! LET'S MOVE.
WE'LL HAVE YOU OUT IN TWO SHAKES, FELLAS.
KA-THUG
CHASE! HAS ANYONE SEEN CHASE?
WHO IS THAT? A CREWMAN?
NO, HE'S THE DIVER THAT CAME DOWN HERE FIRST.
HE LAUNCHED THE MISSILES, MUST HAVE BEEN FIFTEEN MINUTES AGO.
HAVEN'T SEEN HIM SINCE. FIGURED ONE OF YOU WAS HIM.
SHWUUNK
WE CAN'T LEAVE HIM.
MORGAN, WE DON'T HAVE A CHOICE. THE SUB IS ROLLING, SHE'S DECIDING FOR US.
LET'S MOVE!
DAMMIT.

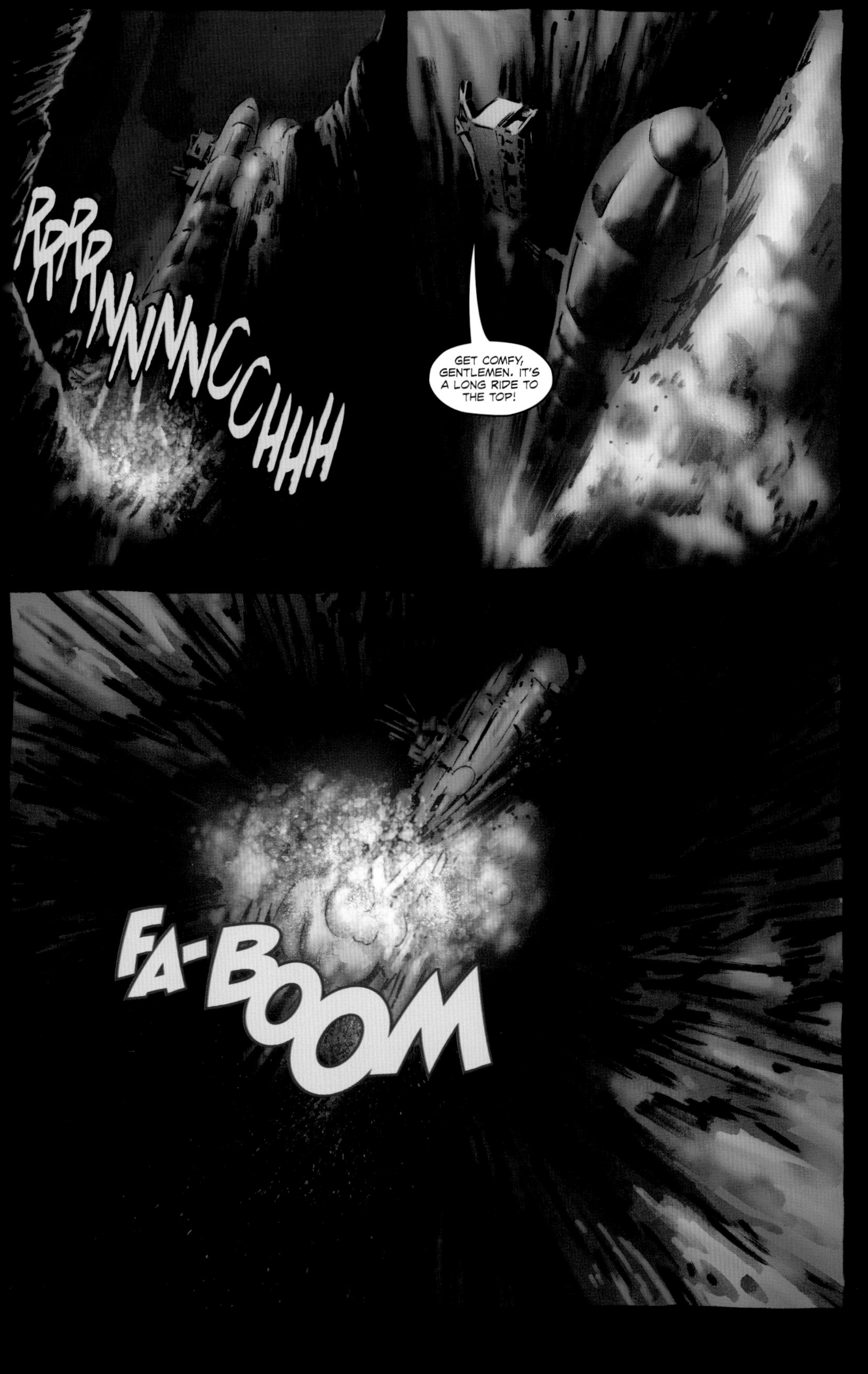
RRRRNNNNCCHHH
GET COMFY, GENTLEMEN. IT'S A LONG RIDE TO THE TOP!
FA-BOOM

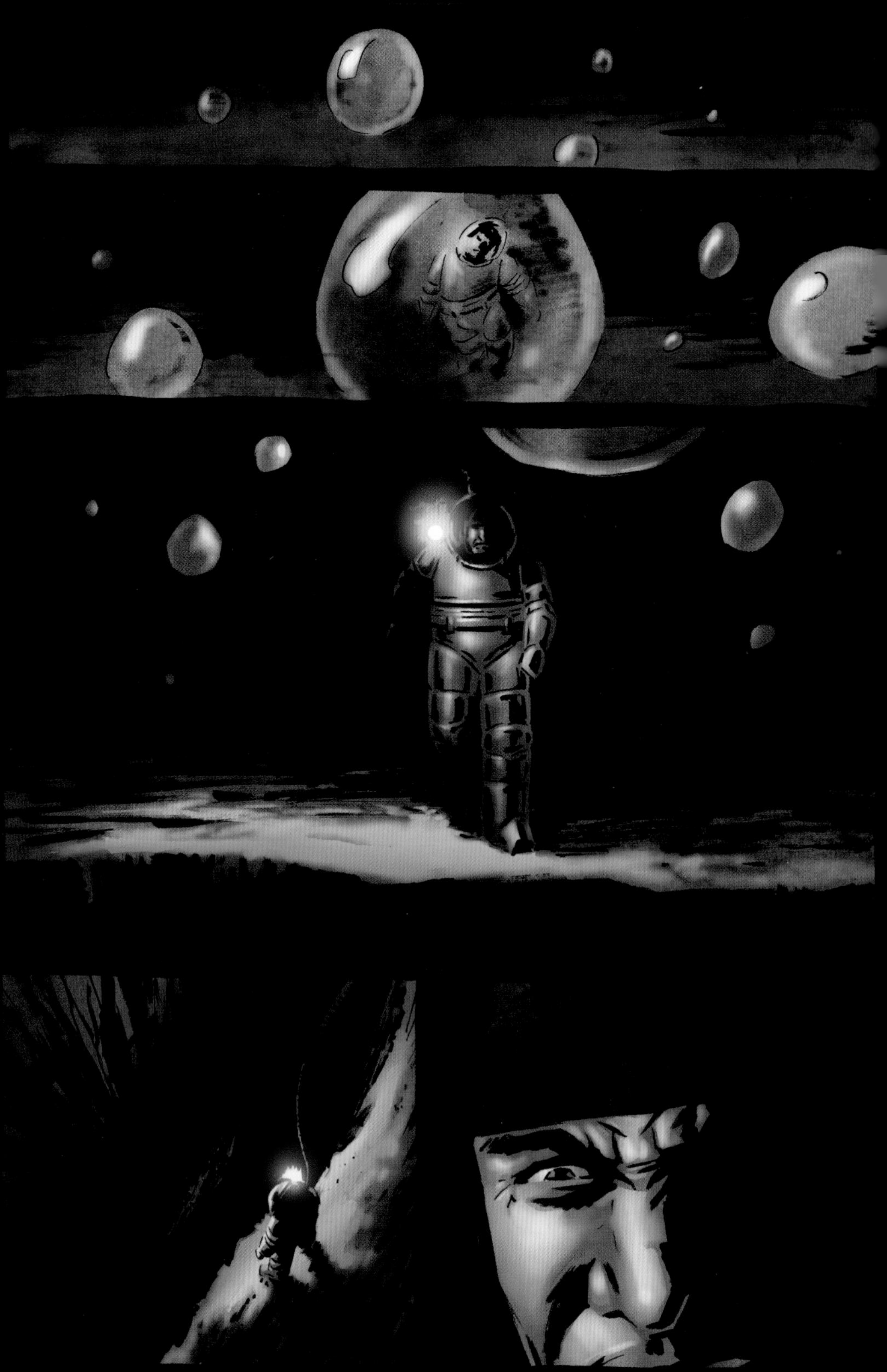

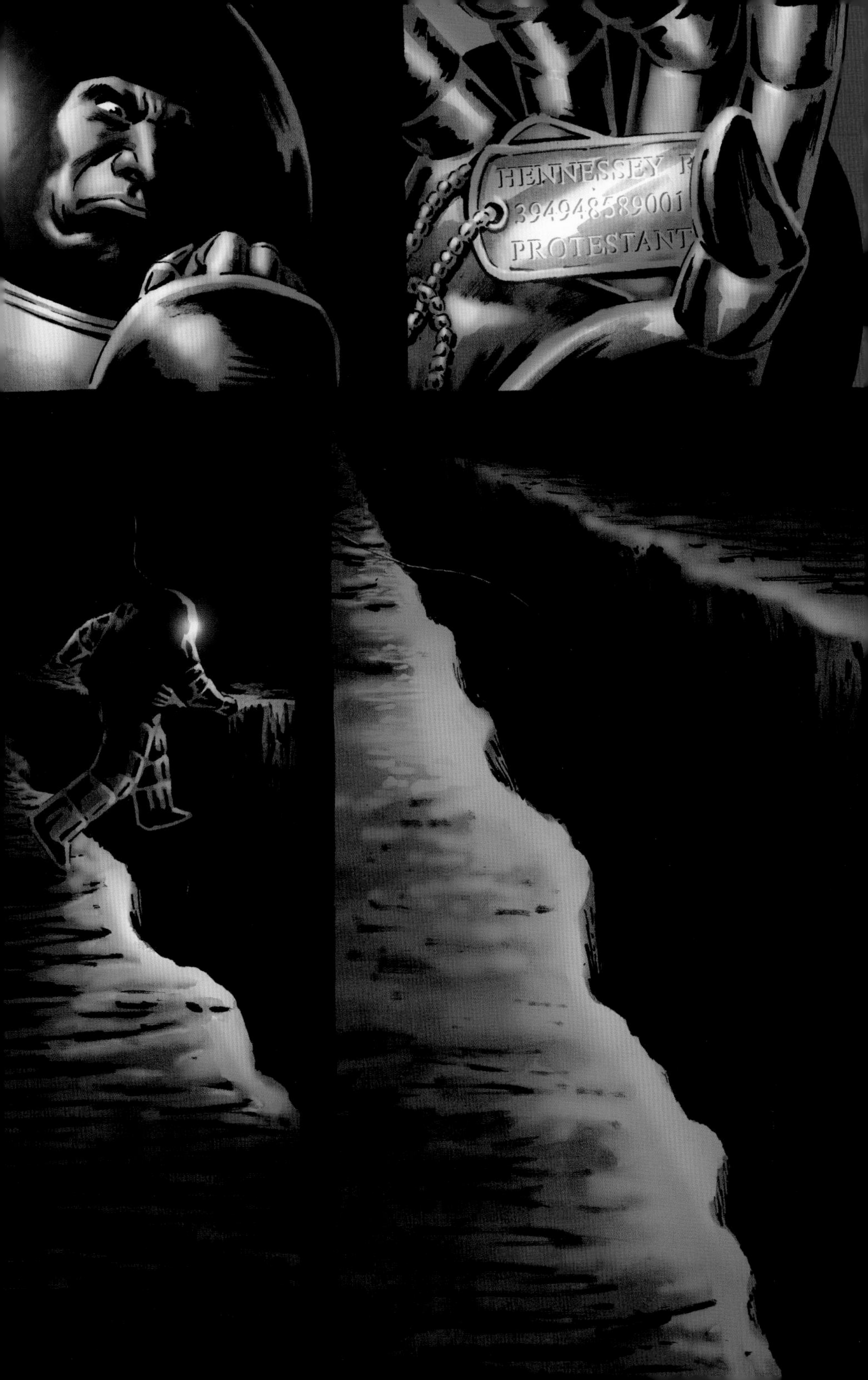
HENNESSEY
394948589001
PROTESTANT

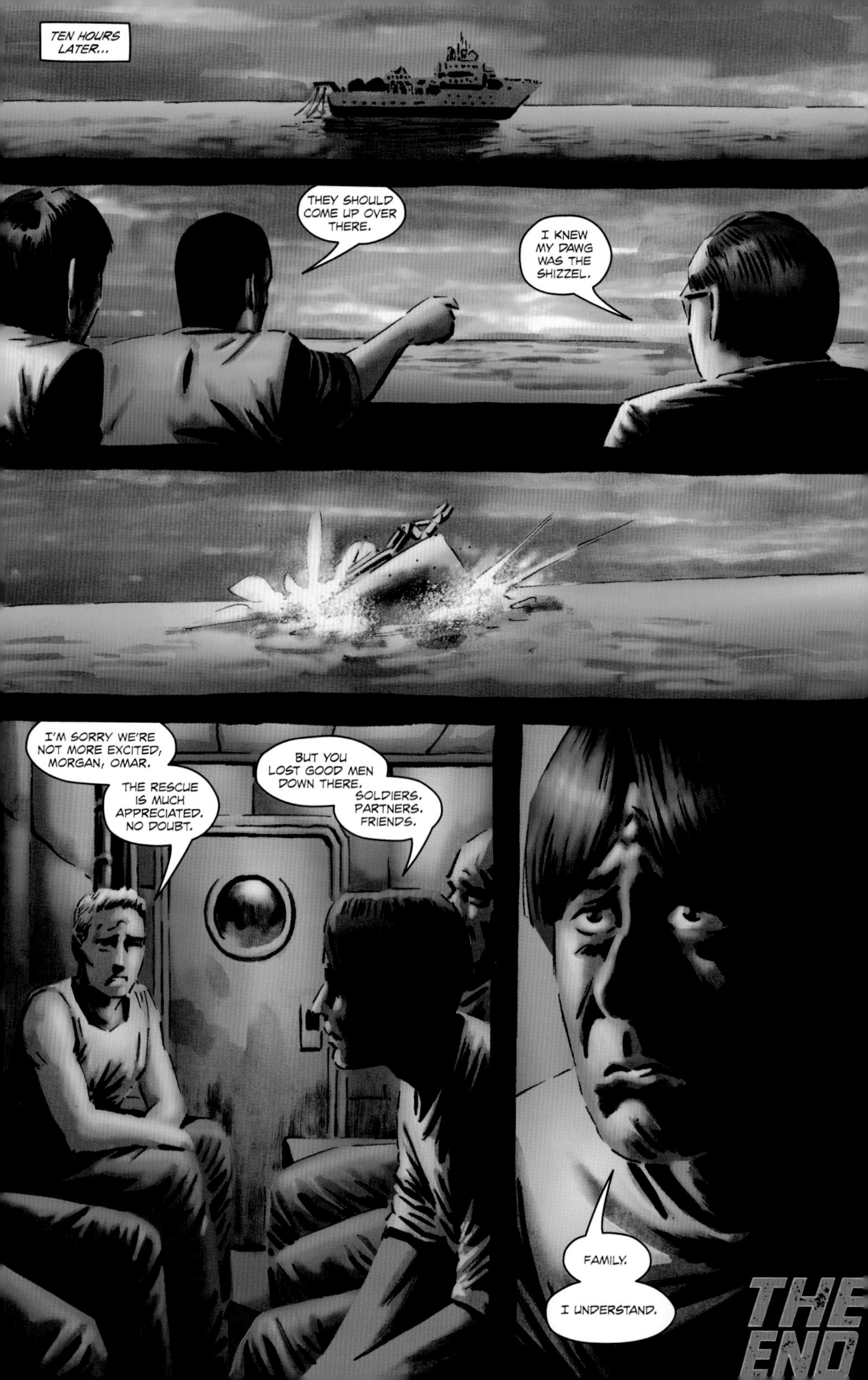
TEN HOURS LATER...
THEY SHOULD COME UP OVER THERE.
I KNEW MY DAWG WAS THE SHIZZEL.
I'M SORRY WE'RE NOT MORE EXCITED, MORGAN, OMAR.
THE RESCUE IS MUCH APPRECIATED. NO DOUBT.
BUT YOU LOST GOOD MEN DOWN THERE.
SOLDIERS. PARTNERS. FRIENDS.
FAMILY.
I UNDERSTAND.
THE END

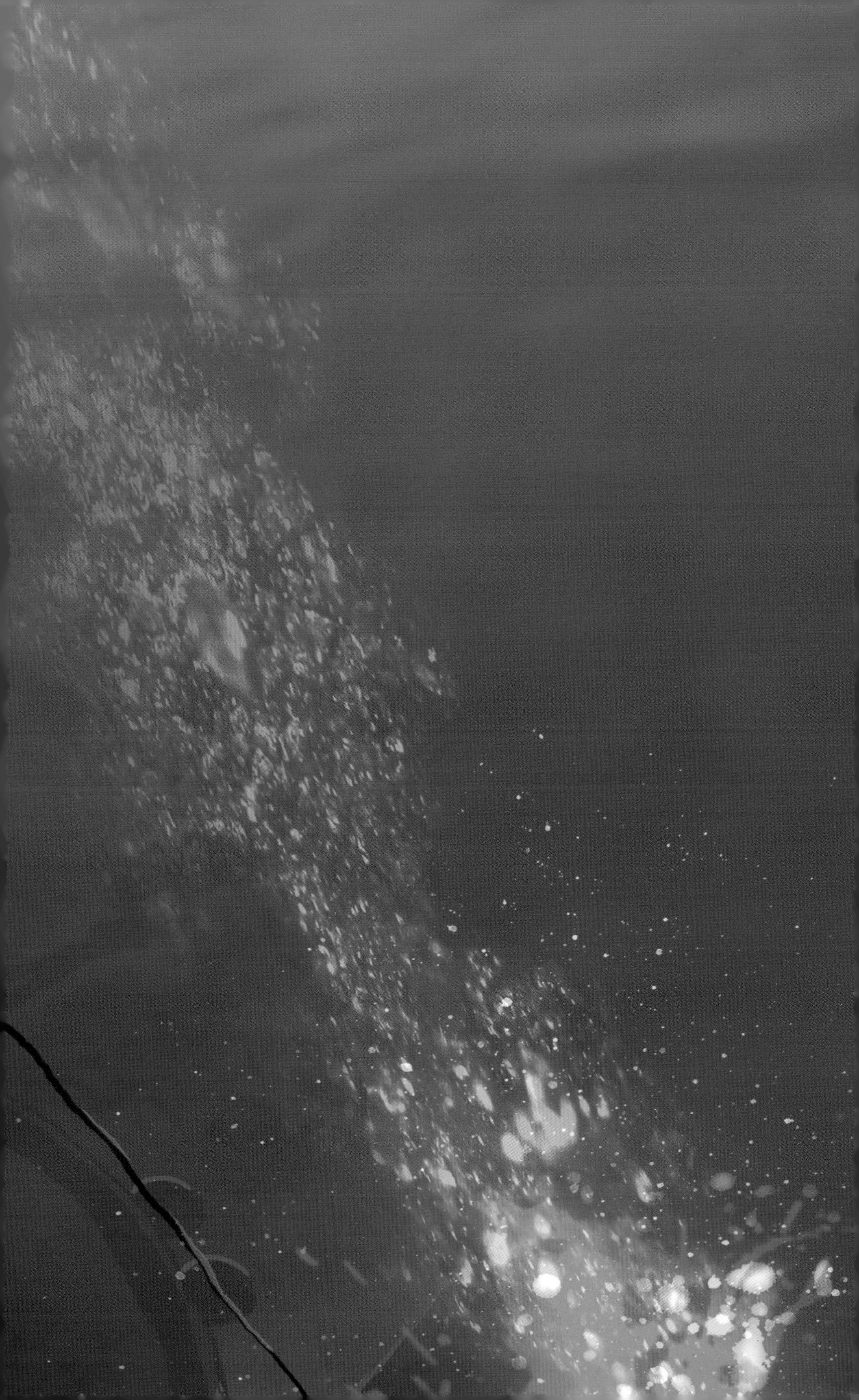

# ORIGINAL ART

ART BY CHEE

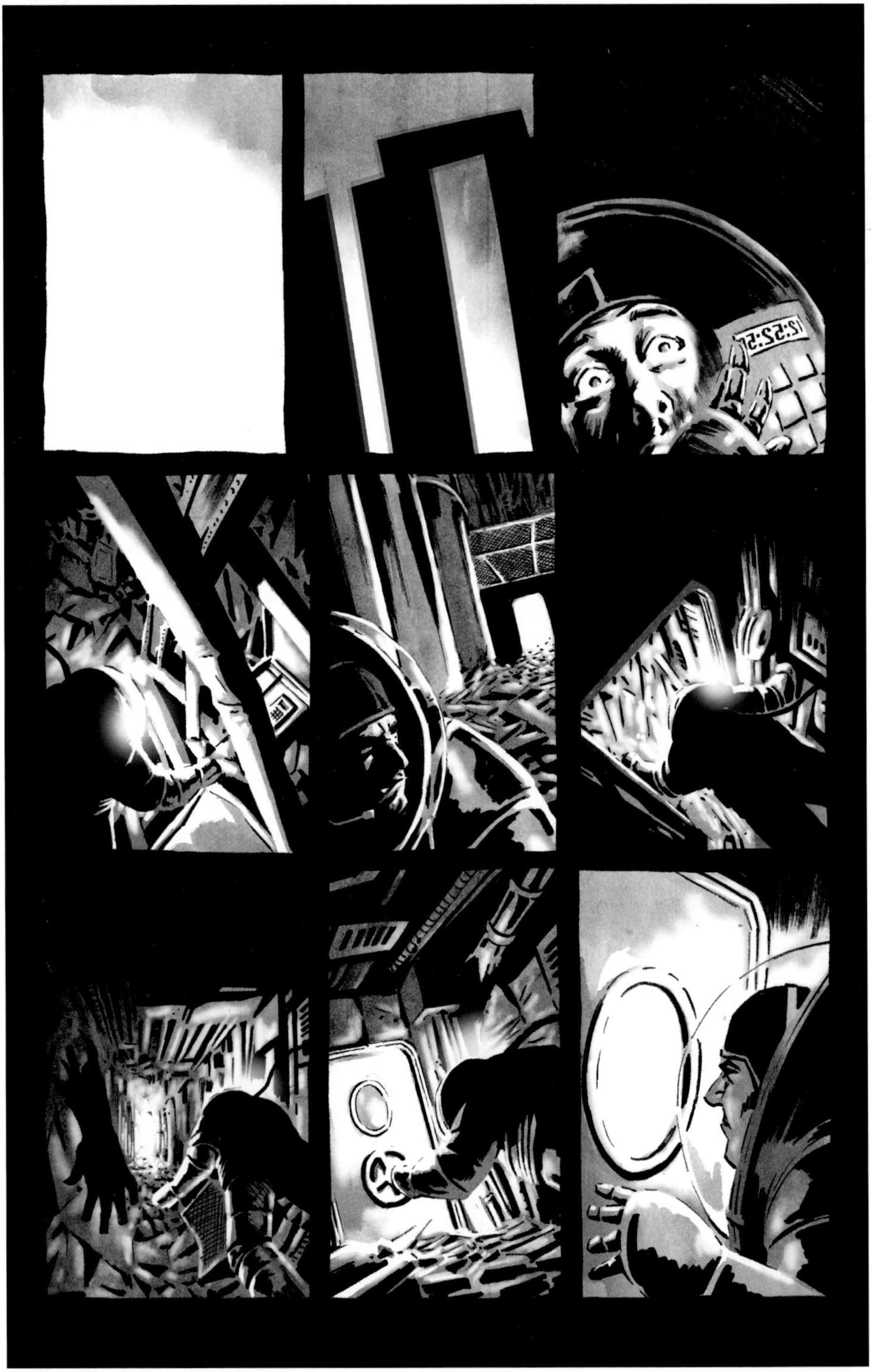

# ORIGINAL ART

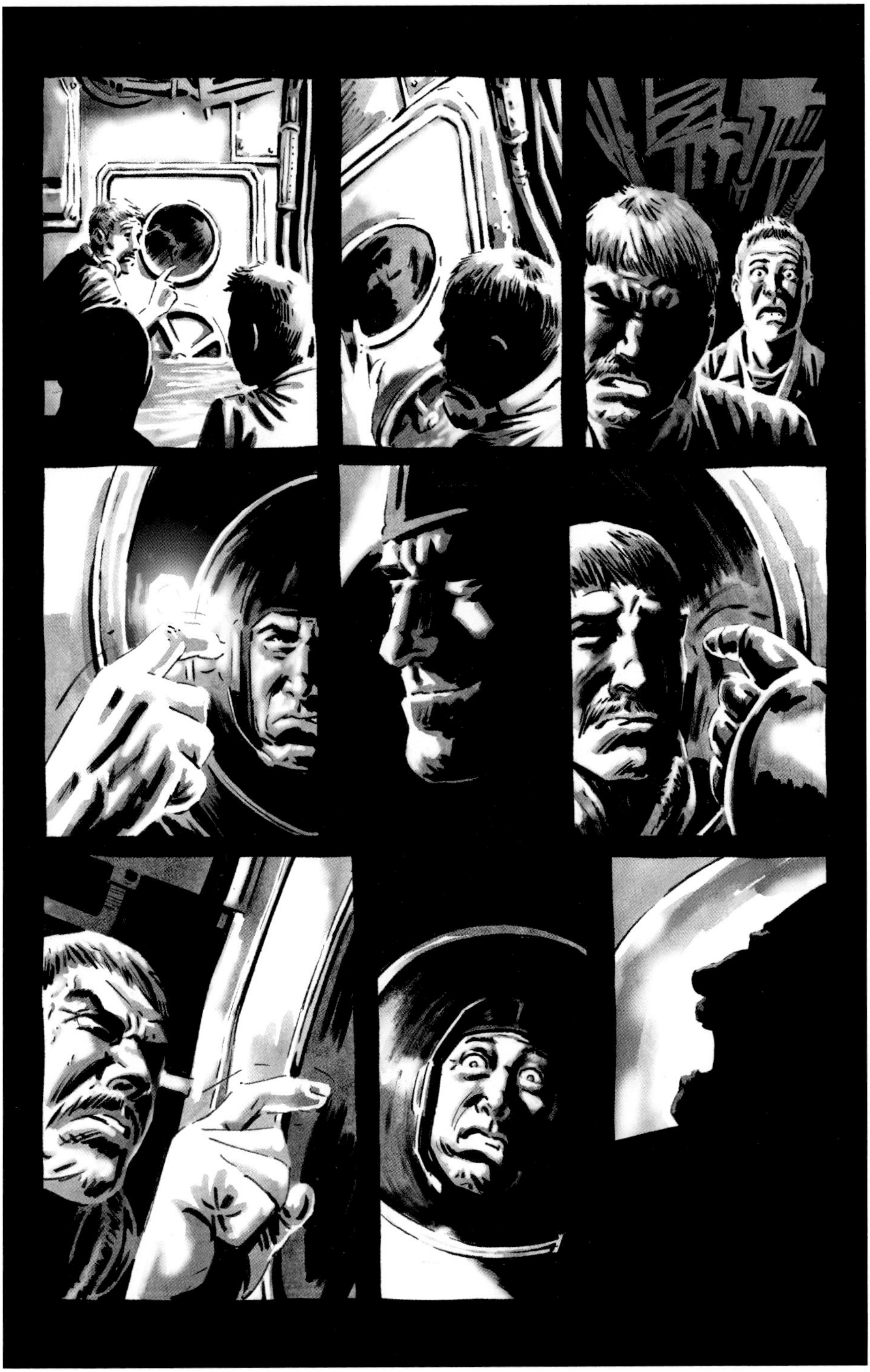

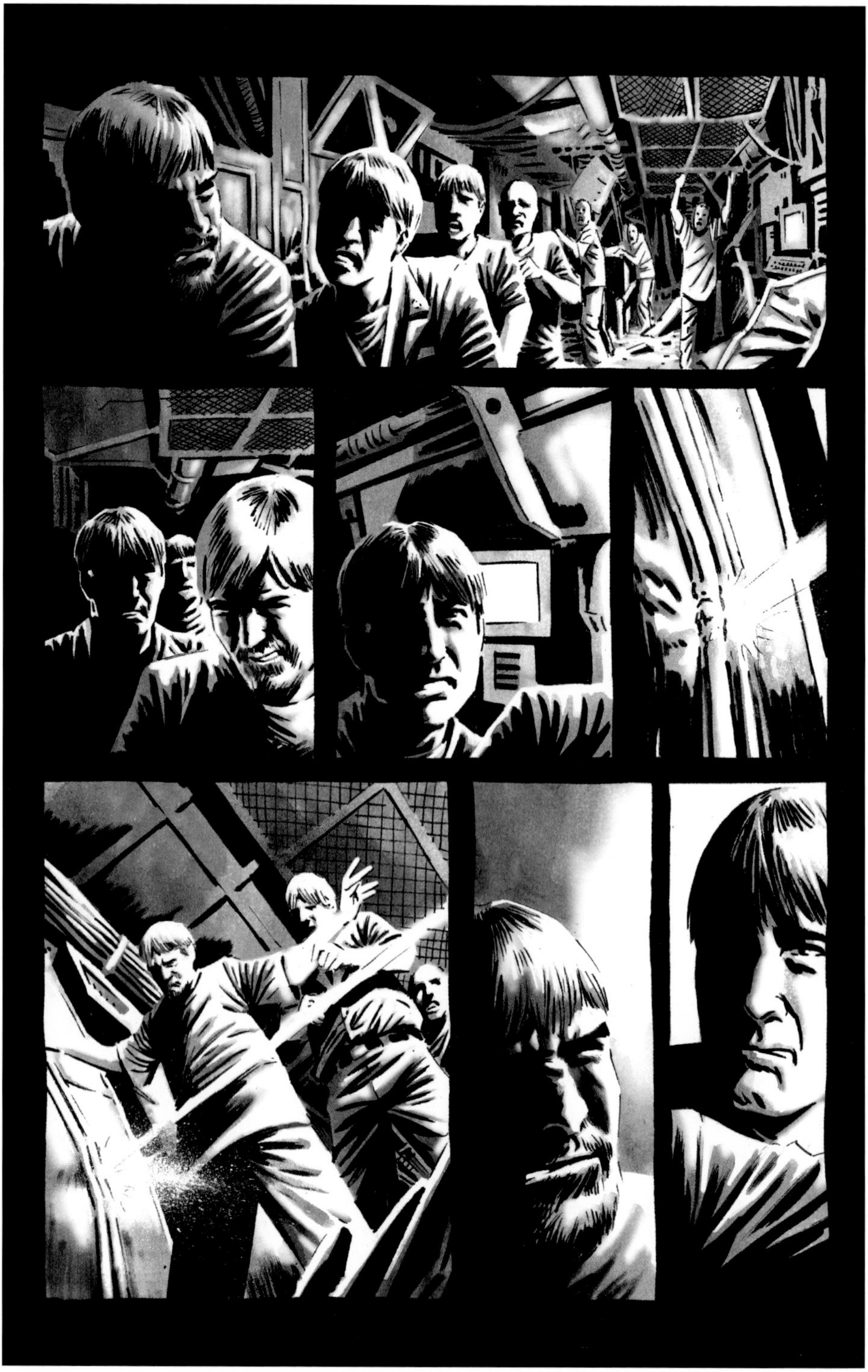

ART BY CALL

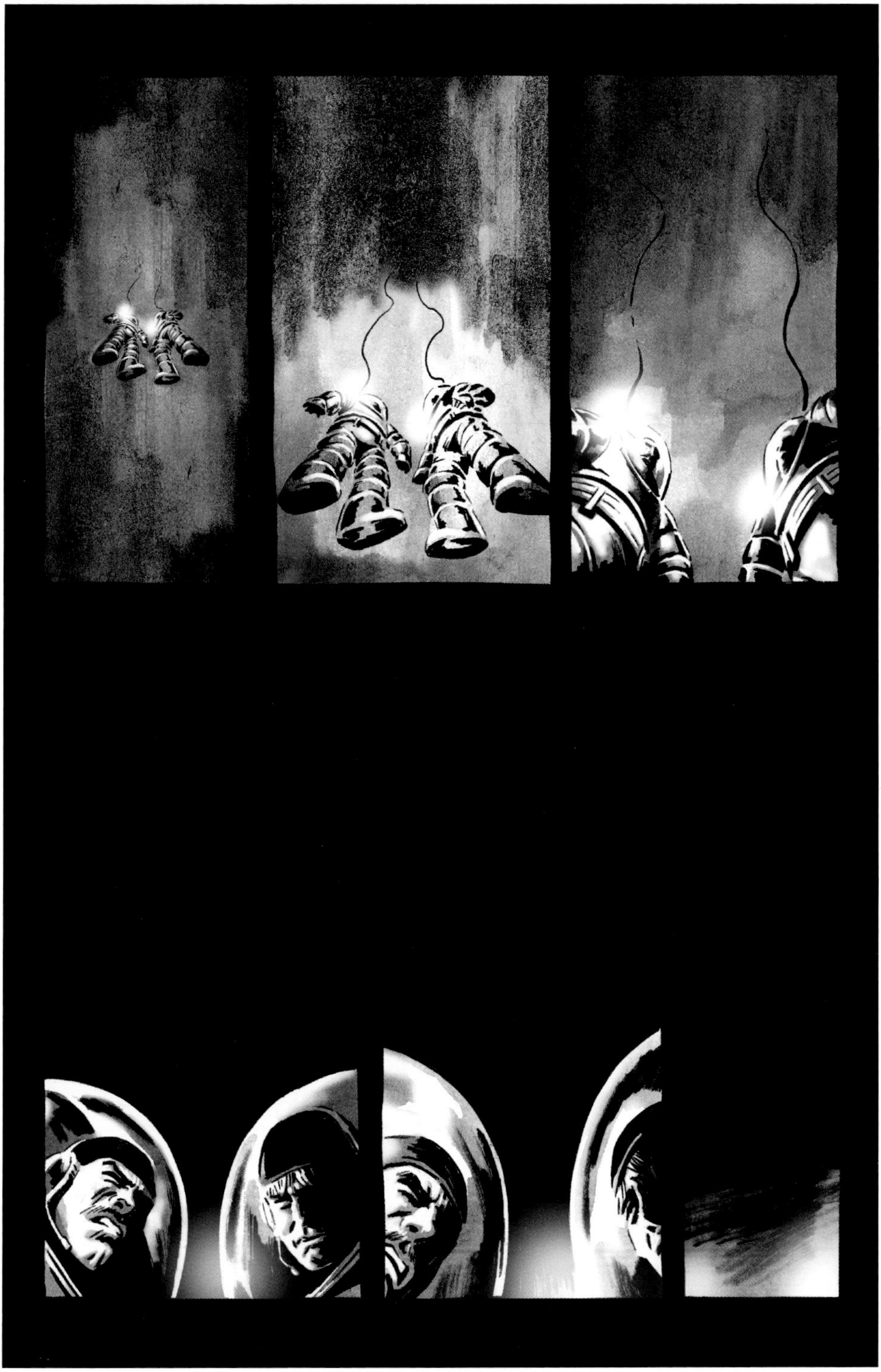

# ORIGINAL ART

ART BY CHEE

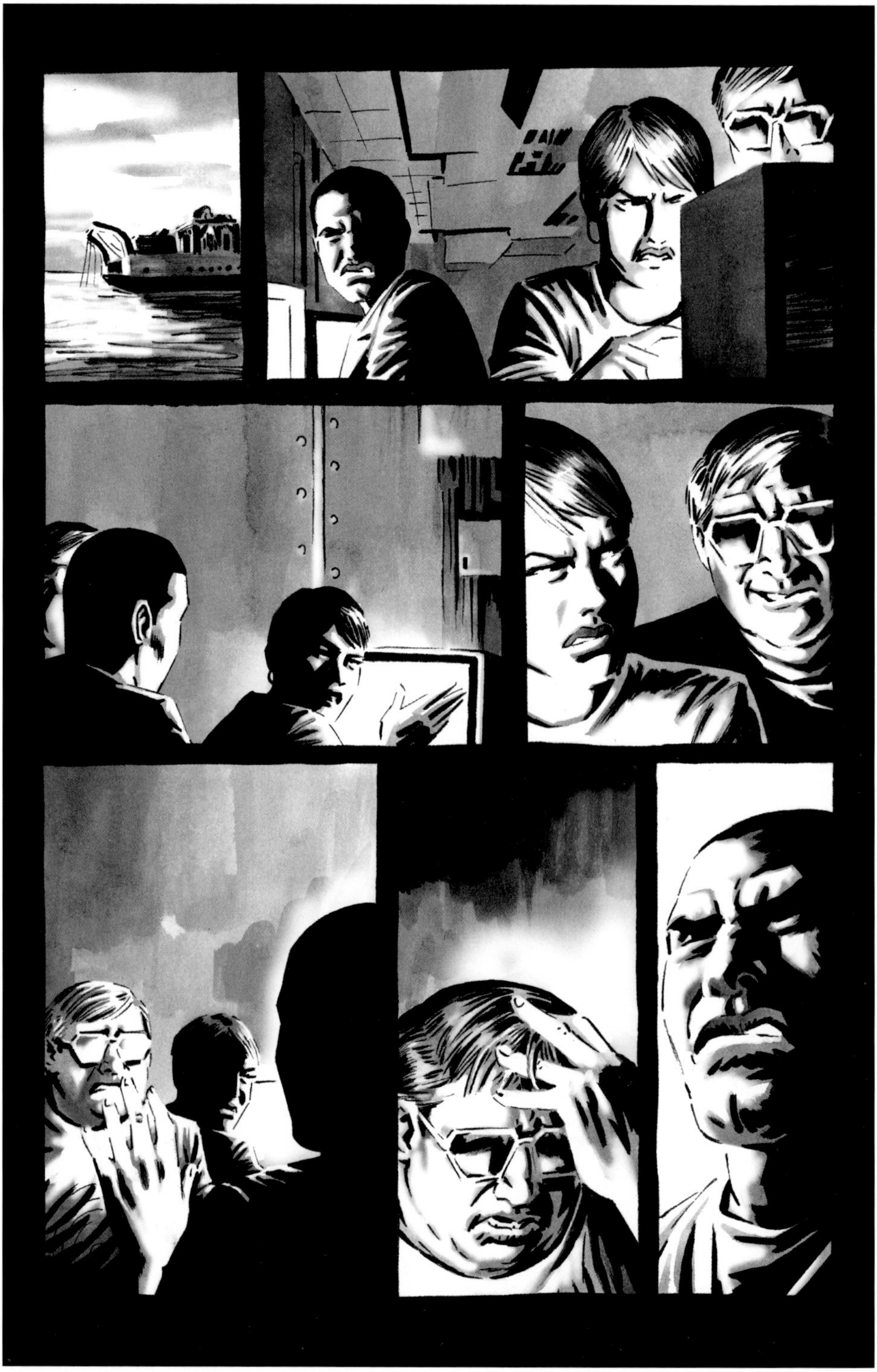

# ORIGINAL ART

ART BY CHEE

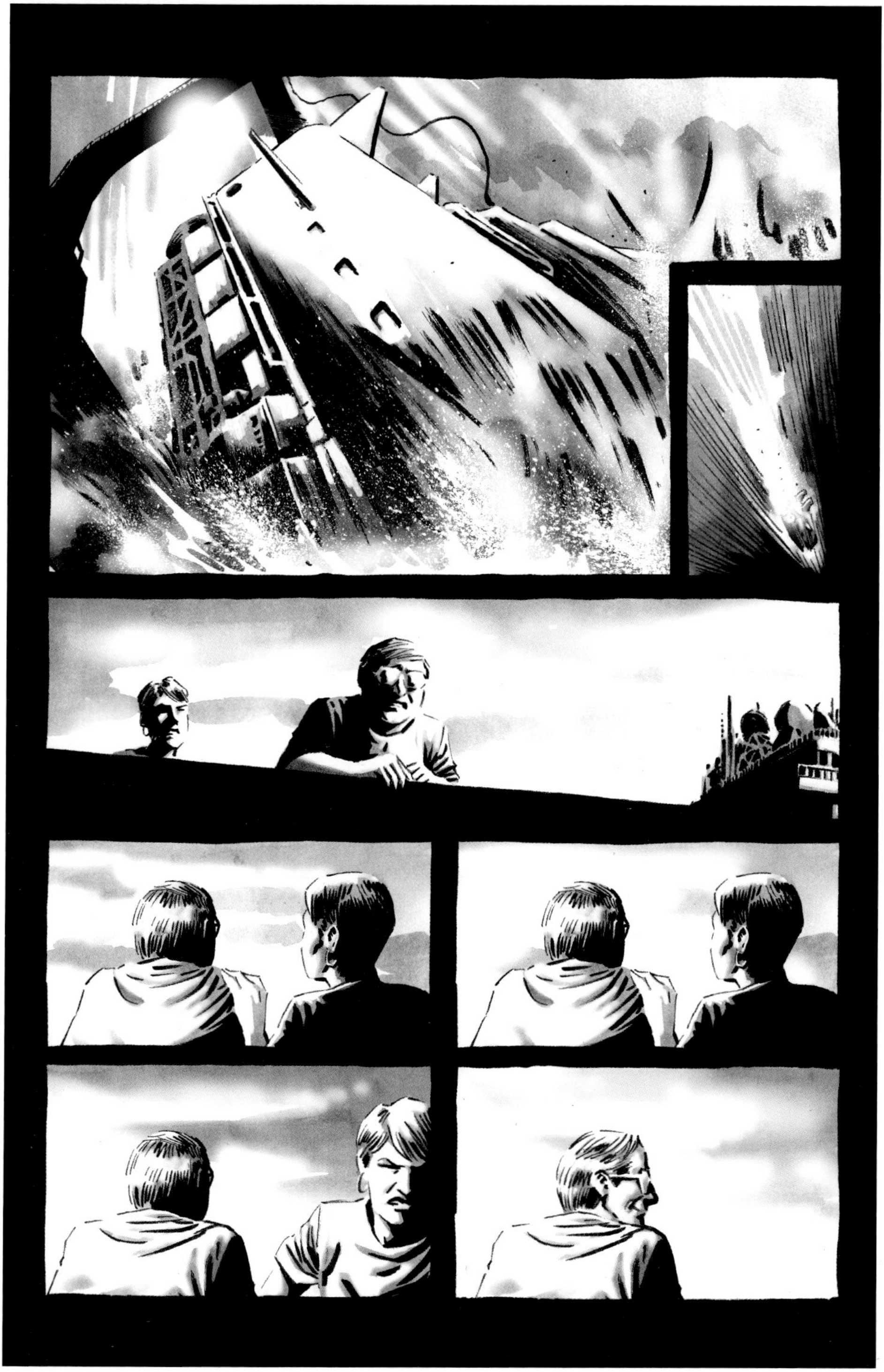

ART BY CHEE

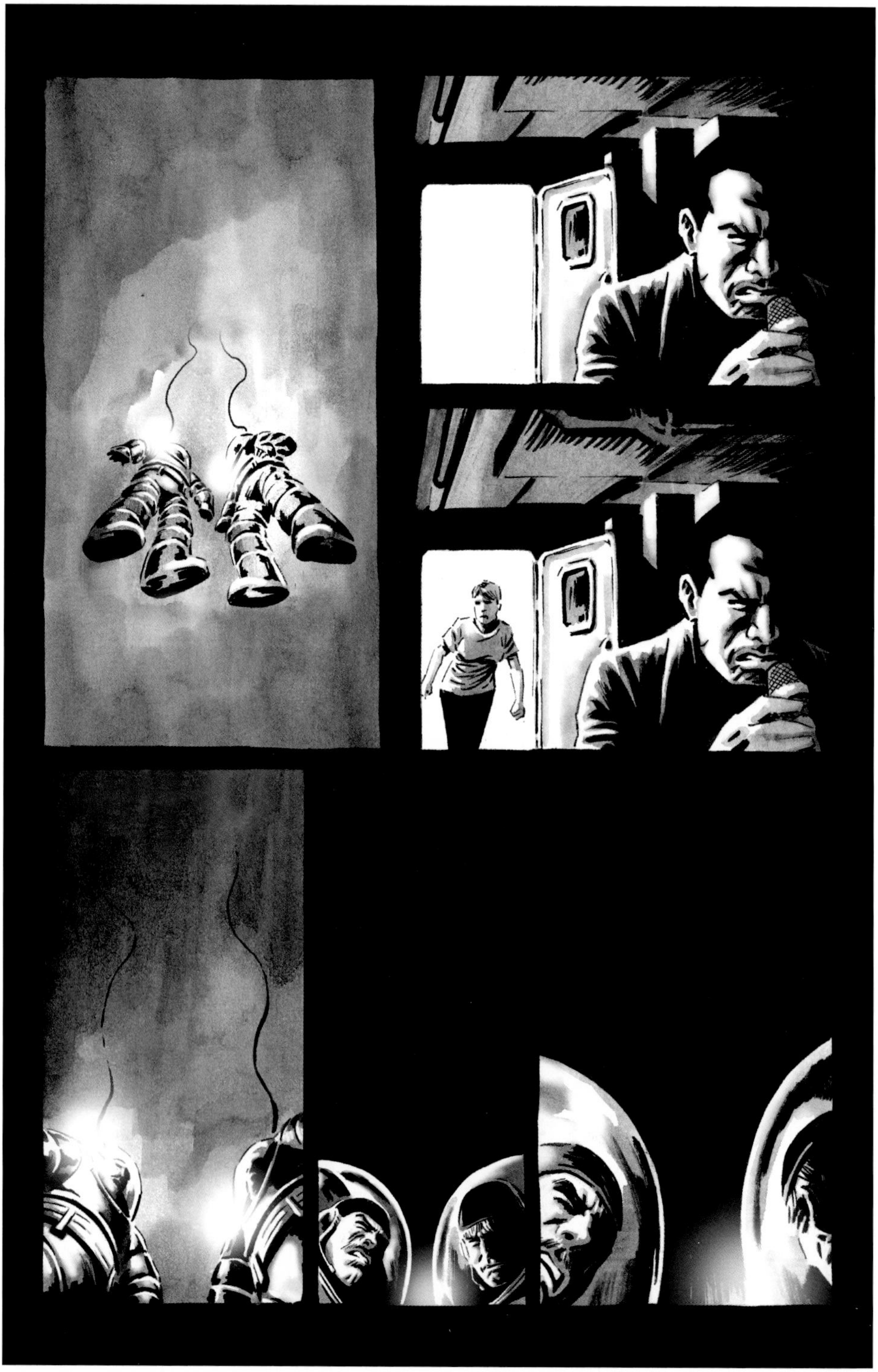

# ORIGINAL ART

ART BY CHEE

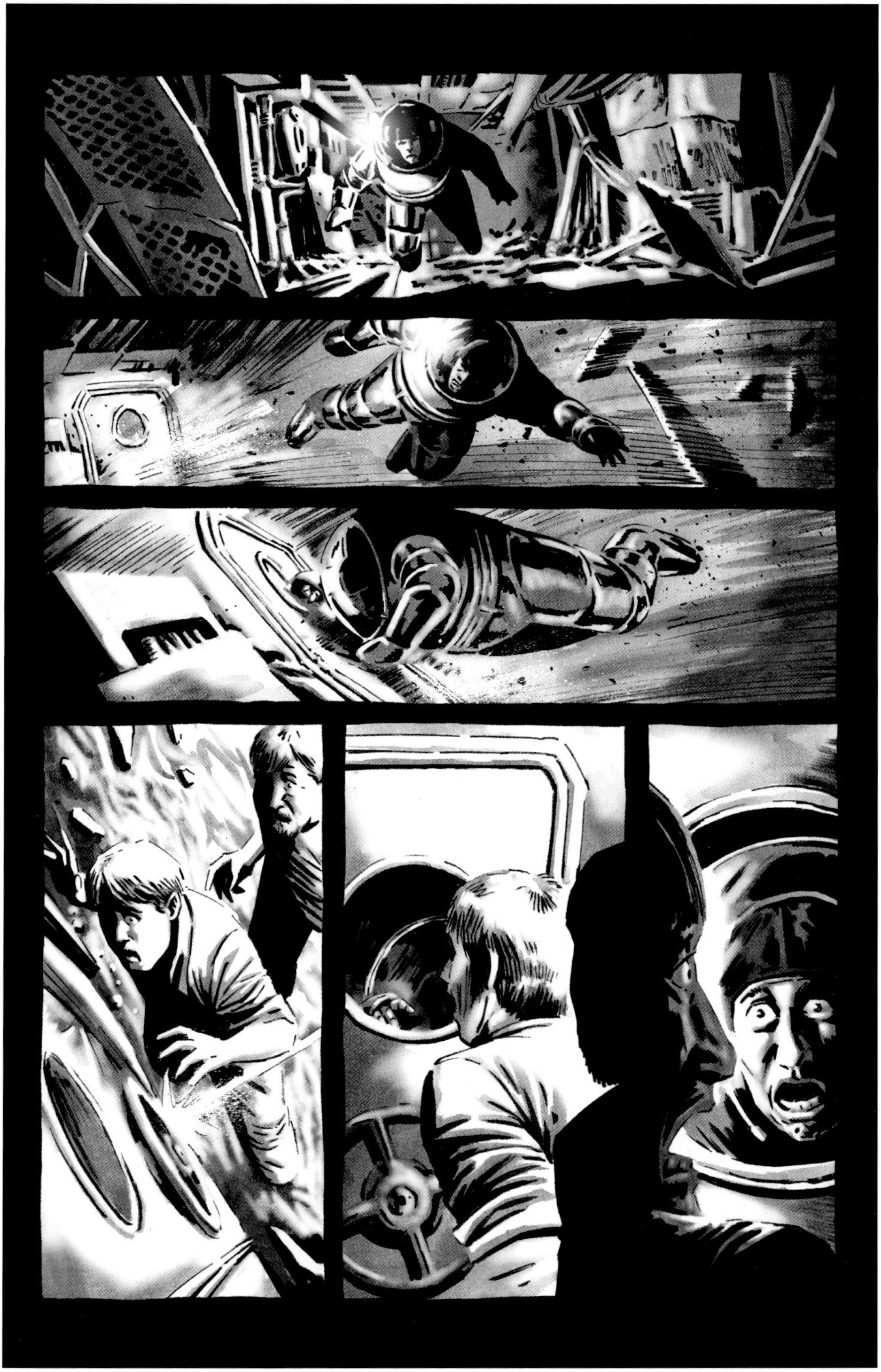

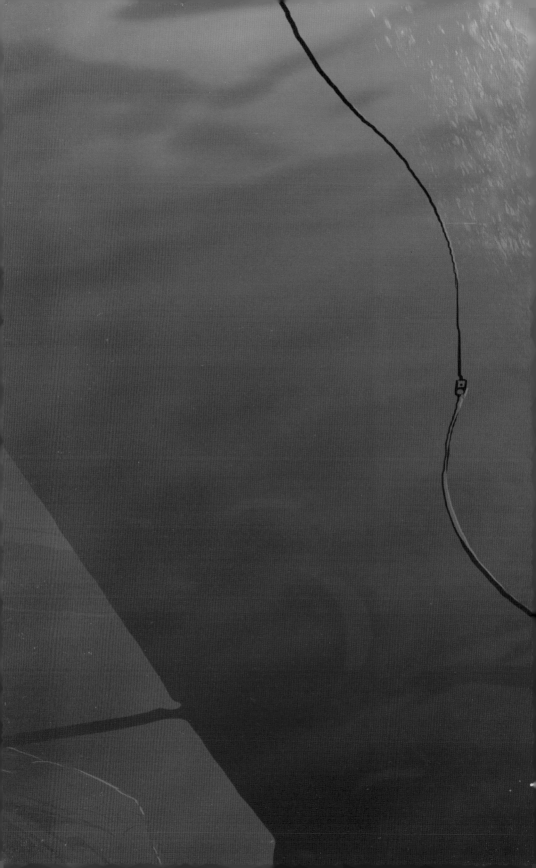